Semantic Service Provisioning

Dominik Kuropka • Peter Tröger •
Steffen Staab • Mathias Weske
Editors

Semantic
Service
Provisioning

 Springer

Editors

Dominik Kuropka
alfabet AG
Leibnitzstr. 53
10629 Berlin
Germany
dominik@kuropka.net

Steffen Staab
University of Koblenz
Institute for Computer Science
Universitaetsstr. 1
56016 Koblenz
Germany
staab@uni-koblenz.de

Peter Tröger
Blekinge Institute of Technology
Department of Systems and
Software Engineering (APS)
PO Box 520
37225 Ronneby
Sweden
peter.troger@bth.se

Mathias Weske
Universität Potsdam
HPI - Hasso Plattner Institute
Prof.-Dr.-Helmert-Str. 2-3
14482 Potsdam
Germany
mathias.weske@hpi.uni-potsdam.de

ISBN 978-3-642-09735-5   e-ISBN 978-3-540-78617-7

DOI 10.1007/978-3-540-78617-7

ACM Classification: D.2.11, D.2.12, H.4, J.1

© 2010 Springer Berlin Heidelberg

Cover design: KünkelLopka GmbH, Heidelberg

Printed on acid-free paper

9 8 7 6 5 4 3 2 1

springer.com

Preface

Information systems play an increasingly important role for the realisation of products that companies provide to the market. Typically, the functionality of several heterogeneous information systems needs to be combined to realise a particular product. Therefore, the seamless integration of information systems plays a key role in the development and maintenance of products. In today's dynamic market environments, change is the rule rather than the exception. Consequently, the ability to change products in an effective way and to adapt products to a changing information technology landscape, are important competitive advantages of a successful company.

Service oriented architectures are regarded as the main technology to provide well specified business functionality realised by information systems. Services allow effective re-use of existing functionality. The vision is to capture business relevant functionality of existing software systems as services and use service composition to plug services to larger, composite applications or products. Unfortunately, this vision has yet to be achieved. Today it is generally accepted that syntactic specifications of services are not sufficient to provide the high degree of flexibility for finding and composing services in an efficient manner.

Therefore research activities have been conducted in this context to investigate how the need for flexibility can be met by service oriented architectures in practical applications. One example for such kind of research activities is the European integration project *Adaptive Services Grid (ASG)* with 21 partners from academia and industry. From 2004 to 2007, the project developed a prototype of an automated service composition and enactment platform for semantically described services. The ASG approach for semantic service provisioning is blueprint to implement agility and adaptiveness promised by service oriented architectures.

This book presents the consolidated research results from the ASG project and other ongoing research activities. Rather then focusing only on technology and implementation details, the book aims at presenting the core concepts and illustrating their application with concrete examples. This book is well suited for researchers and practitioner who want to catch the idea and get a concrete overview on semantic service provisioning concepts. References to more detailed literature on particular research aspects and implementation standards are given in this book, where applicable.

ASG C-D Dissemination   Holger Krause
Arbeitsgemeinschaft tranSIT GmbH Ilmenau
TCC Medienwerkstatt Zella-Mehlis

Contents

List of Contributors

Joachim Bayer
Hessische Zentrale für
Datenverarbeitung
Mainzer Strasse 29
65185 Wiesbaden
Germany
joachim.bayer@
joachimbayer.de

Emilia Cimpian
STI/University of Innsbruck
Technikerstr. 21a
6020 Innsbruck
Austria
emilia.cimpian@sti2.at

Steffi Donath
University of Leipzig
Marschnerstr. 31
04109 Leipzig
Germany
sdonath@wifa.uni-leipzig.de

Michael Eisenbarth
Fraunhofer Institute for Experimental
Software Engineering
Sauerwiesen 6
67661 Kaiserslautern
Germany
michael.eisenbarth@
iese.fraunhofer.de

Thomas Hering
University of Leipzig
Marschnerstr. 31
04109 Leipzig
Germany
hering@wifa.uni-leipzig.de

Marek Kowalkiewicz
SAP Research
Level 12, 133 Mary Street
Brisbane, QLD 4000
Australia
marek.kowalkiewicz@sap.com

Dominik Kuropka
alfabet meta-modeling AG
Leibnitzstr. 53
10629 Berlin
Germany
dominik@kuropka.net

Guido Laures
Software AG
Uhlandstr. 12
64297 Darmstadt
Germany
guido.laures@softwareag.com

Theresa Lehner
Fraunhofer Institute for Experimental
Software Engineering
Sauerwiesen 6
67661 Kaiserslautern
Germany
theresa.lehner@
iese.fraunhofer.de

Andre Ludwig
University of Leipzig
Marschnerstr. 31
04109 Leipzig
Germany
ludwig@wifa.uni-leipzig.de

Harald Meyer
Hasso Plattner Institute
University of Potsdam
Prof.-Dr.-Helmert-Str. 2-3
14482 Potsdam
Germany
harald.meyer@
hpi.uni-potsdam.de

Mariusz Momotko
Rodan Systems S.A.
465 Puławska Street
02-844 Warszawa
Poland
Mariusz.Momotko@rodan.pl

Kai Petersen
Blekinge Institute of Technology
Fridhemsvägen 21
372 38 Ronneby
Sweden
kai.petersen@bth.se

Andreas Polze
Hasso Plattner Institute
University of Potsdam
Prof.-Dr.-Helmert-Str. 2-3
14482 Potsdam
Germany
andreas@polze.de

Christoph Ringelstein
University Koblenz-Landau
Institute for Computer Science
56016 Koblenz
Germany
cringel@uni-koblenz.de

Dumitru Roman
STI/University of Innsbruck
Technikerstr. 21a
6020 Innsbruck
Austria
dumitru.roman@sti2.at

Alexander Saar
Day Software AG
Barfüsser Platz 6
4001 Basel
Schweiz
alexander.saar@day.com

Jan Schaffner
Hasso Plattner Institute
University of Potsdam
Prof.-Dr.-Helmert-Str. 2-3
14482 Potsdam
Germany
Jan.Schaffner@hpi.uni-
potsdam.de

Adina Sirbu
STI/University of Innsbruck
Technikerstr. 21a
6020 Innsbruck
Austria
adina.sirbu@sti2.at

Steffen Staab
University Koblenz-Landau
Institute for Computer Science
56016 Koblenz
Germany
staab@uni-koblenz.de

Christian Stamber
IDS Scheer AG
Altenkesseler Str. 17
66115 Saarbrücken
Germany
christian.stamber@ids-scheer.com

Sebastian Stein
IDS Scheer AG
Altenkesseler Str. 17
66115 Saarbrücken
Germany
sebastian.stein@
ids-scheer.com

Nathalie Steinmetz
STI/University of Innsbruck
Technikerstr. 21a
6020 Innsbruck
Austria
nathalie.steinmetz@sti2.at

Ioan Toma
STI/University of Innsbruck
Technikerstr. 21a
6020 Innsbruck
Austria
ioan.toma@sti2.at

Peter Tröger
Blekinge Institute of Technology
Fridhemsvägen 21
372 38 Ronneby
Sweden
peter@troeger.eu

Mathias Weske
Hasso Plattner Institute
University of Potsdam
Prof.-Dr.-Helmert-Str. 2-3
14482 Potsdam
Germany
mathias.weske@
hpi.uni-potsdam.de

1

Introduction

Mathias Weske

1.1 State-of-the-art and Motivation

While service oriented computing has recently gained extensive momentum in both industry and academia, reality lags far behind expectations. Major software vendors hook on the service paradigm and tailor their software systems towards services, but a thorough and consistent design of applications based on loosely coupled services has yet to be achieved.

From its beginning, standardisation has been an important factor in service computing. However, rather than being integrated, standardisation efforts are rather independent from each other, so that the complex interplay between the various aspects in service computing is not accounted for by standardisation efforts.

While there are service based software applications in place, they realise just a minimal potential of service oriented computing, for instance standardised data and message formats. While Burbeck [37] has already identified dynamic binding of services at runtime as a core functionality of service based environments in 2000, dynamic binding of services has yet to be achieved. The main reason is the lack of rich service specifications, concepts, and tools to process them. The limitations of state-of-the-art service oriented systems can be characterised as follows:

- *Static Discovery and Binding*: Static binding of services means that an application invokes a service during execution time. The service is hard wired to the application, so that when the service fails, the application will also fail, unless additional measures are taken. Static binding of services can be realised by syntactic service specifications during the development of service based applications.

  These services are discovered manually by browsing and searching facilities, typically provided by a dedicated software component, called service registry. Services are then hard-wired to the application, which effectively realises a strong coupling, which contradicts the intended service paradigm of loose coupling.

The main reason for this limitation is the lack of rich specifications of services as well as proper domain ontologies that would facilitate dynamic service discovery and binding. Service description languages like *Web Services Description Language (WSDL)* [44] can only specify the technical syntactic interface of a service. Thus, what the service actually does, the semantics of the service, remains unspecified.

- *Fixed Service Landscape*: Static service binding restricts service based applications to a fixed service landscape. This means that new and improved services that become available after the application was developed but before the application is executed, cannot be used without modifying the application. This is a severe limitation, because adapting existing applications to use new services requires changing the application code and, thus, incurs considerable overhead.

- *Static Service Composition*: To fulfil particular goals, multiple services need to be performed according to underlying execution constraints. These execution constraints are specified in service compositions. Static service composition characterises the composition of existing services as a manual task. The service based application is more flexible and can adapt to changing service landscape with reduced effort, if services are composed dynamically, based on rich semantic specifications.

- *Poor Service Level Agreement Specification*: The service based application needs to define non-functional parameters for externally invoked services, for instance, related to response time or cost of using the services. As a result, service platforms need to be aware of non-functional quality of service parameters. Currently available platforms do not have these required capabilities. There is also no established interoperable specification language for defining, agreeing on, and monitoring such contracts between the consumer and provider of services.

This book introduces advanced concepts in service provisioning and service engineering, including semantic concepts, dynamic discovery and composition, and illustrates them in a concrete business use case scenario. To prove the validity of the concepts and technologies, a semantic service provisioning reference architecture framework as well as a prototypical implementation of its subsystems and a prototypical realisation of a proper business scenario are presented. The book goes way beyond current service based software technologies by providing a coherent and consistent set of technologies and systems functionality that realises advanced concepts in service provisioning.

In particular, the following advanced topics are addressed in this book. These are features on the technological level, which are appointed by the application of a compliant platform for service provisioning. On a business level, these achievements lead to a reduction of costs in development and maintenance. Furthermore the semantic service provisioning platform supports continuous adaptation of service centric applications towards environmental changes and upcoming business needs.

- *Seamless integration of heterogeneous existing services*: Service integration is achieved by the provision of an elaborated methodological approach embedded into a set of integrated tools. These tools assist the user in her task of integrating existing heterogeneous services into the platform. Starting point for integration is a domain-specific ontology from which a specific type system is derived. The semantic service provisioning platform supports the mapping to this specific type system. Integrated services are augmented with semantic descriptions regarding service functionality and non-functional properties. In terms of the business dimension, this achievement reduces the maintenance and modification costs for large numbers of available services. It has the potential to ease integration of services and data formats. The envisaged architecture allows an easy discovery and interoperability of integrated services.

- *On-demand creation of service compositions*: Automated semantic-enabled service composition allows creation of new services by composing existing services on-demand and at run-time for individual user requests. For this purpose, the semantically described functionality of services is used. Current service integration approaches base on manual programming, making it hard to cost-effectively maintain and modify the complex service world. Therefore, the interface to services is lifted from a manual to a logical level, and supports service composition based on automated tools. The adaptive service composition implies a cost reduction in service provisioning.
- *Reliable service provision with assured quality of service*: The semantic service provisioning platform supports the description, negotiation, and realisation of non-functional service quality parameters. In cases of service failures or violations of agreed quality parameters, the platform reacts adaptively through re-enactment, re-binding or re-composition activities. The future service world will be based on global and dynamic services, which can be composed to answer the needs of complex service requests. Dynamic service re-enactment, re-binding or re-composition provide alternative solutions for non-reliable services, thus provides the end-customer with a reliable service delivery.

1.2 Scope and Organisation

This book introduces concepts and technologies in semantic service engineering and provisioning. A use case scenario illustrates the concepts and shows the validity of the technologies used. The organisation of this book follows roughly the lifecycle of a service based application, from the specification of concepts and services to service integration, composition, and finally enactment.

Chapter 2 introduces the foundation of this book by providing common terminology and a use case scenario that is used throughout the book. Finally, the phases involved in service provisioning are discussed.

Chapter 3 introduces semantic concepts in service engineering based on ontologies. In particular, ontology languages are introduced to capture the main concepts and their relationships. These ontology languages are used to express domain ontologies and service ontologies. Domain ontologies represent the semantic concepts of the particular domain of a service based application, while service ontologies define

how services are specified. A section on matchmaking explains how semantic specifications of services and domain ontologies can be used to generate new knowledge
in service engineering, for instance, to decide which service actually fulfils the needs
of a given service specification.

Service enabling is studied in Chap. 4. At a technological level, the generation of
code for legacy integration is essential to service enabling, because it allows efficient
legacy integration. Concepts and technologies in software generation are used to
develop wrappers to existing software that realise the integration of services. Based
on the specification of domain ontologies, the semantic specification of services is
introduced.

One of the most important concepts in service provisioning is the composition of
services to value-added service compositions. Chapter 5 looks at various techniques
to compose services, ranging from manual composition to assisted composition and,
finally, to runtime composition. To provide a broad perspective on research work
in this area, Chap. 5 completes with a section on service composition and binding
as developed in the Integrated Project SUPER, supported by the EU in the Sixth
Framework Programme.

The enactment of service compositions is addressed in Chap. 6. Based on a set
of enactment strategies, service monitoring and service profiling is addressed. The
chapter completes with technologies to handle faults, based on the rich specification
of services.

The service infrastructure is presented in Chap. 7, starting with middleware concepts and technologies, and proceeding to Web services technologies and a discussion of the service infrastructure for semantic service provisioning.

A service engineering methodology is introduced in Chap. 8. This methodology
explains in detail the steps involved in the conceptual design and technological development of service based applications using the approach presented in this book.

While the introduced use case scenario is used to illustrate the concepts and solutions in the chapters, a consistent and sufficiently complete discussion of the realisation of this scenario is provided in Chap. 9.

2

Core Concepts and Use Case Scenario

Dominik Kuropka, Guido Laures, and Peter Tröger

2.1 Terminology

This chapter starts the discussion on semantic service provision by establishing a common terminology. Furthermore, we are introducing a non-trivial use case scenario, which acts as a base for the following explanations in the book. Based on both the terminology and the use case, this chapter defines the semantic service provision lifecycle based on the introduced core building blocks.

2.1.1 What is the Service?

The term service is widely adopted by the business and the software engineering community. However, both communities have a different understanding about what services are. This is usually a source for many misunderstandings in practice.

A *service oriented architecture (SOA)* [37] describes the architectural concept to organise applications and infrastructures in a business environment. Gartner defines a SOA as a technical software infrastructure which enables an interaction between service provider and service requester based on interface descriptions [139]. The granularity of a service corresponds to the granularity of the provided business function. The *Organization for the Advancement of Structured Information Standards (OASIS)* reference model defines SOA as a paradigm for the organisation and usage of distributed business capabilities [123]. Melzer et al. define SOA as the abstract concept of a software architecture which focuses on the provision, discovery and usage of services over a network [64].

Three participant roles are the crucial aspect in service oriented business: The service provider, the service broker, and the service requester respectively *service consumer* (see also Fig. 2.1).

Both terms, requester and consumer, are used to the same amount in SOA literature and standards. Therefore, both terms are used also in this book by the different authors. The SOA reference model only sticks with the service consumer term,

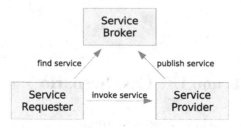

Fig. 2.1. Service oriented architecture

while other sources reason the usage of service requester with the missing exhaustion resources, which is typical in an consumption activity. Service requesters are sometimes also wrongly named as service clients, customers, or requestors.

The service requester utilizes the service through its *service interface*. A service may have several different technical interfaces. These interfaces are exposed by the service provider to give the requester access to the functionality encapsulated by the service. To properly access a service, a requester has to do specific technical things in a specific order, like sending a well structured message to a proper computer which is aligned to a predefined data format. Therefore the service providers have to publish a *service specification* to enable access to their services.

The *service broker* has the role of yellow pages, it acts as a repository for service specifications. Service providers publish their service specifications in the repository. In addition, service broker offer searching and matching tools to facilitate efficient finding of services. Common technologies to implement a service repository are *Repository for Universal Description, Discovery and Integration (UDDI)* [148], ebXML [60] and LDAP [39]. They allow a standardised storage of service specifications, natural language descriptions of the services and a semi-formal classification of the services.

In some cases, research publications also refer to the term *service oriented computing (SOC)*. The SOC approach is meanwhile widely accepted as a cross-disciplinary paradigm for distributed computing, where services act as basic building blocks for computational applications [92, 151]. Here, a service is a well-specified unit of computational work, which is again offered by a service provider. This work might be in the simplest case just the addition of two numbers; more sophisticated services offer functionalities like charging of credit cards or the initiation of a human activity for example the transportation of physical goods.

At this point, the difference between the service term in the business and the software engineering community comes to the fore. In the business community, the whole process of acquiring delivery information, physical transportation of goods and the final delivery and payment are usually seen as one (transportation) service. In SOC such an interpretation is not valid, since services have to be computational work. The physical transportation of goods as a whole therefore cannot be a service, since it can not be delivered by pure computational work. But the collection of delivery information can be a service, as long as computer based interfaces are used. The same holds for the charging, as long as it includes some computational work like the charging of a credit card. In sum, services in SOC can only represent the computational subset or parts of real-world services in the sense of the business community. SOC could therefore be ranked as substantial part of the SOA research and paradigms.

The general crucial point of SOA approaches is the intended support of a late and dynamic service binding. The service requester should not need to bind itself at design-time to only one of the service provider. Instead, the service requester can query the broker for the most suitable services during execution time.

In theory, the resulting business competition encourages a continuous improvement of the offered services. In practice, most attempts to realise such a dynamic binding showed technical obstacles. A major challenge in finding the proper service is the derivation of service functionality from a pure syntactical specification. These descriptions only contain information about input and output data formats, but not about the service functionality and the meaning of the data structures. This is usually not a big issue with a manual integration of services at the design time of the requester application. In this case, the programmer can read additional natural language documentation or directly contact the service provider representatives. However it becomes a major obstacle with *automated late binding* of services.

A solution for this challenge is the concept of a semantic service, which is the main topic of this book. The idea behind semantic services is to extend the syntactical specification of a service by a semantic specification. This semantic specification formally describes the functionality and the meaning of the data used by the service interface. Formats and languages for a semantic specification of services are presented in Sect. 3.4, while techniques to specify existing services and to ensure a proper data integration (service grounding) are discussed in Sect. 4.3.

Another aspect also discussed in this book is the composition of services. A service composition is a partially ordered set of services in the sense of a workflow or business process [204]. It could also be understood as service based application. Today, service compositions have to be created manually which is a laborious and thus expensive task. Referring to this point semantic services also provide a benefit. With semantic services the costs for the composition of services can be reduced if assisted or automated service composition approaches are used. This topic will be discussed in detail in Chap. 5. Since service compositions offer their functionality also through a service interface, we distinguish here between a *atomic service* and a *composed service* (often also called composite service). The latter one represents the combination of different atomic services in a workflow, which itself is usable over a service interface.

For the implementation of SOA environments, many different technologies are provided by industry vendors. Web service technologies like *SOAP* and *Web Services Description Language (WSDL)* are the usual, but not the only promising technology to implement the SOA concepts. Chapter 7 discusses their technical details.

2.1.2 Service Quality

The consideration of the quality of service provisioning usually focuses on two categories of metrics: performance metrics and dependability metrics. While performability is naturally specific for the according middleware area (e.g. computational clusters vs. business service environments), dependability has a mature terminology from the history of distributed systems [16]. We therefore re-use some basic terms for dependability in our understanding of service oriented systems. Other service quality aspects beside dependability are discussed specifically in Sect. 6.3.

First, we define a correct service to deliver a functionality according to its specification, in contrast to an incorrect service, which misbehaves in comparison to its specification. A service failure is the event in time, when the delivered service functionality deviates from its specified functionality. All failures have *failure symptoms*, which might or might not be observable. This demands some understanding of a correct service behaviour, and the possibility for monitoring and rating the service behaviour to detect a failure symptom. With the existence of a service failure, the underlying system has some kind of error state. The cause of this error state in the system is called a fault.

An incorrect service shows up by a failure in the service functionality or its interface. It is caused by a system error state, which itself results from a (maybe nonobservable) causing fault. It has to be noted that a service can either be a single atomic service or a composed service, consisting of several other services. The dependability concepts remain the same for both types of services.

Since the overall goal of a dependable (service oriented) system is an integrated concept [116], it consists of several sub-topics based on the above terminology. The alternation of correct and incorrect service functionality in time is used for some of the sub-concepts to describe according metrics:

- availability: The readiness of a system to provide a correct service. An according measure is the relationship between correct and incorrect service functionality over time.
- reliability: The continuity of a correct service provisioning in all cases. An according measure is the time to failure.
- safety: The absence of an catastrophic consequence on the user and the environment. As a special case, it expresses the reliability according to catastrophic failures.
- confidentiality: The absence of unauthorised information disclosure.
- integrity: The absence of improper state alteration.
- maintainability: Ability to undergo repairs and modifications. A measure is the time to restoration of the correct service after a detected failure.

Dependable system research is aware of many other dependability concepts and terms, some of them are used inflationary in the SOA research. A popular example is the notion of security as quality metric, which expresses the intend to avoid unauthorised access to service functionality. In terms of the generic dependability concepts, security represents a combination of availability for authorised users only, confidentiality regarding unauthorised users, and integrity in terms of unauthorised usage. There are four major technologies for achieving dependable service functionality:

- fault prevention prevents the introduction or occurrence of faults.
- fault tolerance delivers a correct service even in the presence of faults, by combining error detection with system recovery.
- fault removal reduces the number or severity of faults.
- fault forecasting estimates the present or future number of faults, and their incidence.

system recovery denotes the movement from a faulty system state to a correct system state. The recovery from faults can be performed by error handling (roll-back, compensation, roll-forward) or fault handling (diagnosis, isolation, reconfiguration, re-initalization).

In SOA environments, dependability approaches usually concentrate on service compositions as unit of dependability. The system term here can be mapped to the different atomic services forming the composition. For fault tolerance, error handling works on the system (= service composition) state during runtime, while the fault handling concentrates on identifying and isolating a faulty atomic service.

In this book, we will see both error handling approaches: fault handling for service compositions, as well as fault handling strategies for atomic services. Fault removal is accompanied by manual tasks during development time (verification, validation, fault injection) or runtime (corrective maintenance, preventive maintenance), and will therefore not be in focus in this book. Also fault prevention is mainly attained during development time. Fault forecasting maps to the concept of service profiling, where the analysis of historical service behaviour is used to compute and consider dependability measures for a service.

2.1.3 Service-Level Agreements

The term of a *Service Level Agreement (SLA)* originates from an industrial context. It is frequently (mis-)used by research and industry people in SOA discussions and publications. Different communities, such as networking, multimedia, grid computing, or agent technology people, use the SLA-term in their own environment in different manners.

In networking environments, data centres and independent software vendors have several standards and technologies to deal with performance objectives for network connections [142], such as data rate, packet delay, latency, error rate, or network uptime. The multimedia community defined quality models for adaptive multichannel information systems, which are implemented by resource partitioning techniques. The Grid computing community sees SLA simply as formulation of resource requirements [12], while the agent community sees SLA as subject of negotiation between different software agents, in order to support full-automated agreement creation.

Due to this widespread, but unspecified application of SLA terminology, we try to give here common base for the SLA discussions in this book. An *agreement* in general can be seen as the concordant declaration of some intention. It includes at least some kind of statement about the agreement, and the exchange of contractual documents. In real world, these contractual agreements can regulate purchases, leasing activities, a permanent work relationship—or some kind of service.

When we interpret SOA as the mapping of business environments and conditions to the world of software, *service-level* agreements define the conditions under which a business service is provided to a consumer. This can relate to performance, cost, reliability, security, or other issues relevant for the service consumer. Obligations and provided functionalities are defined for both partners, but also penalties if the negotiated properties are not fulfilled [120].

The service requester has specific requirements and expectations on the service. The level of fulfilment for these requirements relates to the costs of the service— cheaper services have a lower level of expectable service quality metrics. The service provider has the task of fulfilling all negotiated contracts, while maximising the utilisation of the resources and minimising the costs for contract penalties. Typical service-level agreements contain quality guarantees in different granularity levels, which potentially have a stochastic definition:

> The maximum response time for 95 percent of the requests should be below 2 seconds.

Technical properties of such a specification are usually named as service-level specification or service-level objective. The promised behaviour is formulated as logical expression, which is checked through measured values during runtime. Beside these technical aspects, also organisational requirements (e.g. violation notification) or commercial aspects (e.g. price for SLA violation) can be a part of a SLA definition.

2.2 Use Case Scenario

This section introduces a use case common to all chapters of this book. Concepts and technologies for semantic service provision will be illustrated by referring to this use case. It is settled in the hosting services industry. However, it is important to keep in mind that this is just one specific example. Semantic service provision and the concepts described in this book are independent from industrial domains.

2.2.1 Introduction

The use case presented in this section bases on the *business-to-business (B2B)* wholesale model of an Austrian *Internet Service Provider (ISP)* called Hostit. It specialises on products like domain registration, web hosting solutions and messaging services, but not on providing the Internet access itself.

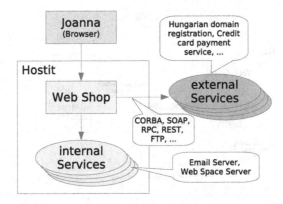

Fig. 2.2. The available B2C solution

Let us consider the Hostit *business-to-consumer (B2C)* hosting product shop solution shown in Fig. 2.2. *Joanna*, an Hungarian woman, wants to become a Hostit customer. She uses her browser to access the Hostit web shop and order the hosting solution she desires. She is interested in registering her own domain (joanna.hu) with e-mail addresses and web space. She wants to use her credit card to pay for the products. Using the Hostit web shop she is able to specify all configuration items needed for the order processing like the intended domain name, the payment method, and so on. To process an order the Hostit web shop application accesses the needed company-internal services as well as services from external partners. The service selection highly depends on the order configuration, respectively the service invocation order is determined by Hostit's business processes.

To process Joanna's order Hostit has to make use of external partner services for domain registration, operating and maintaining of *Domain Name Server (DNS)* information, web hosting configuration, and payment. Which services to use highly depends on the customer's demands. For instance, the service used for domain registration depends on the customer's desired top-level domain. Assignment of domains with .com or .org endings are governed by *Internet Corporation for Assigned Names and Numbers (ICANN)* while for example national domains like .de or .at are assigned by *Deutsches Network Information Center (DENIC)* in Germany or *nic.at* in Austria. In Joanna's case, the domain registration service to use is *Network Information Centre (NIC)* Hungary. Internet service providers accredited by the supervising registrars can register domains by using dedicated interfaces of the registrars domain database. Web hosting services of internet providers encapsulate interfaces for web hosting systems. They allow allocation of web space to users while enforcing fine-grained restrictions on data volume, traffic and e-mail configuration.

Hostit is interested in expanding into the German market. Thus, its cooperates with a German newspaper named Heidelberger Zeitung. This company wants to bundle a newspaper subscription with a web hosting and e-mail product. The idea is that subscribers automatically get their own e-mail address and domain for a one year subscription as a free add-on. To enable Heidelberger

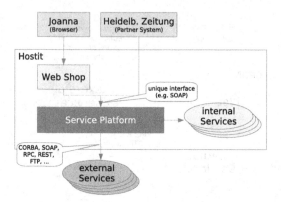

Fig. 2.3. Extension for B2B scenarios

Zeitung to order Hostit products without having to manually order them using the web client, Hostit expands its existing end-customer-centric application
to a more flexible platform that can be used through various front-end solutions
operated by resellers. The goal is to develop a B2B solution that reuses already
available elementary business capabilities. This service reuse reduces customer acquisition and support costs for Hostit. The underlying internet service provision
system requires extensions to support a more generalised B2B approach instead
of a restricted B2C application. Currently, the complexity of interweaved subtasks
of product ordering in the web shop and provisioning of these products through a
back-end system hinders the reuse of provisioning capabilities through varying order
processes.

Figure 2.3 illustrates Hostit's system architecture that supports both, the B2C
and the B2B access using a central service platform. The benefit of unifying and
channelling the access to the company-internal and -external services is an increased
flexibility and maintainability. To integrate a new service, it is published in the service platform. Access control rights can now be centrally managed in the service
platform.

2.2.2 Drawbacks in State-of-the-art Service Provision

Using a state-of-the-art service provision platform has a number of drawbacks. To
integrate a new service not only the service needs to be published in the platform but
also the platform clients need to be changed to benefit from the new service. This
is the case because the clients of the service provision platform explicitly invoke
specific services and hence will not notice newly available services on the platform
automatically. Another drawback is that the service invocation order is hard-coded in
the clients. Thus, clients need to be changed to implement new or adapted business
processes that might be useful because of the newly available services. Last but not
least a state-of-the-art service provision platform does not provide fall-back solutions
in case of a service invocation error. Thus, if the invocation of a specific service fails

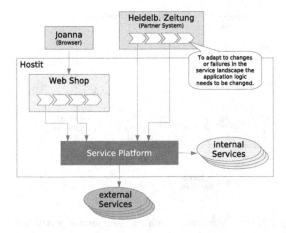

Fig. 2.4. State-of-the-art service provisioning

for instance because of a network problem on the provider side, the platform does not know if there might be another service available with an equivalent functionality.

Figure 2.4 illustrates the service invocation logic inside the web shop and the B2B systems. The little white shapes inside the web shop and the Heidelberger Zeitung application symbolise the steps that form the internal application logic. Some steps invoke company-internal or partner services on the service platform. The binding of steps to services is hard coded inside the application. Thus, the application logic will not make use of newly available service unless it is changed. The steps of the application logic are duplicated in the web shop and the Heidelberger Zeitung partner application. Thus, all these applications need to be adapted if they want to benefit from changes in the service landscape. If a service in the platform fails the application logic needs to cope with this failure. Thus, it needs to know if there are functionally equivalent services available in the landscape and how they are invoked.

2.2.3 Semantic Services

Semantic services promise to overcome the drawbacks of traditional service provision approaches. Therefore, Hostit engages *Steve*, an expert in semantic services, to plan a Hostit service provision architecture that leverage innovative technologies and methodologies from that area. Steve's first draft of a new Hostit architecture looks much alike the current solution. However, there are a few changes that aim at an improved flexibility, adaptability and maintainability of the entire architecture. Figure 2.5 shows Steve's first high-level plan for the semantic service solution.

One of the main differences compared to the architecture shown in Fig. 2.4 is the reduced complexity of the clients of the Hostit service platform. The clients now access the service by providing semantic service requests. They do not have to state explicitly which services to use but describe their needs using semantics and

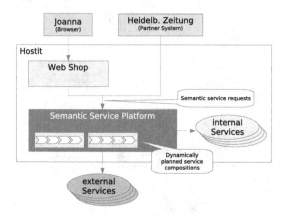

Fig. 2.5. Draft architecture with semantic service provisioning

let the platform find out which of the available services to use for the fulfilment of this request. Thus, the logic of composed services that together implement an order processing is now in the platform, not in the client. Even more important, the logic is not hard coded but it is composed at runtime and thus, capable of dealing with changes in the service landscape. As soon as a new service is published in the platform, it is considered as a candidate to be used in a service composition. Furthermore, if a service fails the platform is able to identify semantically equivalent services or service compositions and use these instead.

The components of such a semantic service provisioning platform, how it uses semantics for dynamic service compositions and which technologies are available for building up such a platform are the topics of this book. Thus, having read this book you will understand how Hostit can set up a platform that offers all the benefits mentioned above.

2.3 Adaptive Service Provision Approach

The *traditional approach* for using (Web) services in SOA bases on static binding of services. During design-time of the application the developer selects proper services and binds them to the applications. This implicates that the applications can only adapt in a very limited manner to changes in the service environment. For intra-organizational scenarios this deficiency is often tolerable, since the service environment is under full control of one organisation and unplanned changes are rather infrequent. In contrast to this, static binding of services is problematic when it comes to inter-organisational scenarios where major parts of the service environment are not under control of one entity. Static binding of services suffer from the following drawbacks:

- *Poor utilisation of new services*: Static service binding enforces a manual adaptation of existing applications to include new, cheaper or better services. This causes additional costs in the maintenance of applications and it limits the timeliness of adaptations as well as the ease of implementation of new business models which usually are combined with new services.

• *Poor reliability*: In inter-organisational scenarios services my fail or disappear at any time for a large variety of reasons: communication and network failures, overload, internal failures or simply disappearance of the providing organisation. In all these cases, the static binding of services causes a (partly or even total) failure of the depending applications. In situations where it is impossible to simply sit such a failure out (e.g. because of running costs) a time consuming and costly manual adaptation of the applications is needed.

In this book we propose an approach which avoids the above mentioned drawbacks by enabling a dynamic binding of services which leads to an *adaptive service provisioning*. Instead of simply binding services to applications at design-time we propose a sophisticated and adaptive service delivery life-cycle as shown in Fig. 2.6. The entry or initial point of this delivery life-cycle is a semantic service request. In contrast to a static service binding the semantic service request does consist of a description of what shall be achieved and not which concrete service has to be executed. The semantic service request describes the initial and goal state and consist therefore among other things out of the given data, data types, and conditions which are met by the data as well as the desired type of data and desired effects beyond. The data types, conditions and, effects are all specified in relation to a common set of concepts—the domain ontology. Referring to the book's use case scenario from Sect. 2.2.1 a semantic service request (here formulated in natural language) might be:

> Given the domain joanna.hu (initial state) check if this domain is available (goal state).

a more complex semantic service request might look like this:

> Given the domain joanna.hu and the credit card with the number 1234 5678 9999 0000, registered for Joanna, expiry date 1st of January 2010 (initial state) register the domain and charge the credit card with 19.99 €.

A detailed explanation of the formalisation, its structure, and the semantic evaluation of a semantic request is presented in Chap. 5. Whereas ontologies are discussed in Chap. 3.

Now we want to give a brief overview on the various steps and cycles shown in Fig. 2.6. The *planning sub-cycle* is the first step in processing of the semantic service request. At the beginning the semantic service provision platform tries to find a service, which perfectly matches the semantic service request. Perfectly matching means that the service is able to process the given data as input, that all preconditions for the execution of the service are fulfilled and that the service output fits to the desired type of data and effects. In case of successful matchmaking, the Planning Sub-Cycle is completed. Otherwise the platform tries to find an abstract composition of services, which is able to meet the semantic service request. Abstract composition means that the composition does not directly bind to services.

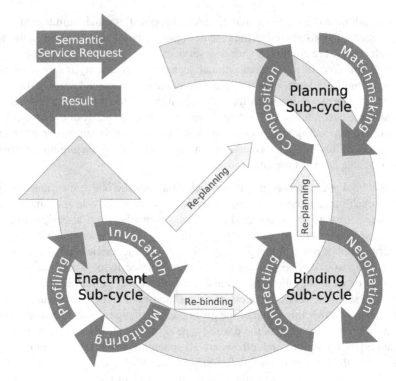

Fig. 2.6. The service delivery life-cycle

Rather the services are represented by semantic service specifications which act as place holders for the real services. This proceeding allows a late binding of services and features a better re-usability of service compositions which is useful for performance issues (e.g. by caching of compositions). The composer starts composing from the initial state of the service request. Given this state the composer searches for services, which are executable in this state. By taking their results and effects into account, the composer searches successively for executable services until either the goal state of the semantic service request is met or a further composition is not possible or reasonable. In case of successful composition or a perfect matching of an individual service, an abstract service composition representation is created and forwarded to the next sub-cycle. Otherwise the processing of the semantic service request is aborted. Details on service matchmaking are provided in Sect. 3.5 and on composition in Sect. 5.4.

Abstract service compositions are transformed into enactable service compositions by the *binding sub-cycle*. This happens by binding the semantic service specifications—which act as place holders—to concrete services. For each place holder the platform starts a negotiation on negotiable service properties with all matching services. The platform tries to find a combination of services which fit as good as possible to the desired properties of the semantic service request. It is worth mentioning that the properties of services which are discussed now are not the semantic functionality of the service like the above mentioned input, pre-conditions, output and effects of a service. Rather the properties describe qualities of the service execution like for example the duration or the costs per execution. These properties are limited insofar that they are not allowed to depend on the concrete input data. When an agreement with a particular service is achieved a digital contract it is set up and signed by both parties. Details on service binding including negotiation and contracting are presented in Sect. 5.5. Services do not necessarily need to support negotiation mechanisms. In such cases, the platform simply selects services by their given service properties without conducting a negotiation procedure.

The third step in processing of semantic service requests is the *enactment sub-cycle*. It receives enactable service compositions from the Binding Sub-Cycle and enacts them by successively or—where possible—invoking the scheduled services in parallel. The invocation of services is monitored by the platform for two reasons: On the one hand it is monitored to verify if the previously contracted peculiarities of properties are met. On the other hand the monitoring data is passed to a profiler which aggregates the data to a service-specific profile. This profile contains an aggregate of experiences made during past invocations of a service. It contains information like the average service execution time or reliability in the sense of observed probability of failure. This profile information can be used by the Planning and Agreement Sub-Cycles to avoid unreliable services. Further details on invocation, monitoring and profiling of services are introduced in Chap. 6. After successful enactment of the service composition the result is collected and it is send back to requester.

As already mentioned in the beginning of this section, service environments are quite dynamic when inter-organisational scenarios come into play. The service delivery life-cycle as shown in Fig. 2.6 on page 16 includes two mechanisms to handle the dynamics when it comes to explicitly considered or unconsidered failures of services: re-binding and re-planning. The definition of the term failure which is used here has already been presented in Sect. 2.1 and is compliant to the definition in [16].

Considered failures are well known failures which might occur during the execution of a service and are therefore explicitly specified as possible (even though not desired and therefore hopefully seldom) results of a service. One example for such an considered failure is the rejection of a credit card by a credit card charging service, which might occur if the credit card data is invalid or expired. Another example is the physical loss of a package by a package shipping service (for example by accident). Considered failures are handled in our platform by conducting *re-planning*. In case a considered failure occurs during the invocation of a service, the Planning Sub-Cycle is triggered to find a new composition. The composer tries to find a solution which takes the already achieved results into account including the specified undesired results of the failure. The new composition is required to reach the goal specified in the original semantic service request notwithstanding the occurred failure. (Refer to Sect. 5.4) Referencing the package shipping service this might mean that a new package is seized and send. Naturally not all considered failures can be handled by re-composition. In case of the credit card charging service a recovery is not possible and it is even not useful if a credit card is invalid. Someone may ask why we propose to handle considered failures by re-composition instead of simply handling them by considering them directly in the original composition as it is usual in common workflow applications. There are several reasons for using our approach:

- The limitation of the composing algorithm to an optimistic composition reduces the composition time. Optimistic composition means that all specified considered failures are ignored as possible results during the composition. This reduces the number of path through a composition and thus limits the size, complexity, and search space of a composition.
- The proceeding of optimistic composition avoids infinite loops to handle failure cascades. In the package shipping service example the recovery of the package loss failure is simply done by resending a new package. However, the resent package might get lost as well. This new failure has to be recovered once again and so on.
- The flexibility is higher when compositions are re-planned at the time of failure instead of predefining static recovery mechanisms. Referring to the package shipment example, a different shipment strategy or simply a different service of a different provider might be chosen by the Planning Sub-Cycle or the following Binding Sub-Cycle if the first or second shipment fails.

In contrast to the considered, are the *unconsidered failures* not explicitly specified for a service. Unconsidered failures are usually low-level issues like network failures which are raised before or during the invocation of a service. The platform has no detailed information about semantic effects of such failures except that these failures just happen at a given point in time. For this reason it assumes in such cases of failure, that the according service simply has not been executed and thus its desired results and effects are not achieved. Such unconsidered failures are handled in up to two phases. In the first phase the platform tries to recover the failure by re-binding. This triggers a new pass of the Binding Sub-Cycle. Here an search for an alternative equivalent service to the already invoked and failed service is conducted by negotiation with proper services. If the search is successful, the new service is invoked in substitution for the old one. Else the second phase is conducted. In this second phase the platform tries to recover the unconsidered failure by re-planning the composition in the Planning Sub-Cycle. Similar to the handling of considered failures, a search for a new solution with different services is conducted which nevertheless reaches the specified goal. In case this search is successful, the Binding Sub-Cycle is invoked. After the outstanding service place holders have been bound to concrete services the new composition is enacted in the Enactment Sub-Cycle.

As a summary of this section we should adhere, that the challenges on adaptiveness and reliability of a global and thus dynamic service environment can be met by a three-staged semantic-enabled adaptive provision of services as proposed here. The next chapter will go into more details regarding the semantic aspects of service specification and service matchmaking.

3

Ontologies and Matchmaking

Emilia Cimpian, Harald Meyer, Dumitru Roman, Adina Sirbu, Nathalie Steinmetz, Steffen Staab, and Ioan Toma

3.1 Overview and Motivation

The word ontology is used with different meanings in different communities. We distinguish between Ontology (uncountable reading and capital initial) and *an* ontology (countable reading and lower-case initial). In the first case, we refer to a philosophical discipline, namely the branch of philosophy which deals with the nature and the organisation of reality. Unlike the special sciences, each of which investigates a class of beings and their determinations, Ontology regards all the species and tries to answer the question: *What is being?*, or *What are the features common to all beings?* In the second case, we refer to an information object and engineering artefact as the most prevalent use in the computer science communities.

Ontologies are a means to formally model a specific universe of discourse. The ontology engineer analyses relevant entities and classifies them. The backbone of an ontology consists of a concept hierarchy, i.e., a taxonomy. Associations define relationships between concepts and can be instantiated accordingly. In a domain of software engineering "actor", "end user", and "use case" might be relevant concepts, where the first is the super-concept of the second. "participatesIn" may be considered a crucial association holding between actors and use cases. A concrete requester participating in a concrete use case would then be an instance of its corresponding concept.

Practically speaking, ontologies exhibit many similarities to existing conceptual modelling techniques, e.g., the Entity Relationship Model or *Unified Modeling Language (UML)*. Therefore, many best practices from these methodologies can and should be applied to ontologies and vice versa. However, ontologies also differ from these approaches in the following dimensions:

1. The primary goal of ontologies is to enable agreement on the meaning of specific vocabulary terms and, thus, to facilitate information integration across individual applications;

2. Ontologies are formalised in logic based representation languages. Their semantics are thus specified in an unambiguous way.
3. The representation languages come with executable calculi enabling querying and reasoning at run time.

While logic based representations and corresponding calculi are bread and butter for computer scientists, what is less obvious is the item of agreement. Gruber originally defined the notion of an ontology as an "explicit specification of a conceptualization" [77, 78]. This definition was later on often extended to include the sharing of the conceptualization between a group of people, e.g: "An ontology is a model of linguistic means of expression on which several actors have agreed on and which are (or can be) used by those actors." [114]

Thereby, a conceptualisation or *model* abstracts from the situations that arise in a domain of interest. It constraints the situations that may hold in this domain. For instance, in the domain of software engineering we may constrain that each instance of the concept actor must be involved in at least one use case. We may also constrain the binary relation "participatesIn" to hold only between the domain concept "actor" and the range concept "use case". The conceptualisation may also include more complex rules as well as instances. For example, we may require that "Java" and "C" are instances of the concept "programming language" and exist in the conceptualised software engineering domain.

Such a conceptualisation may be specified in any sufficiently expressive formal language. In Sect. 3.2, we will give a few examples that are widely used in the ontology community. By formally specifying such a shared conceptualisation of a domain, the vocabulary terms become accessible for precise discussion by the ontology stakeholders as well as for automatised use via formal calculi. By both means, terminological disagreements and misunderstandings may be reduced significantly, though—one must concede—not entirely.

Use of Ontologies

The usage of an ontology is of interest whenever the costs that arise through terminological disagreements and misunderstandings while not using ontologies exceed the costs for providing ontologies and formalised descriptions of situations. There are a number of characteristics of settings where use of ontologies appears promising:

1. *Important heterogeneous (and possibly imprecise) vocabularies:* When vocabularies constitute an important asset by itself, the value of formalising the domain tends to increase, too.
2. *Small to medium sized domain:* Open domains, e.g. the content of general web pages, cannot be appropriately formalised and change too often. Small and medium sized domains naturally exhibit boundaries between what should and what should not be part of a conceptualisation.
3. *Multitude of participants with overlapping interests:* In such a situation the need for agreement rises.

4. *Long-term interest in understanding of vocabulary and corresponding data:* Over a longer period of time the increased benefits of improved understanding tend to outweigh the costs of providing ontologies with corresponding data.
5. *Many and/or (rather) expensive transactions:* More frequent and/or more valuable transactions, e.g. exchange of data, naturally generate more benefit through preciseness implied by the use of an ontology.

To give a concrete example, let us illustrate these points for management of service oriented architectures.

Ontologies for the Service Lifecycle

The value proposition for ontologies used to manage the service life cycle lies in reducing errors, failures, and time-to-manage via ontologies that (i) increase agreement about core concepts in service provisioning and (ii) provide (semi-)automation of crucial service lifecycle management tasks.

Service provisioning may be conceptualised as a complex sub-domain of software and systems engineering. The issue is of utmost monetary or other value to the service lifecycle stakeholders, i.e. its service providers and service users (cf. characteristics above). Service provisioning touches upon many different aspects of the world and implements models of the world. Thereby, the core domain of services that describes services as software entities and that describes the working of and interrelationships between services is of moderate size, while the application domain of services that describes what services are about (e.g. about payment, customer relationships) may be very large—though circumscribed by the boundaries of what the software accomplishes. Hence, the different ontologies that are relevant for service modelling, i.e. (at least) one for modelling the software aspects and (at least) one for modelling application aspects remain of small to moderate size (2). At the same time each service management platform has many stakeholders (3) with long-term interests (4) that often attribute many valuable transactions (5) with the services performed on the service platform (e.g. large numbers of business transactions).

In the remainder of this chapter let us now survey possibilities for formally specifying conceptualisations of the domain of services and service application domains and illustrate their automatised exploitation by reasoning tasks such as service matchmaking.

3.2 Ontology Languages

The foundations of formal approaches for specifying domain conceptualisations, i.e. ontology languages, date back to work on (i) knowledge representation and reasoning, (ii) database management, (iii) logic programming, and (iv) object oriented programming. In the following we will elucidate work on description logics and logic programming, two paradigms with orthogonal concerns.[1]

---

[1] The reader may note that for a long time the two paradigms seemed to be incongrueable, but very recently a theoretical framework has been presented for joining them into a coherent theory [135].

3.2.1 Description Logics

The primary purpose of the knowledge representation and reasoning community was the representation of knowledge about *specific* situations and intelligent inference of consequence implied by these situations, e.g. diagnosis, theorem proving, natural language understanding or intelligent game playing. An important strand of research in this area adopted some ideas from object oriented programming. WOODS and BRACHMAN represented knowledge about situations in so-called semantic networks, which basically constituted graphs of labelled nodes for entities and labeled edges for relationships. In their most seminal work [206, 31] they asked and answered the question, *what is the formal meaning of a semantic network irrespective of the algorithm that interprets it?* BRACHMAN proposed to formalise the meaning of the previously informal graph nodes and edges. He recognised that a basic set of patterns in first order predicate logics formally captures the intuitive meaning of different links very well—in fact, he re-discovered core patterns of logical reasoning described over 2000 years before by Aristoteles (cf. [181]).

Core to this approach is the distinction of a knowledge base into a terminological box (T-Box) and an assertional box (A-Box). The terminological box captures reasoning patterns that are restricted to knowledge about the class level, i.e. which are independent from a given situation, like the following:

Given	Every *service* has at least one *hasServiceDescription*	(3.1)
Given	A *paymentFunction* has at least one *hasServiceDescription* that is a *PaymentDescription*	(3.2)

Concluded	Every *paymentFunction* is a *service*	(3.3)

In contrast, the A-Box captures reasoning patterns that concern knowledge about specific instances, i.e. knowledge about specific situations, like the following:

Given	*MyFavoritePaymentWay hasServiceDescription* "This service does this and this."	(3.4)
Given	"This service does this and this." is instance of *PaymentDescription*	(3.5)

Concluded	*MyFavoritePaymentWay* is a *paymentFunction*	(3.6)
Concluded	*MyFavoritePaymentWay* is a *service*	(3.7)

Though some patterns mix the two levels of A-Box and T-Box, e.g. the class of Italians is defined by all people that are citizens of the *specific* country *Italy*, overall this distinction is useful for many modelling purposes and corresponds closely (though not completely) to the distinction between the formalisation of a conceptualisation in the T-Box and the formalisation of a situation in the A-Box.[2]

---

[2] *Italy* might be an instance required in every conceptualisation of a specific domain of interest, e.g. about EU government.

Early research in description logics was heavily influenced by building practical systems for the above mentioned purposes. Systems like KL-One [33] or Classic [32] have been extremely influential in the 1980s. In spite of their successes, scalability and predictability of these systems was low. Predictability was low, because these systems would come with incomplete reasoning procedures[3] that would return with unexpected results or would not stop at all when reasoning, even when the size of the knowledge base was limited up to a few hundred concepts (cf. [83]).

These two drawbacks were tackled by two lines of research. First, people investigated the formal properties of the description logics languages. Each description logics language is defined by the exact set of logical patterns it includes. It was found that some simple reasoning patterns turn out an undecidable description logics language [173], while other useful combinations yield *decidable* fragments of first-order predicate logics. Second, Horrocks [91] exploited progress made in the field of theorem proving (more specifically in tableaux reasoning) for an expressive description logics in order to scale sound and complete reasoning in description logics by two orders of magnitude. Thereby, the decidability of the language proved to be crucial in order to find and exploit optimisation procedures for the common reasoning problems in description logics that would be intractable in the worst case even for small problems—but that hardly ever turn out to come even close to the worst case.

Standardisation Efforts

Web Ontology Language (OWL) [209] is a Web Ontology Language, and defines Web vocabularies, the meaning of terms in the vocabularies and the relationships among these terms. Different from the languages (e.g. HTML), which are designed for presenting Web contents to humans, the goal of OWL is to enable the Web for machines and allow the automated processing and integration of data from the Web. The OWL syntax supports such processing and integration, as it distinguishes the core aspects of a conceptual model, i.e. its classes, associations and objects, in a Web compatible model, i.e. with the help of globally unique and (often) de-referencable identifiers, the *Unified Resource Identifier (URI)*'s or unique resource identifiers. For this purpose of syntax, much of the preceding Web knowledge representation language RDF [210] has been reused. The OWL semantics is mostly inherited from work in description logics. Reasoning engines that realise OWL semantics may perform useful reasoning tasks on (Web) data. For example, OWL provides vocabulary for describing properties and classes, including relations between classes, characteristics of properties, rich typing of properties, enumerated classes, equality and cardinality. OWL consists of three increasingly expressive sub-languages:

1. *Web Ontology Language Lite (OWL Lite)* primarily provides a classification hierarchy and simple constraints. For instance, OWL Lite supports cardinality constraints, but it only allows cardinality values of 0 or 1. OWL Lite is less expressive but has a lower complexity, thus it is simpler to provide reasoning support

---

[3] Some of which turned out to be faulty, once their theoretical properties were better understood.

for OWL than *Web Ontology Language with description logics (OWL DL)* and *Full Web Ontology Language (OWL Full)*.

2. OWL DL (DL stands for description logics) provides maximum expressiveness and supports computational completeness (all conclusions are guaranteed to be computable), and decidability (all computations will be finished in finite time) of a reasoning system, but has a higher worst-case complexity than OWL Lite. OWL DL includes all OWL language constructs with certain restriction, e.g. the restriction of type separation: a class can neither be an individual nor be a property, and a property can neither be an individual nor be class. OWL DL has been developed to draw on the rich experience of research in description logics and to provide maximum expressiveness while remaining a decidable language. Current efforts towards OWL 1.1 will push the envelope a bit in order to accommodate most recent findings, but OWL 1.1 will still remain close to OWL DL and decidable.

3. OWL Full supports maximum expressiveness and the syntactic freedom of *Resource Description Framework (RDF)*, but without computational guarantees. As an example, in OWL Full a class can be considered as a collection of individuals and simply as an individual at same time. OWL Full allows an ontology to augment the meaning of the pre-defined vocabulary. Because of such freedom OWL Full allows for formulating logical theories that are undecideable. Therefore it is impossible to support sound and complete reasoning for OWL Full.

The following rules describe the relations among three sub-languages, with respect to the soundness of expression and validity of conclusion:

- Each sound OWL Lite ontology is a sound OWL DL ontology.
- Each sound OWL DL ontology is a sound OWL Full ontology.
- Each valid OWL Lite conclusion is a valid OWL DL conclusion.
- Each valid OWL DL conclusion is a valid OWL Full conclusion.
- Each conclusion reached in OWL DL about an OWL Lite ontology is also reached with an OWL Lite reasoner.

However, the last sentences does not apply analogously for OWL DL and OWL Full, i.e. there are ontologies formulated in OWL DL which lead to sound conclusions in OWL Full that could not be reached with an OWL DL reasoner.

3.2.2 Logic Programming

Research and practice in database management is motivated by efficient, yet powerful access to a consistent, non-redundant database. With the adoption of the relational algebra (cf. [47]) as a means to store and access data, the previous approach to data management by implicitly imperative, hierarchical navigation turned into a declarative approach that described what data were to be accessed. The relational algebra approach requires the provisioning of a relational schema that describes which *types* of data may *be instantiated* in which places. Chen [43] developed the Entity-Relationship model that would allow the user to capture a conceptualisation of the

Table 3.1. Extensional definitions of two example database relations

Service		
ID	Name	Location ID
s1	myFavoritePaymentWay	l1
s2	MumsFavoritePaymentWay	l2

Deploy	
Location ID	Location
l1	HPI, Potsdam
l2	Transit, Illmenau

domain and that could be translated—with some loss of information—into a relational schema.

When investigating the properties of the relational algebra researchers like H. Gallaire soon recognised that the relational algebra was close to using a first-order predicate logics (PL1) formula as a query to a set of extensionally defined predicates. For instance, the two queries 3.8 and 3.9 executed on the example relations from Table 3.1 are equivalent; the two queries 3.9 and 3.10 just constitute denotational variants:

$$\text{Relational Algebra:} \qquad \pi_{Name, LocID}\text{Svc} \bowtie \text{Deploy} \tag{3.8}$$

$$\text{PL1 Formula:} \qquad \exists x, y\ \text{Svc}(x, Name, y) \land \text{Deploy}(y, Loc)) \tag{3.9}$$

$$\text{Prolog Query:} \quad : -\text{Svc}(\_1, Name, \_2), \text{Deploy}(\_2, Loc) \tag{3.10}$$

$$\text{Prolog Rule: RunsAt}(N, L)\text{:-Svc}(\_1, N, \_2), \text{Deploy}(\_2, L) \tag{3.11}$$

The generalisation of this approach includes intensional Horn rules in addition to the first-order query formula, such as also used in Prolog. Initially, the logic programming community investigated the optimised computation of Prolog by inclusion of procedural aspects. The database management community and—for a long time now—the logic programming community have been more interested in set processing of facts, i.e. in deriving *all* facts to which a query would apply when considering the extensionally defined relations and the intensional Prolog-like rules.

This approach came with particular problems when treating negation in Prolog rules. Prolog uses the strategy of negation-by-failure, i.e. when a part of the premise of a rule is negated, Prolog (i) requires that all variables in the negated part of the premise be fully instantiated and (ii) that such an atomic and ground fact can either be proven—then its negation is false—or it can not be proven, then its negation is assumed to hold. While this assumption may not hold in general, this does not pose a problem for the rule modeller when he is aware of the assumption and it is useful under many circumstances, e.g. when one may assume that one's database of services is complete. This strategy, however, poses a problem for set-oriented processing with recursion and negation in rules. Several specific semantic models and strategies have been proposed to deal with this model, among which stratification

[121], stable model semantics [70] and well-founded semantics [199] are the most popular ones.

Finally, the need for object oriented modelling primitives has been recognized in these communities. One important result, F-Logic [104], which is presented below in more details, was the development of syntactic extensions on top of logic programming approaches in order to capture the relationship between classes and/or relationships in a more intuitive manner.

As a result, the formal specification of a conceptualisation was made possible by the definition of classes, relationships and intensional Prolog-like rules (e.g., (3.11)). The specification of situations was found in the extensional definition of relations, such as depicted in Table 3.1.

Standardisation of Rule Languages

W3C recently started an initiative to provide a standard for rules on the Web. The *Rule Interchange Format (RIF)* Working Group[4] was formed at the end of 2005, with the aim to produce a core rule language plus extensions which together allow rules to be translated between rule languages and thus transferred between rule systems. As of August 2007, the group has published two drafts:

- *RIF Use Cases and Requirements*[5]: it presents a set of use cases that are representative of the types of application scenarios that the RIF is intended to support.
- *RIF Core Design*[6]: it develops the core of RIF through a set of foundational concepts shared by all RIF dialects; the overall RIF design takes the form of a layered architecture organised around the notion of a *dialect* (i.e. a rule language with a well-defined syntax and semantics). As currently defined, RIF Core corresponds to the language of definite Horn rules with equality. Syntactically, however, RIF Core has a number of extensions to support features such as objects and frames, URIs as identifiers for concepts, and XML Schema data types.

Although the RIF specification is far from being finalised, RIF Core already provides an interoperability basis for future core RIF dialects, which are expected to cover a number of important paradigms in rule based specification and programming, such as production rules, logic programming, FOL based rules, reactive rules, and normative rules (integrity constraints).

3.2.3 Combining Description Logics and Logic Programming

When comparing the two paradigms of description logics and frame logics, one may recognise that the two paradigms share a number of characteristics:

- They both allow for the specification of a conceptualisation and a situation.
- They both support some kind of rules.

---

[4] http://www.w3.org/2005/rules.

[5] http://www.w3.org/TR/rif-ucr.

[6] http://www.w3.org/TR/rif-core.

Table 3.2. Comparing OWL-DL and F-Logic

Characteristic	Common Description Logics (OWL-DL)	Common Logic Programming Approach
Computational Complexity	Decidable	Undecidable
Expressiveness	PL1 formulas restricted to two variables	Turing Powerful
Reasoning	Terminology driven	Data driven
Semantics	More natural PL1 semantics	Fixed-point semantics
Overall Strength and Focus	T-Box reasoning	A-Box reasoning

- They both (can) adopt some frame-like structures as found in object oriented modelling and programming.
- They both allow for querying the (combined) formalisation.

However, they also exhibit significant differences as can be seen in Table 3.2.

Ontology Language Paradigms

F-Logic [105] is a formalism that combines two successful approaches for modelling and manipulating data: deductive databases and object oriented approaches. It adopts the declarative semantics of deductive databases and adds the rich modelling support offered by object oriented approaches. F-Logic has a model theoretic semantics and a sound and complete proof theory. By analogy with predicate calculus, F-Logic stands in the same relation with to the object oriented paradigms as predicate calculus stands to relational programming. There are two flavours of F-Logic: (1) *a first-order flavour and* (2) *a logic programming flavour.* The first-order flavour is a syntactic materialisation of the classical first-order logic. The logic programming flavour is a subset of the previous flavour but as in other logic programming languages adopts negation-as-failure or other non-classical strategies for negation, such as fixed-point semantics.

In the rest of this section we are going to give an overview of the main constructs in F-Logic and furthermore we are going to exemplify them using the book's use case scenario.

- *Objects* are fundamental constructs in F-Logic. They are the representation of real word entities being identified by object identifiers (OIDs). F-Logic uses first-order variable-free terms to represent object identity. For the example scenario, real entities that can be modelled as objects in F-Logic are Joanna or credit-CardOwner(JoannaCreditCard1). Objects usually have attributes. For example:
Joanna[firstName -> "Joanna", lastName -> "Solyom"].

Following the principles of object oriented approaches objects IDs are not visible to users. Objects are referenced by their names not by their OIDs. In F-Logic, one object may also have multiple values for one of its attributes.[7] For example:
```
Joanna[hasCreditCard -> {JoannaCreditCard1, JoannaCreditCard2}].
```

- *Variables* are a fundamental concept in F-Logic. Every alphanumeric set of characters prefixed by ? is consider a variable. For example in the following expression, that might be part of a query, the firstName and lastName attributes are not bound. This is expressed by using the variables ?X and ?Y:
```
Joanna[firstName -> ?X, lastName -> ?Y].
```

- atoms in F-Logic are expressions of the form object[attribute -> value]. For example:
```
Joanna[firstName -> "Joanna"]. and Joanna[lastName -> "Solyom"].
```

- molecules are used to express in a more condensed way the information from different atoms. For example the information expressed before can be written in a single molecule:
```
Joanna[firstName -> "Joanna", lastName -> "Solyom"].
```

- *Methods* are also allowed in F-Logic. They are functions that take arguments and return values. For example the following expression
```
Joanna[creditBalance(JoannaCreditCard1) -> 1000].
```
says that Joanna has a method creditBalance, which for the argument JoannaCreditCard1 has the value 1000. Methods can also return set values.

- *Classes* are introduced by class signatures. For example:
```
person[firstName => string, lastName => string].
```
Please notice that the symbol => is used instead of ->, the symbol used to indicate the value of an attribute in an object. The *class membership* relation is introduced by ':'. For example: Joanna:person. , while the subclass relation is introduced by '::'. For example: male::person.

WSML

The *Web Services Modeling Language (WSML)*[8] [54] is a language for the specification of different aspects of Semantic Web services. It provides a formal language for the *Web Services Modeling Ontology (WSMO)* [163] which is based on well-known logical formalisms, specifying one unifying language framework for the semantic description of Web services, starting from the intersection of Datalog and the Description Logic $\mathcal{SHIQ}$. This core language is extended in the directions of Description Logics and Logic Programming in a principled manner with strict layering.

WSML is a Web language. Therefore it makes use of *Internationalized Resource Identifier (IRI)* as identifiers. WSML defines XML and RDF serialisations for interoperation. WSML distinguishes between conceptual and logical modelling in order to support users who are not familiar with formal logic, while not restricting the expressive power of the language for the expert user.

---

[7] Minor syntactic variances have been used for F-Logic use over the years.
[8] http://www.wsmo.org/wsml.

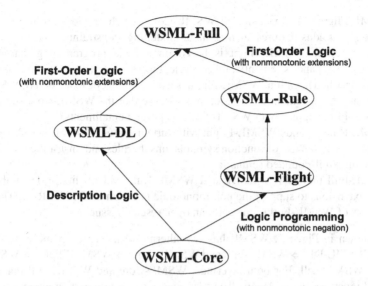

Fig. 3.1. The WSML language variants

WSMO [163] provides a conceptual model for the description of various aspects of services towards such *Semantic Web Services (SWS)*. In particular, as we shall see in the sections below, WSMO distinguishes four top-level elements: Ontologies, Goals, Web services, and Mediators. The WSML takes into account all aspects of Web service descriptions identified by WSMO.

A concrete goal in the development of WSML is to investigate the usage of different formalisms, most notably description logic and logic programming in the context of ontologies and Web services. Three main areas can benefit from the use of formal methods in service descriptions: *Ontology description, Declarative functional description of Goals and Web services*, and *Description of dynamics*.

WSML defines a syntax and semantics for ontology descriptions. The underlying formalisms which were mentioned earlier are used to give a formal meaning to ontology descriptions in WSML. Figure 3.1 shows the variants of WSML. These variants differ in logical expressiveness and in the underlying language paradigms and allow users to make the trade-off between provided expressiveness and the implied complexity for ontology modelling on a per-application basis.

- WSML-Core is based on by the intersection of the Description Logic $\mathcal{SHIQ}$ and Horn Logic, based on Description Logic Programs [75]. It has the least expressive power of all the WSML variants. The main features of the language are concepts, attributes, binary relations and instances, as well as concept and relation hierarchies and support for data types. with respect to OWL, WSML-Core can be seen as a semantic subset of OWL Lite.
- WSML-DL captures the Description Logic $\mathcal{SHIQ}(\mathbf{D})$, which is a major part of the (DL species of) OWL [21] (OWL DL).

- WSML-Flight is an extension of WSML-Core, which provides a powerful rule language. It adds features such as meta-modelling, constraints, and non-monotonic negation. WSML-Flight is based on a logic programming variant of F-Logic [105] and is semantically equivalent to Datalog with inequality and (locally) stratified negation. WSML-Flight is a direct syntactic extension of WSML-Core and it is a semantic extension in the sense that the WSML-Core subset of WSML-Flight agrees with WSML-Core on ground entailments).
- WSML-Rule extends WSML-Flight with further features from Logic Programming, namely the use of function symbols, unsafe rules and unstratified negation under the Well-Founded semantics.
- WSML-Full unifies WSML-DL and WSML-Rule under a first-order umbrella with extensions to support the non-monotonic negation of WSML-Rule. The semantics of WSML-Full is currently an open research issue.

As shown in Fig. 3.1, WSML has two alternative layerings, namely, WSML-Core ⇒ WSML-DL ⇒ WSML-Full and WSML-Core ⇒ WSML-Flight ⇒ WSML-Rule ⇒ WSML-Full. For both layerings, WSML-Core and WSML-Full mark the least and most expressive layers. The two layerings are to a certain extent disjoint in the sense that inter-operation in WSML between the Description Logic variant (WSML-DL) on the one hand and the Logic Programming variants (WSML-Flight and WSML-Rule) on the other, is only possible through a common core (WSML-Core) or through a very expressive superset (WSML-Full).

WSML is an ontology language which distinguishes itself from other ontology languages (i.e. RDFS and OWL) in the following aspects. WSML is an extension of a significant part of RDFS through the possibility of specifying local attributes, range and cardinality constraints for attributes and attribute features such as symmetry, transitivity and reflexivity. Moreover, WSML (in its rule based variants) provides an expressive rule language which can be used for the manipulation of RDF data. With WSML one can capture both Description Logics and Logic Programming paradigms in one coherent framework. For a complete description of the language, we refer the reader to [54].

3.3 Domain Ontologies

3.3.1 Tools and Approaches for Creation and Maintenance

As any other new technology, ontologies need tool support in order to proceed from a research innovation to a wide spread knowledge representation. Numerous approaches in modelling and representing ontologies have emerged during the last years, from the very simple syntax highlighting to the newly proposed multidimensional visualisation tools. Simultaneously, several tools have been built to allow easy creation, visualisation and manipulation of ontologies.

In this section, we describe the general ontology creation approach and some of the most well-known ontology modelling and visualisation tools. As we are interested in this book, in the domain of Web services, we will focus on tools that allow the modelling and visualisation of ontologies like OWL and WSMO.

Ontology Engineering Mechanisms

Several methodologies for ontology engineering have been elaborated during the last decades. [29] conducted a study based on more then 20 such methodologies, concluding that the majority of them propose 6 steps for ontology creation and maintenance, as follows:

1. Domain/Requirements analysis;
2. Conceptualisation;
3. Implementation;
4. Evaluation;
5. Population;
6. Evolution and maintenance.

The first phase, domain analysis, consists of the detailed analysis of the domain that is going to be modelled, having as result a clear understanding of those aspect of the domain that are going to be represented in the ontology and a set of requirements. This step also includes knowledge acquisition in terms of re-usage of existing ontological sources or performing ontology learning operations. The second step, conceptualisation, consist of the definition of the concepts, relations and instances that are going to be used in representing the domain; the result is the corresponding conceptual model. The *implementation* phase consists of representing the conceptual model in an ontology representation language with the adequate expressiveness. The forth phase consists of the *evaluation* of this initial ontology against the previously identified requirements. The evaluation may trigger modifications of the conceptual model, and as a consequence of the implementation as well. The population phase deals with the alignment of concrete application data to the implemented ontology. Further modifications or even complex re-engineering tasks are performed in the last phase, *evolution and maintenance*.

Protégé-OWL Editor

Protégé [71] is an ontology engineering environment that can be extended to support different ontology formats. The Protégé-OWL editor is an extension of Protégé[9] that supports the Web Ontology Language. Some of the editor's functionalities are:

- Load and save OWL and RDF ontologies.
- Edit and visualise classes, properties and *Semantic Web Rule Language (SWRL)* rules.
- Define logical class characteristics as OWL expressions.

---

[9] http://protege.stanford.edu.

- Execute reasoners such as description logic classifiers.
- Edit OWL individuals for Semantic Web markup.

Being a Protégé plug-in, the Protégé-OWL editor can also benefit from the generic services provided by the core platform, such as an event mechanism or undo capabilities [110]; another advantage is that the already existing plug-ins can be used for OWL (either directly or updated with very little effort). The Protégé-OWL plug-in has, in its turn, several ontology visualisation extensions, like OWLViz, TGVizTab [9] and Jambalaya [184], that allow different visualisation of the ontologies (like graph-structures or graphical representations).

WSMT

Web Service Modeling Toolkit (WSMT)[10] is a modelling environment for the WSMO, offering support for modelling ontologies, goals, Semantic Web services, and mediators.

Currently WSMT contains the WSMO Ontology Editor/Visualizer plug-in, the Ontology Mapping plug-in, and the Monitoring plug-in. WSMT relies on WSMO API and uses WSMO4j as its reference implementation. The Ontology Editor and Visualizer is a tool for creating, publishing, and visualising WSMO elements; additionally it offers an embedded reasoner and an interface for querying the WSMO descriptions under development. The Ontology Mapping tool provides semi-automatic mechanisms for creating alignments between heterogeneous ontologies [132]. Such alignments can be stored and later used for run-time mediation requests inside *Web Service Modeling Execution Environment (WSMX)*. Finally, the Monitoring tool is used in monitoring both the WSMX itself (together with its components) and the execution of the Semantic Web services through WSMX. Another tool for modelling WSMO ontologies is WSMO Studio,[11] which provides similar functionalities.

3.3.2 A Domain Ontology Example

This section presents an example ontology for the domain of Internet Service Providers (ISPs), described in the book's use case scenario. The main purpose of a domain ontology is to capture the concepts, relations, instances, and axioms of the chosen domain. Our aim in this section is to provide at the same time an overview of the ontology, and concrete examples of how each of the ontology elements can be modelled.

For exemplification we have chosen the WSML, and from the five variants presented in Sect. 3.2, the WSML-DL variant has been selected. The main advantage of using WSML-DL is the decidability and the possibility to perform complex reasoning tasks that are not supported or very costly in case of a rule based language.

Every WSML specification should start with the `wsmlVariant` keyword, followed by an identifier for the WSML variant. For WSML-DL this is:

[10] http://sourceforge.net/projects/wsmt.
[11] http://www.wsmostudio.org/.

http://www.wsmo.org/wsml/wsml-syntax/wsml-dl

The specification of the WSML variant is optional, but recommended, as it facilitates the work of tools (which can recognise the intention of the author and react to it).

Next comes an optional block for namespace references, preceded by the keyword namespace. Each namespace reference, except the default namespace, consists of a namespace prefix and the IRI which identifies the namespace. The default namespace does not contain a namespace prefix.

An ontology declaration starts with the keyword ontology optionally followed by an identifier. If no identifier is specified, the locator of the ontology serves as identifier. As for almost any WSMO element, a set of non-functional properties can be specified, providing information that does not affect the functionality or the element, like title, description, language etc. The majority of the recommended non-functional properties are properties defined in the Dublin Core Metadata Element Set.[12] Importing other ontologies or use of mediators are also part of the header.

Listing 3.1 is an example prologue of a WSML-DL ontology. This ontology is called "dsc4isp", since it defines the necessary terminology for describing dynamic supply chains for Internet service providers like in the use case scenario. The full source code of the ontology can be downloaded at:

http://kuropka.net/ssp-book/dsc4isp.wsml

An WSML ontology specification may contain concepts, relations, instances, relation instances and axioms:

Concepts

Concepts are defined by their subsumption hierarchy and their attributes, including range specification. The range of the attributes can be a datatype or another concept. There are two kinds of attribute definitions: constraining definitions, using the

Listing 3.1. An example ontology header

```
wsmlVariant "http://www.wsmo.org/wsml/wsml-syntax/wsml-dl"
namespace {"http://www.example.org/ontology#",
    dc _"http://purl.org/dc/elements/1.1#",
    wsml _"http://www.wsmo.org/wsml/wsml-syntax#"}

ontology dsc4isp
  nonFunctionalProperties
    dc#title hasValue "ISP Domain Ontology"
    dc#description hasValue "An ontology for describing
        knowledge related to Internet service providers"
    dc#format hasValue "text/x-wsml"
    dc#language hasValue "en-us"
  endNonFunctionalProperties
```

[12] http://dublincore.org/documents/dces/.

Listing 3.2. A concept example

```
concept contact
concept domainName
  name ofType _string
  tld impliesType TLD
  isRegisteredTo impliesType contact
```

keyword ofType and inferring definitions using the keyword impliesType. In the first case, the values of the attribute are constrained to having the mentioned type, while in the latter, the values of the attribute are inferred to have the mentioned type.

In the case of WSML-DL, the constraining definitions may only be used for data type ranges. This means that attribute definitions of the form A ofType D are only allowed if D is a data type identifier. Listing 3.2 is an example of a concept definition valid in WSML-DL.

The concept hierarchy of our ontology example is presented in Fig. 3.2. All the figures representing different aspects of the domain ontology are snapshots taken using the WSML Visualizer, a graph based ontology editing and visualising solution for WSMO. The WSML Visualizer belongs to the Web Services Modeling Toolkit, introduced in Sect. 3.3.1.

The concepts presented in the figure can be grouped into three categories: concepts related to persons, to domains, and to payment operations.

1. The concepts related to persons are: *person, phone, fax, address,* and *contact*. A contact specifies the contact information for a person, and this information refers to the person's phone, fax, address, but also other data, like e-mail or organisation.
2. The basic concepts related to domains are: *domainName, TLD* (representing the top-level domain extension of a domainName), *domainState* and *nameServer* (with the corresponding *nameServers*, defined as a list of name servers). The *genericTLD* is a sub-concept of TLD, and represents those TLDs used by a particular class of organizations (for example, .com for commercial organisations). Further on, the *verisignTLD* is defined as a genericTLD operated by VeriSign Global Registry Services (.com, .net). The *countryCodeTLD* is a two letters long TLD used by a country or a dependent territory, for example .at for Austria. Correspondingly, we have defined the *genericDomainName* (a domain with a genericTLD) and the *ccDomainName* (a domain with a countryCodeTLD) as subconcepts of the domainName.
3. With respect to payment, the basic concepts are *paymentData, paymentTransactionData* (a handle to the paymentData, containing also its *validity*), *invoiceNumber, amountOfMoney*. A *creditCard* is defined as a subconcept of paymentData, having the type specified by a *creditCardType*. Two subconcepts to paymentTransactionData are defined: *payPalTransactionId* and *saferpayTransactionHandle*. The *saferpayTransactionInformation* extends the handle with information relative to the transaction, for example: an authorisation code, a time stamp, the state of the payment (having the type *paymentState*) etc.

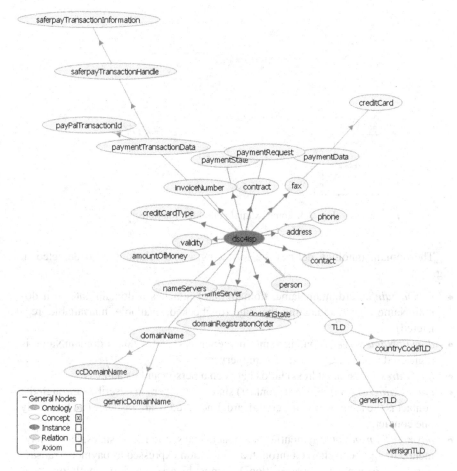

Fig. 3.2. A concept hierarchy

Listing 3.3. A relation example

```
relation hasDomainState(impliesType domainName,
         impliesType domainState)
```

Relations

A relation definition starts with the keyword `relation`, followed by an identifier. A relation can be defined as `subRelationOf` another relation. The usage of `impliesType` and `ofType` for parameter type definitions corresponds to the usage in attribute definitions. In WSML-DL relations are binary, and the parameters are strictly ordered. Also, the `ofType` keyword is only allowed in combination with a datatype and only the second parameter may have a datatype at its range. Listing 3.3 is an example of a relation valid in WSML-DL.

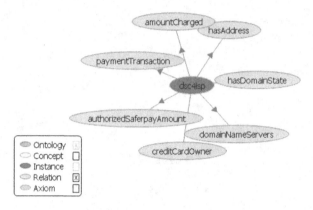

Fig. 3.3. Some example ontology relations

The domain ontology defines the following set of relations, also depicted in Fig. 3.3:

- *hasDomainState*(domainName, domainState) attaches a domainState to a domainName object, indicating the state (unchecked, available, unavailable, registered).
- *domainNameServers*(domainName, nameServers) states that a domainName is registered with the given list of nameServers.
- *hasAddress*(person, address) holds between a person and its address.
- *creditCardOwner*(creditCard, contact) states that a person described through the contact is the legal owner of a creditCard. Each creditCard instance can have only one contact.
- *paymentTransaction*(paymentData, paymentTransactionData) states that the paymentData has been charged through a transaction expressed as paymentTransactionData. Each paymentTransactionData must be associated to exactly one paymentData. However, one paymentData (i.e. a credit card) can relate to more than one paymentTransactionData in a sense that it has been used for different payments.
- *amountCharged*(amountOfMoney, paymentTransactionData) states that the handle expressed as paymentTransactionData has charged a certain amount of money.
- *authorizedSaferpayAmount*(saferpayTransactionHandle, amountOfMoney) the relation is specifically designed for Saferpay atomic services. Since the services provided by Saferpay split the payment process into authorization and actual payment, the payment must know the amount of money a previous authorisation has allowed.

Instances

A concept may have an arbitrary number of instances associated to it. Instances can either be explicitly defined in an ontology or they can exist outside the ontology in a private database. An instance starts with the `instance` keyword, followed by an

Listing 3.4. An instance example

```
instance JohnDoe memberOf person
  firstName hasValue "John"
  lastName hasValue "Doe"
```

Listing 3.5. An example of a relation instance

```
relationInstance hasDomainState(fooDomain, registeredState)
```

identifier, the `memberOf` keyword and the name of the concept to which the instance belongs (all these definitions being optional). The instance definition can be followed by the attribute values associated with the instance. Listing 3.4 is an example of an instance declaration.

Besides specifying instances of concepts, it is also possible to specify instances of relations. Such a relation instance definition starts with the `relationInstance` keyword, followed by an identifier, the `memberOf` keyword and the name of the relation to which the relation instance belongs. This definition is followed by the values of the parameters associated with the relation instance. Listing 3.5 is an example of an relation instance declaration.

The example ontology contains a limited set of instances. They have been provided for every concept having a finite set of extensions, where by extension we understand every object that falls under the definition of the concept. This has been the case for the following concepts:

- *domainState*, with four possible instances: uncheckedState, availableState, unavailableState, registeredState
- *validity*, having only three instances: valid, invalid, unknown
- *paymentState*, with possible instances: completedState, abortedState, and unknownState
- *creditCardType*, with the instances: VisaType, MCType, AmexType, DiscoverType, JCBType, DinersType

Axioms

An axiom definition starts with the keyword `axiom`, followed by (optionally) an identifier, the `definedBy` keyword and a logical expression. Such axioms can be used to refine the definitions already given in the conceptual syntax, e.g. the subconcept and attribute definitions of concepts.

Our ontology defines several axioms describing equivalence or disjointedness of concepts. The WSML-DL axiom in Listing 3.6 states that a generic domain is equivalent to a domain with a generic Top-Level Domain extension.

Listing 3.6. An axiom example

```
axiom GenericDomainNameDef
  definedBy
    ?domain memberOf genericDomainName equivalent
      ?domain memberOf domainName
      and exists ?tld (?domain[tld hasValue ?tld]
        and ?tld memberOf genericTLD).
```

3.4 Service Ontologies

Domain ontologies serve the purpose of defining how a domain is formalised and what situations are hold regarding the content that is to be communicated in a network of Web services. However, such domain ontologies are not sufficient in order to characterise what a service does, how it proceeds or what its implications are.

If we consider the definition of a Web service, we will find that there are several issues we want to know about a Web service before we may consider it to be appropriate for a particular task. We want to know about technical issues, e.g. its way of communication (e.g. HTTP), but we also want to know about the linkage between technical issues and domain issues, e.g. how to communicate a specific domain request in the protocol (e.g. via a particularly defined interface providing parameters for my domain need specifications), and we want to know about further implications that the Web service may have, e.g. on my checking account or on the time I have to wait until I get the desired result.

Handling these issues in a fully integrated framework is not possible if the semantics of these technical and domain-specific functional and non-functional requirements is not specified in a common model. Ontologies for Web services appear here as a natural solution in order to capture domain and technical needs together.

In the following sections, we will illustrate and substantiate this idea by the example of WSMO, a concrete ontology for describing services in a fully integrated framework that is tied together with exchangeable domain ontologies.

3.4.1 WSMO as Example for Service Ontologies

WSMO [163] provides ontological specifications for the core elements of SWS. In fact, SWS aim at an integrated technology for the next generation of the Web by combining Semantic Web technologies and Web services, thereby turning the Internet from an information repository for human consumption into a world-wide system for distributed Web computing. Therefore, appropriate frameworks for SWS need to integrate the basic Web design principles, those defined for the Semantic Web, as well as design principles for distributed, service oriented computing of the Web. WSMO is therefore based on the following design principles:

- *Web Compliance*: WSMO inherits the concept of URI for unique identification of resources, it adopts the concept of namespaces, supports XML and other W3C Web technology recommendations.
- *Ontology-based*: Ontologies—a widely accepted state-of-the-art representation of knowledge—are used as the data model throughout WSMO.
- *Strict Decoupling*: WSMO resources are defined in isolation, each resource is specified independently without regard to possible usage or interactions with other resources).
- *Centrality of Mediation*: It addresses the handling of heterogeneities that naturally arise in open environments; it can occur in terms of data, underlying ontology, protocol or process.
- *Ontological Role Separation*: The underlying epistemology of WSMO differentiates between the desires of users or clients and available services.
- *Description versus Implementation*: WSMO differentiates between the descriptions of SWS elements (description) and executable technologies (implementation).
- *Execution Semantics*: In order to verify the WSMO specification, the formal execution semantics of reference implementations like WSMX as well as other WSMO-enabled systems provide the technical realisation of WSMO.
- *Service versus Web service*: A Web service is a computational entity which is able (by invocation) to achieve a users goal, and a service in contrast is the actual value provided by this invocation; WSMO is designed as a means to describe the former and not to replace the functionality of the latter, i.e. WSMO provides means to describe Web services that provide access to services.

The following text briefly outlines the conceptual model of WSMO. The elements of the WSMO ontology are defined in a meta-meta-model language based on the Meta Object Facility (MOF).[13] In order to allow complete item descriptions, every WSMO element is described by non-functional properties. These are based on the Dublin Core (DC) Metadata Set [203] for generic information item descriptions, and other service-specific properties related to the quality of service.[14]

Ontologies

Ontologies provide the formal semantics for the terminology used within all other WSMO components. A set of non-functional properties are available for characterising ontologies; they usually include the DC Metadata elements. *Imported ontologies* allow a modular approach for ontology design and can be used as long as no conflicts need to be resolved between the ontologies. When importing ontologies in realistic scenarios, some steps for aligning, merging and transforming imported ontologies in order to resolve ontology mismatches are needed. For this reason ontology mediators are used (ooMediators). Concepts constitute the basic elements of the agreed

---

[13] http://www.omg.org/technology/documents/formal/mof.htm.
[14] For a detailed description of all the elements defined in WSMO, we refer the reader to [164].

terminology for some problem domain. Relations are used in order to model inter-dependencies between several concepts (respectively instances of these concepts); *functions* are special relations, with a unary range and a *n*-ary domain (parameters inherited from relation), where the range value is functionally dependent on the domain values, and *instances* are either defined explicitly or by a link to an instance store, i.e., an external storage of instances and their values.

Web Services

WSMO provides service descriptions for describing services that are requested by service requesters, provided by service providers, and agreed between service providers and requesters. Within the service class the non-functional properties and *imported ontologies* attributes play a role that is similar to that found in the ontology class, with the addition of an extensible set of Web service-specific non-functional properties. An extra type of mediator to deal with protocol and process related mismatches between Web services is also included.

The final two attributes define the two core WSMO notions for semantically describing Web services: a capability which is a functional description of a Web Service, describing constraints on the input and output of a service through the notions of preconditions, assumptions, postconditions, and effects; and *Web service interfaces* which specify how the service behaves in order to achieve its functionality. A service interface consists of a choreography which describes the interface for the client-service interaction required for service consumption, and an orchestration which describes how the functionality of a Web Service is achieved by aggregating other Web services.

Goals

A goal specifies the objectives that a client may have when consulting a Web Service, describing aspects related to user desires with respect to the requested functionality and behaviour. Ontologies are used as the semantically defined terminology for goal specification. Goals model the user view in the Web service usage process and therefore are a separate top level entity in WSMO. The *requested capability* in the definition of a goal represents the functionality of the services the user would like to have, and the *requested interface* represents the interface of the service the user would like to have and interact with.

Mediators

The concept of mediation in WSMO addresses the handling of heterogeneities occurring between elements that shall interoperate by resolving mismatches between different used terminologies (data level), on communicative behaviour between services (protocol level), and on the business process level. A WSMO Mediator connects elements and provides mediation facilities for resolving mismatches. The description elements of a WSMO Mediator are its source and target elements, and the mediation service for resolving mismatches. WSMO defines different types of mediators for connecting the distinct WSMO elements: *OO Mediators* connect and mediate heterogeneous ontologies, *GG Mediators* connect Goals, *WG Mediators* link Web services to Goals, and *WW Mediators* connects interoperating Web services resolving mismatches between them.

An Example of a Semantic Service Specification

This section provides a concrete specification of one of the services in the book's use case scenario, namely the `Paypal Direct Payment` service. The above mentioned scenario involves a set of services: (1) *domain checking services* which verify if a certain domain is available for registration, (2) *domain registration services* which can register a given domain, (3) *credit card authorisation service*, which verify and authorise credit card payments (4) *payment services* which provide payment functionalities and finally (5) *update name servers services* which are responsible for updating the name servers with name-IP mappings for the newly paid and registered service.

The `Paypal Direct Payment` service, which is used in this section to exemplify the semantic services modelling approach is a *payment service*. In an informal way its functionality can be described as follows. The service processes a credit card payment immediately, without any authorisation. It requires that all input parameters are given, including the users' IP address for tracing credit card fraud.

As described in Sect. 3.4.1, WSMO distinguishes between three aspects in a service description namely: *functional* (i.e. capability)—what the service can do, *non-functional* (i.e. non-functional properties)—annotations and quality of service aspects and *behavioural* (i.e. interface)—how the functionality of the service can be achieved in terms of interaction with the service (choreography) and as well in terms of functionality required from the other Web services (orchestration). This section exemplifies the first two aspects of a WSMO service description. The functional (capability) specifications are provided using both WSML-Flight and WSML-DL, with the purpose of underlining the differences in modelling for the two language variants.

The general rules for writing WSML specifications apply as well to service specification. More precisely a WSML service specification has a header block containing a variant specification and a namespace references blocks. The header block should start with the `wsmlVariant` keyword, followed by an identifier for the WSML variant. For WSML-Flight this is:

http://www.wsmo.org/wsml/wsml-syntax/wsml-flight

For WSML-DL this is:

http://www.wsmo.org/wsml/wsml-syntax/wsml-dl

The specification of the WSML variant is optional, but recommended, as it facilitates the work for tools. The next block, optional as well, is the namespace references block. This block is preceded by the keyword `namespace`. Each namespace reference, except the default namespace, consists of a namespace prefix and the IRI

Listing 3.7. Paypal direct payment service header

```
wsmlVariant _"http://www.wsmo.org/wsml/wsml-syntax/wsml-flight"

namespace {_"https://asg-platform.org/dsc4isp#",
    dO _"https://asg-platform.org/dsc4ispOntology#",
    qosP _"https://asg-platform.org/dsc4isp/qosParameters#",
    dc _"http://purl.org/dc/elements/1.1#"}

webService paypalDirectPaymentService
    nfp
        dc#title hasValue "Paypal direct payment service"
        qosP#executionDuraton hasValue _double("0.4")
        qosP#responseLatency hasValue _double("0.5")
    endnfp
    importsOntology {_"https://asg-platform.org/dsc4ispOntology",
    _"https://asg-platform.org/dsc4isp/qosParameters#"}
```

which identifies the namespace. The default namespace does not contain a namespace prefix. The Paypal Direct Payment service header is listed in Listing 3.7.

A service declaration starts with the keyword `webService` optionally followed by an identifier. If no identifier is specified, the locator of the service serves as identifier. The `webService` declaration might be followed by non-functional properties block and other blocks for importing ontologies or use of mediators.

Non-functional Properties

Non-functional properties description of a service in WSML include both annotations and quality of services properties. Annotations are usually specified using the properties defined in the Dublin Core Metadata Element Set.[15] In our particular example, the `dc#title` element is used to specify the title of the service, information which does not specify neither the functionality neither the behaviour of the service. The other non-functional properties specify quality of service (QoS) values of the services. The QoS notions are defined in a QoS ontology which is imported in the service specification. Two QoS values are specified, for the Paypal Direct Payment service namely the duration of the service invocation `qosP#executionDuration` and the response latency of the service `qosP#responseLatency`.

Capability

In WSML, the capability of a Web service defines its functionality in terms of pre- and postconditions, assumptions and effects. Only one capability is allowed. The WSML-Flight description of the service capability is presented in Listing 3.8 and the WSML-DL description of the same capability is presented in Listing 3.9.

---

[15] http://dublincore.org/documents/dces/.

Listing 3.8. Paypal direct payment service capability (WSML-Flight)

```
capability paypalDirectPaymentCapability
  sharedVariables {?amount, ?card, ?tranId}
  precondition
    definedBy
      ?card memberOf dO#creditCard and
      ?contact memberOf dO#contact and
      dO#creditCardOwner(?card, ?contact) and
      ?invoiceNumber memberOf dO#invoiceNumber and
      ?amount memberOf dO#amountOfMoney.
  postcondition
    definedBy
    ?tranID[dO#hasValidity hasValue ?validity] memberOf
    dO#payPalTransactionId.
  effect
    definedBy
    dO#paymentTransaction(?card, ?tranID)
    and dO#amountCharged(?amount, ?tranID).
```

Listing 3.9. Paypal direct payment service capability (WSML-DL)

```
capability paypalDirectPaymentCapability
  sharedVariables {?paymentReq, ?tranID}
  precondition
    definedBy
        ?paymentReq memberOf dO#PaymentRequest
        and ?paymentReq[dO#paymentData hasValue ?creditCard]
            and ?creditCard memberOf dO#CreditCard
            and dO#creditCardOwner(?creditCard, ?contact)
                and ?contact memberOf dO#Contact
        and ?paymentReq[dO#invoiceNumber hasValue ?invoiceNr]
            and ?invoiceNr memberOf dO#InvoiceNumber
        and ?paymentReq[dO#amount hasValue ?amount]
            and ?amount memberOf dO#amountOfMoney.
  postcondition
    definedBy
    ?tranID[dO#hasValidity hasValue ?validity] memberOf
    dO#PayPalTransactionId.
  effect
    definedBy
    dO#paymentTransaction(?card, ?tranID)
    and dO#amountCharged(?amount, ?tranID).
```

A capability declaration starts with the keyword `capability` optionally followed by an identifier. The `capability` declaration might be followed by non-functional properties, imported ontologies, used mediators, and shared variables declarations. In our examples only the shared variables sections are specified. These variables are implicitly all-quantified and their scope is the whole Web service capability.

The four major blocks of a capability description in WSML are the preconditions, postconditions, assumptions and effects. They are all represented as logical axioms and can be seen as conditions that are met in (1) information space, before (preconditions) and after (postconditions) the execution of the service, and (2) world state, before (assumptions) and after (effects) the execution of the service. In our example a credit card, an invoice number and an amount are required to invoke the service. This requirement should be valid before the execution of the service in the information space and therefore it is modelled as a precondition. When finished, the service returns a `payPalTransactionId`, no matter if the payment was successful or not. This represents an item generated in the information space and therefore the previous statement is modelled as a postcondition. In case of successful service invocation, the associated validity object has a value of "valid", else it will be set to "invalid". Only when payment was successful, the association `amountCharged` will express that the credit card connected with the `payPalTransactionId` has been charged the amount specified in the precondition. In this case something changed in the state of the world after the execution of the service, thus it is modelled in the effect block.

The differences between the WSML-Flight and WSML-DL versions of the service capability are relatively minor at a first look. However in the DL version a payment request is used as core concept which groups the necessary data to initiate a payment operation.

Please notice that the service descriptions provided in this section are relying on the terminology provided by the domain ontology which was described in Sect. 3.3.

3.4.2 Related Work

OWL-S: OWL-based Web Service Ontology

OWL-S [125], part of the DAML program,[16] is an OWL-based Web service ontology; it aims at providing building blocks for encoding rich semantic service descriptions, in a way that builds naturally upon OWL. Very often it is referred to the OWL-S ontology as a language for describing services, thus reflecting the fact that it provides a vocabulary that can be used together with the other aspects of the OWL to create service descriptions.

The OWL-S ontology mainly consists of three interrelated sub-ontologies, known as the *profile*, *process model*, and *grounding*. The profile is used to express "what a service does", for purposes of advertising, constructing service requests, and matchmaking; the process model describes "how it works", to enable invocation, enactment, composition, monitoring, and recovery; and the grounding maps the constructs of the process model onto detailed specifications of message formats, protocols, and so forth (normally expressed in WSDL). All these sub-ontologies are linked to the top-level concept Service, which serves as an organisational point of reference for declaring Web services.

---

[16] http://www.daml.org.

Although OWL-S was the first approach to SWS, its design was inappropriate in some aspects. First, OWL-S is based on OWL; OWL was not developed with the design rationale in mind to define the semantics of processes that require rich definitions of their functionality, thus inherently limiting the expressiveness of OWL-S. Moreover, OWL-S inherits some of the drawbacks of OWL: lack of proper layering between RDFS and the less expressive species of OWL and the lack of proper layering between OWL DL and OWL Lite on the one side and OWL Full on the other. OWL-S provides the choice between several other languages, e.g. SWRL, KIF, etc. By leaving the choice of the language to be used to the user, OWL-S contributes to the interoperability problem, rather than solving it. In OWL-S, the interaction between the inputs and outputs, which have been specified as OWL classes, and the logical expressions in the respective languages, is not clear. Furthermore, the logical language used for the specification of Web service preconditions and postconditions is an integral part of the language, thus the overall Web service description and the logical expressions which specify the pre- and postconditions are connected for free. Approaches such as WSMO and SWSF tackled such drawbacks in various ways.

SWSF: Semantic Web Services Framework

Semantic Web Services Framework (SWSF) [19] is one of the newest approaches for Semantic Web Services, being proposed and promoted by Semantic Web Services Language Committee (SWSLC)[17] of the Semantic Web Services Initiative (SWSI).[18] It is based on two major components: an ontology and the corresponding conceptual model by which Web services can be described, called *Semantic Web Services Ontology (SWSO)* and a language used to specify formal characterisations of Web services concepts and descriptions called *Semantic Web Services Language (SWSL)*.

SWSO presents a conceptual model for semantically describing Web services and an axiomatisation, formal characterisation of this model given in one of the two variants of SWSL: SWSL-FOL based on First Order Logic or SWSL-Rules based on Logic programming. The resulting ontologies are called: FLOWS—First-Order Logic Ontology for Web Services, which relies on First Order Logic semantics, and ROWS—Rule Ontology for Web Services, which relies on Logic Programming semantics. The development of SWSO was influenced by the OWL-S ontology and the lessons learned from developing this ontology; it can be seen as an extension/refinement of OWL-S ontology with a special focus on providing interoperability or semantics to existing standards in Web services area (e.g. *Web Services Business Process Execution Language (WS-BPEL), Web Services Description Language (WSDL)*, etc.)

SWSL is a language for describing, in a formal way, Web services concepts and descriptions of individual services. SWSL comes in two variants which are based on two well-known formalisms: First-Order Logic and Logic Programming. The two sub-languages are: SWSL-FOL and SWSL-Rules. The design of both languages

---

[17] http://www.daml.org/services/swsl.
[18] http://www.swsi.org.

was driven by compliance with Web principles, like: usage of URIs, integration with XML built-in types and XML-compatible namespaces and import mechanisms. Both languages are layered languages where every layer includes a number of new concepts that enhance the modelling power of the language.

IRS III: Internet Reasoning System

IRS-III [59] is a framework and implemented platform which acts as a broker mediating between the goals of a user or client and available deployed Web services.[19] The IRS uses WSMO as its basic ontology and follows the WSMO design principles.

The overall framework of IRS is composed of three core components, which communicate through *SOAP*:

- *IRS Server*: The server holds descriptions of Semantic Web Services at two different levels. A knowledge level description of components is represented internally in Operational Conceptual Modelling Language (OCML).[20] Additionally, two sets of mappings are used to connect the knowledge level descriptions to a specific Web service.
- *IRS Publisher*: The publisher plays two roles in the IRS framework: it links Web services to semantic descriptions within the IRS server, and it automatically generates a wrapper which allows standalone Lisp or Java code to be invoked as well as a Web service through its WSDL description.
- *IRS Client*: A key feature of IRS is that Web service invocation is capability driven. An IRS user simply asks for a task to be achieved and the server selects and invokes an appropriate Web service.

WSDL-S: Web Service Semantics

WSDL-S [8] proposed a mechanism to augment the Web service functional descriptions, as represented by WSDL, with semantics. This work is a refinement of an initial proposal developed by the Meteor-S group, at the LSDIS Lab, Athens, Georgia.

Starting from the assumption that a semantic model of the Web service already exists, WSDL-S describes a mechanism to link this semantic model with the syntactical functional description captured by WSDL. Using the extensibility elements of WSDL, a set of annotations can be created to semantically describe the inputs, outputs, and the operation of a Web service. By this the semantic model is kept outside WSDL, making the approach agnostic to any ontology representation language. The advantage of such an approach is that it is an incremental approach, building on top of an already existing standard and taking advantage the already existing expertise and tool support. In addition the user can develop in WSDL in a compatible manner both the semantic and operational level aspects of Web services. WSDL-S work is

---

[19] http://kmi.open.ac.uk/projects/irs.

[20] http://kmi.open.ac.uk/projects/ocml.

guided by a set of principles, the most important of them being: building on existing Web services' standards, annotations being agnostic to the semantics representation language, and support annotation of XML Schema data type.

SAWSDL: Semantic Annotations for WSDL and XML Schema

Standardisation of semantic Web services technologies in W3C is in early stages, reflecting the relative youth of the research field. In 2004, the W3C started receiving submissions for specifications for semantic descriptions of Web services (OWL-S, WSMO and others). In June 2005, the W3C held a Workshop on Frameworks for Semantics in Web Services,[21] to organise a discussion on the proposed steps. The workshop identified that there was a lot of disagreement on what Semantic Web Services should do; yet there was consensus on the fact that semantics are necessary in Web service descriptions, and that building on the existing Web Services Description Language WSDL, as proposed by WSDL-S, would be a good start. In April 2006, a working group was formed to standardise Semantic Annotations for WSDL,[22] which resulted in a Recommendation (W3C standard) called "Semantic Annotations for WSDL and XML Schema", short name SAWSDL, published in August 2007 [66].

SAWSDL builds mainly on WSDL 2.0 (W3C Recommendation, June 2007), but also supports the still prevalent WSDL 1.1. On the semantic side, SAWSDL is independent of any ontology technology, assuming that semantic concepts can be identified by URIs. RDF and OWL from W3C are example technologies that can be used in SAWSDL. Along with the SAWSDL specification, the working group has produced a companion Usage Guide note,[23] to provide more examples on how SAWSDL can be used.

COWS: The Core Ontology of Web Services

The Core Ontology of Web services is an approach somewhat orthogonal to the work described so far. It has been started with an analysis of OWL-S [130], which revealed that OWL-S—in spite of its seminal role in the inception of Semantic Web services—exhibited several ontological mistakes that would render the reuse and integration of OWL-S into a broader perspective difficult if not impossible. For instance, a common problem that would arise was that OWL-S was too ambiguous to lead to a sound conceptual modelling of Web services by its users.

To resolve this issue a comprehensive analysis of a conceptualisation of software, its embedding into a sound foundational ontology, i.e. DOLCE, and its use for middleware management at large has been performed. The results have indicated economic benefit of the use of semantics for means such as configuration [205]. However, COWS has not targeted yet the automatic composition of Semantic Web services as demonstrated in this book.

---

[21] http://www.w3.org/2005/01/ws-swsf-cfp.html.

[22] http://www.w3.org/2002/ws/sawsdl.

[23] http://www.w3.org/TR/sawsdl-guide.

The corresponding analysis and ontology definitions of COWS and its foundations may be found comprehensively in [146], the use with application servers and Web services is demonstrated in [147], and the overall realisation is described in [145].

3.5 Service Matchmaking

A common task in service oriented systems is the finding of services. Finding services is important when building applications or creating processes as the services implement the actual functionality.

Finding services is a difficult task without the existence of service and domain ontologies (Sects. 3.3 and 3.4). Without these ontologies, services can only be identified by their name, their syntactical interface, and the textual documentation. In such a case finding a service mostly relies on text search. Since natural language text is informal, service names and documentations can be ambiguous.

In the book's use case scenario, multiple different kinds of *payment* happen. First of all the customers of Hostit have to pay for the hosting. Second, Hostit has to pay for the usage of most partner services (e.g. domain registration). If a process designer of Hostit wants to find a process to charge customers, several issues arise:

Is *charging* the same as *payment*? Does the payment service charge the customer or is it used to pay for utilized services from other partners?

To sum up, finding services is difficult as service name and documentation do not sufficiently describe the service and different terminologies allow for misunderstandings. While a human can overcome these problems by asking a colleague or calling the service provider, this is not possible if services are to be found during run-time without human involvement. The computer cannot guess search terms to find a service or understand the service documentation. It can also not ask somebody for assistance (actually it can by crashing, but this not a desired behaviour). It must always find the correct services. Without service ontologies, finding services at run-time is limited to finding services implementing the exact same interface.

This limitation to matching based on purely syntactical features is not desirable. Hardly two services share the same interface even if they implement the same functionality. Services do not match syntactically as soon as their names differ or they use different data representations (e.g.: Is a credit card just the credit card number or does it include the validity date as well? Is the credit card number a number, a string, or a string containing only digits?).

Here, service ontologies come into play. They can be used to describe the functionality or capability of a service. Given this knowledge, a human process designer can find services even if a pure text search would not have shown it. Also false positives are prohibited (e.g.: What would have happened in our example if each service's documentation contained a *Payment Details* section?). As the service and domain ontology define a shared terminology, misunderstandings are unlikely (except if there are disputes about the meaning of the ontology concepts). Service ontologies also allow for finding services at run-time as the functionality of each service is clearly specified. The computer *knows* whether a service *matches* or not. Consequently, this task is called service matchmaking.

In the following we will detail the concept of service matchmaking by first describing different forms of matchmaking and afterwards demonstrating how service matchmaking is actually an application of the aforementioned reasoning tasks.

3.5.1 Aspects of Service Matchmaking

Service matchmaking is the task of finding services for a given *user request* based on their semantic service specification. A user request describes the requirements of the user toward the service in a similar fashion as the semantic service specification describes the functionality of a service. A request consists of an initial state describing the current state of 'the world' as well as available information, and a goal state describing the intended result in terms of world state and information. Figure 3.4 illustrates the matching. To qualify as a match, the precondition must match the initial state of the request and the effect must match the goal state of the request. Precondition matching the initial state, means that in every situation expressed by the initial state (e.g. if disjunction is used) the precondition is fulfilled (i.e. the service is invocable). Correspondingly, effect matching the goal state means, that every possible outcome of invoking the service fulfils the goal.

Actually, matching both the precondition and effect to the request is only one form of matchmaking. It is most useful, if a service for a specific task is required or if run-time binding to concrete services is performed (see Sect. 5.5). We call it *service matchmaking on capabilities* as it matches against the full capability specification. Other forms of matchmaking are useful as well. We can distinguish:

- *Service matchmaking on preconditions*
- *Service matchmaking on effects*
- *Non-functional service matchmaking*

The first two types are mainly of interest for run-time composition approaches (Chap. 5) based on forward chaining (matchmaking on preconditions) or backward

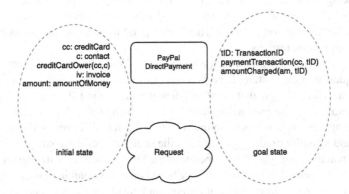

Fig. 3.4. Matchmaking of user requests to semantic service specifications

chaining (matchmaking on effects). When composing services automatically at run-time, matchmaking on capabilities is seldom successful as we will not reach the goal state with just one service. Hence, we need more elaborate selection strategies that will determine which service to select. With forward chaining, matchmaking finds all invocable services. Selection can then, for example, be done using heuristics. Non-functional service matchmaking can be seen as an extension of capability matchmaking. But as different mechanisms are used, it is mentioned here separately. Non-functional properties describe aspects of the services like costs or required security features.

3.5.2 Implementing Matchmaking Using Reasoning

Reasoning is the mental process of looking for reasons to support beliefs, conclusions, actions or feelings [108]. As a result of reasoning new facts, conclusions can be derived given the initial premises. Humans are faced with the necessity of reasoning, and it is a natural question whether this act can be automated. Automated reasoning is the study of Artificial Intelligence using the methods and techniques of computations that automate the process of reasoning. The overall goal is to provide high-level descriptions of 'the world' that can be effectively used to build intelligent systems. This in turn, enables intelligent systems to infer implicit consequence of its explicitly represented knowledge in an automated manner.

The World Wide Web can be seen as the largest knowledge base that has ever existed. This global knowledge base is currently in a transition from a "base of unstructured knowledge" to a "base of structured knowledge". Thus the knowledge representation and efficient automated reasoning are two critical success factors for realizing Semantic Web and Semantic Web Services visions. Offering reasoning support for a Semantic Web Services Language is crucial for the usage and acceptance of the language in the Semantic Web area. Reasoning allows, e.g. to check the consistency of an ontology and of ontology elements and to build classifications of the ontology objects.

In the rest of the section we present two different approaches for the service matchmaking algorithm. The first approach is a service matchmaking algorithm based on the capabilities of the services. The second approach is the service matchmaking algorithm for service composition. They correspond to different phases in the Web service composition process.

The first matchmaking approach is to locate the Web services that directly match a user request in a given state. If no Web services are discovered, the composer can construct a valid solution that fully satisfies the goal using the second approach, which identifies all the executable services in a given state. More specifically, the service composer can construct a solution by successively discovering the executable services and virtually executing them until the state satisfies the goal.

Both matchmaking algorithms operate at the level of rich semantic description of services. As presented in [103], discovery based on rich semantic descriptions takes into consideration the dependence of outputs and effects of the service execution on the concrete input provided by the user when invoking the service. This is accomplished by considering for Web services the preconditions, assumptions, postconditions and effects, and for goals the state of 'the world' reached after the execution of a service, thus only postconditions and effects. In this context, we have not made explicit distinction between effects and postconditions. Together, they represent the outcome of the service execution.

Matching based on Capabilities

The first algorithm for service matchmaking queries for the Web services executable in the given state whose capabilities fully match a requester goal.

Of the four possible types of match described in [103], we are taking into consideration only *exact-match* (the Web service description and the goal description coincide) and *plugin-match* (the sets of objects that the Web service claims to deliver is a superset of the set of objects that are relevant to the requester). The other two cases (*subsumes-match* and *intersection-match*) are not considered valid matches in this context, because the services cannot fully satisfy the goal.

We consider the states of 'the world' to be logical theories. A state of 'the world' comprises the set of registered ontologies and, optionally, an additional set of facts. These facts can be given explicitly by means of an initial state. They can also be the outcome of previous virtual execution of services, because the execution of a service in a given state is considered to change the state of 'the world', resulting in an update to the logical theory.

In order to determine if the capability of a service satisfies a requester's goal, one must reason about the resulting updates. Reasoning about updates raises the frame problem. A solution to avoid the frame problem is offered by Transaction Logic, an extension to First-order Logic that allows to specify the dynamics of knowledge bases in a declarative way. The theoretical approach employing Transaction Logic for Web service discovery that has been used as theoretical foundation for the implementation of this matchmaking algorithm can be found in [103].

The algorithm for service matchmaking based on capabilities implemented in our prototype is presented in Listing 3.10. The ontologies, the services, and the goal are assumed to be loaded prior to invocation of the matchmaking process. An appropriate exception will be thrown in case an unregistered goal is passed as input (lines 7–9).

We consider a "stateless" functioning of the prototype, meaning that the relevant state information is given as input to each state-dependent operation. The state is loaded and respectively unloaded (lines 11, 40).

The available information sources at this point are:

- the set of ontologies referred by both goal and service descriptions
- the knowledge encoded in the state given as input to the matchmaking process
- the information that may be provided by the goal description itself

We select those registered services that are executable (lines 14–18). A service is executable if there exists input information in the available information sources such that the preconditions (what must be valid in order for the service to be executed)

Listing 3.10. Matchmaking algorithm based on capabilities

```
algorithm serviceMatchmakingBasedOnCapabilities
input: state
   goal
output:    set of services with set of variable bindings

begin
   if goal is not registered then
      throw exception
   endif

   register state

   for each registered service
      if holds service.capability.preconditions then

         for each variable binding
            if not holds service.capability.effects(variable binding) and
               not holds service.capability.postconditions(variablebinding)
            then
               insert service.capability.effects(variable binding),
                     service.capability.postconditions(variable binding)

               if holds goal.capability.effects and
                  holds goal.capability.postconditions
               then
                  add variablebinding to variable bindings set
               endif

               delete service.capability.effects(variable binding),
                     service.capability.postconditions(variablebinding)
            endif
         endfor

         if not empty(variable bindings set) then
            add (service, variable bindings set) to result set
         endif
      endif
   endfor

   unregister state

   return result set
end
```

are fulfilled, while the effects and the postconditions (what the service guarantees to hold after its execution) are not yet fulfilled. A variable binding is a set of

$$\langle variable, value \rangle$$

pairs which captures the input information for which the service preconditions hold. More precisely, a variable binding is a complete set of bindings

$$\langle x_1, v_1 \rangle, \langle x_2, v_2 \rangle, \ldots, \langle x_n, v_n \rangle$$

where

$$x_1, \ldots, x_n$$

are the variables occurring in the precondition, and

$$v_1, \ldots, v_n$$

is a set of constants. There can be several variable bindings for the same service, and all further tests on the service effects and postconditions will depend on a particular variable binding (line 16).

Checking that the effects and the postconditions of the service are not satisfied for the input that satisfies the preconditions is necessary due to the fact that in this context we wish to allow only single execution of services for a given input. Note however that a Web service can execute an arbitrary number of times, but with different input information. The assumptions of a service are only assumed to hold, and therefore not checked.

An executable service is considered a match if, for the input information, the outcome of the service satisfies the outcome requested in the goal. We perform this test by assuming the effects and the postconditions of the service for the input and verifying if the effects and the postconditions of the goal hold in the resulting state (lines 20–30). The set of matching services, and for each service all corresponding variable bindings, is then returned (line 42).

Matching for Web Service Composition

The second matchmaking algorithm queries for the executable services in a given state. Listing 3.11 presents the algorithm. The ontologies and the services are assumed to be loaded in the reasoner prior to invocation of the matchmaking process. The state is loaded and respectively unloaded (lines 6, 25).

The available information sources for this second algorithm are:

- the set of the ontologies referred by the service descriptions
- the knowledge encoded in the state given as input to the matchmaking process

A service is considered a match in the context of this algorithm if, for the input information, the service is executable. As already defined, a service is executable if there exists input information such that the preconditions are fulfilled (line 9), while the effects and the postconditions are not yet fulfilled (lines 12, 13). The set of executable services, and for each service all corresponding variable bindings, is then returned (line 27).

Listing 3.11. Matchmaking algorithm for service composition

```
algorithm serviceMatchmakingOnPreconditions
input:     state
output:    set of services with set of variable bindings

begin
  register state

  for each registered service
    if holds service.capability.preconditions then

      for each variable binding
        if not holds service.capability.effects(variable binding) and
           not holdsservice.capability.postconditions(variable binding)
        then
          add variablebinding to variable bindings set
        endif
      endfor

      if not empty(variable bindings set) then
        add (service,variable bindings set) to result set
      endif
    endif
  endfor

  unregister state

  return result set
end
```

After discussing how services can be semantically specified and how a match-making of services works, the next chapter will go into more details about how existing systems, components or applications can be service enabled.

4

Service Enabling

Steffi Donath, Thomas Hering, and Christoph Ringelstein

4.1 Overview and Motivation

Earlier sections introduced the concept of adaptive service provisioning, where semantically described services are combined according to a semantic goal definition.
One of the basic assumptions for such a scenario is the availability of semantically
described service candidates, sometimes, collectively, denoted as service landscape.
The services usually must be derived from existing functional assets in the business
and IT environment. Therefore, the traditional issue of legacy integration still holds
for modern service oriented environments. Not only the technical gap between heterogeneous IT assets must be closed here, but also the creation, maintenance, and
registration of semantic descriptions must be performed.

The integration of existing functional assets in a semantic service provisioning
infrastructure, from now on described as service enabling, is a well-known problem
in industry. Past efforts like the *Enterprise Application Integration (EAI)* [50], Hub-
and-Spoke architectures, and the *Java Business Integration (JBI)* [189] specification
mainly focused on solving technical interoperability issues. For a semantic-enabled
service provisioning, it is also necessary to augment such integrated or newly created services with semantic service specifications. This integration activity must be
accompanied by both tools support and a methodology, in order to coordinate and
reduce development and maintenance efforts.

The following chapter will discuss the problems and current research efforts for
service enabling in a semantic service environment. The technical integration is part
of the overall service enabling, but will be discussed separately as task of the service
infrastructure in Chap. 7. The following chapter focuses on the semi-automated generation of new service functionality or proxy implementations (Sect. 4.2), and on the
semantic description of such atomic service functionality (Sect. 4.3).

4.2 Software Generation For Proxy Development

The need for flexible, automatic, and adaptive orchestration, provisioning and enactment of services forces service developers to produce software that is parameterized
to fit various predefined and hard-to-predict operational contexts and configurations.
Many applications and services are not prepared for this kind of agility. Moreover,
due to the use of different programming languages, development environments and
libraries the customization and modification of service functionalities becomes complicated.

One possibility to overcome this limitation is the utilization of software generation concepts.

4.2.1 Software Generation Concepts

Software generation is the automated or semi automated producing of source code in
a certain programming language. Possible concepts of software generation are *Component Based Software Development (CBSD)*, domain specific languages, software
product lines, and model driven software development:

CBSD suggests building especially large software systems by integrating already
existing functional assets, called software components. Clemens Szyperski, one of
the pioneers on the field of CBSD defines software component as a...

> ... unit of composition with contractually specified interface and explicit
> context dependencies only. A software component can be deployed inde-
> pendently and is subject to composition by third parties. [186]

The core idea of this approach is the re-use of common functionalities, which
are relevant for multiple software products. Instead of developing these common
parts for every software product from the scratch, CBSD suggests to develop such
common parts only once and build larger systems by assembling several common
parts.

Domain-Specific Language (DSL) refers to a concept that becomes more and
more omni-present in recent research and industrial activities. A review of scientific
and best-practice publications shows that there is a large spectrum of definitions for
the term itself. Common definitions contain a number of features for DSLs:

- DSLs are generic languages used not only by typical software developers, but
  also by other kinds of engineers in a specific problem environment. DSLs need
  not to be Turing-complete. Also quite simple specification or parametrization
  languages can be seen as DSLs.
- DSLs are restricted to a domain, i.e. they are specialized languages and problem
  oriented. Domains can be narrow or broad; they can be vertical as well as a
  horizontal domains.
- DSLs provide domain abstractions, i.e. they implement concepts of the respective
  domain and carry a strong expressive power.

- DSLs provide domain-specific notations, i.e. the concrete syntax of a DSL is often close to the syntax to the notations domain experts are familiar with.

The general idea of using a DSL rather than a general purpose programming or description language is to raise the level of abstraction. Instead of expressing the mental model of a solution in a programmers head in low-level-language constructs, it should be possible to be more abstract in the sense of using constructs of the 'natural' language of the problem domain.

The third promising concept for automated and semi-automated software generation are *Software Product Lines (SPL)*. They have emerged as an important approach for software development in the last years. SPL focuses on the production of families of related systems. For the creation of members of one family the same base of development assets is used [144]. The objective of SPL is to increase software engineering effectiveness by exploiting commonalities and managing systematically the variations that exist between members of the software family. Those variations are explicitly and formally represented, e.g. in terms of decision tables, feature diagrams etc., so that they can be easily viewed, reasoned about and automatically or at least semi-automatically processed [113].

A typical life cycle of a process within SPL consists of two major phases, domain engineering and application engineering. Domain engineering consists of the sub phases domain analysis, domain design, and domain implementation. The application engineering phase can be decomposed into application analysis, application design, and application implementation. The overall goal of the domain engineering phase is the creation of the product line infrastructure that consists of assets that are needed for the engineering of concrete members of the product family, i.e. the applications. Within domain engineering the most important things to do are scoping of the domain, creation of reusable requirements, definition a common architecture for all systems of the domain, and implementation of reusable components that can be used for the application creation.

Main objectives of all these approaches are reduction of software development costs and a shortened development time, as well as the re-usability of the resulting components.

4.2.2 Model Driven Approaches

Existing services are realized using different technologies. This hampers their integration. Also on the level of the service execution environment (see also Sect. 7), different technologies are in use. A service enabling strategy should therefore support the separation of service functionality from the implementation technique, in order to free the service developer as best as possible from infrastructure dependencies. One possibility to achieve this goal is the utilization an *Model-Driven Software Development (MDSD)* approach.

The aim of MDSD is the development of software from domain specific models. Key features of MDSD come from the field of domain engineering and software product line engineering. The focus is domain analysis, meta modeling, model driven generation, template languages, domain-driven framework design, the principles for agile software development, and the development and use of Open source infrastructure. The advantage of MDSD is providing the scalability, which is not inherent in agile methodologies [24].

A fundamental concept of MDSD is the partial or complete generation of software from models. These models have to describe the functionality of the software accurate and expressive. For this concern the elements of the model need semantics, which determine a particular run-time behaviour unambiguously [191]. This can be achieved by use of formalized DSL. A DSL raises the level of abstraction. It is intended to be understandable by domain experts and to be at the same time also machine readable. A DSL is defined by a meta model. A meta model is an abstract description of the language and model elements respectively and it contains the rules for composing expressions using the elements of the language [24]. The general MDSD advantages in contrast to typical programming languages are:

- The model language describes the domain and problem more precisely.
- Late binding to specific *Application Programming Interface (API)* and technologies by model transformations is possible.
- Better integration of domain and system analysts.
- Automated code generation instead of copy and paste reuse.
- Better integration of XML or other data exchange languages in the model language.

One very prominent refinement of the ideas of MDSD approaches is *Model-Driven Architecture (MDA)* by the *Object Management Group (OMG)*. MDA has the idea of separating the specification of the operation of a system from the details of the way that the system uses the capabilities of its platform [99]. It has a clearer perception than the MDSD approach. All DSLs within MDA will be defined with *Meta Object Facility (MOF)*. MOF is a meta meta model that was specified by the OMG and it defines amongst others the *Unified Modeling Language (UML)* [191]. With the UML the level of standardization was raised from application implementation to the level of application design.

The goals of MDA are portability, interoperability, and re-usability by way of architectural separation of concerns. The key assets of MDA are models for the description or specification of the system which will be developed. There are several viewpoints on a system. A viewpoint is a technique for abstraction using a selected set of architectural concepts and structuring rules in order to describe particular concerns within that system [99]. One viewpoint is platform independent and for this a *Platform Independent Model (PIM)* is designed with UML. A PIM specifies the system or a part of a system independently of any particular specific platform or language. A MDA model can have multiple levels of PIMs. The PIM on the base level is used to express only business functionality and behaviour. On the next level the PIM includes some aspects of technology (e.g. persistence, transactionality, security).

Another viewpoint is platform specific and can be provided by a *Platform Specific Model (PSM)* expressed in UML, too. A PSM combines the specifications in the PIM with the details of a certain platform in order to specify how that system

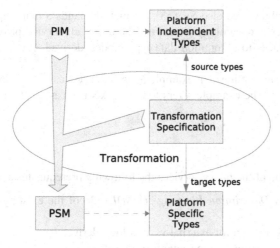

Fig. 4.1. Model transformation [99]

uses a particular type of platform (e.g. run time characteristics and configuration information). The gain of this approach is the possibility of implementation of several platforms from one system and thus cost reduction.

Additionally, an important key part of MDA is model transformation. Model transformation is the process of converting one model into another model using mappings for transforming models. An MDA mapping provides specifications for transformation of a PIM into a PSM for a particular platform. As a last step in MDA the PSM will be transformed to the implementation code for execution of the system.

4.2.3 Example Integration Process with MDA

Overview

This subsection describes one possible way to integrate existing Web services into a certain environment by means of model driven approach. This integration process allows dynamic integration of existing Web services. The goal of the integration process is to enable the use of existing external service within the service oriented environment. Although all Web services rely on XML and the use of *SOAP* as communication mechanism, they may provide different semantics and different data formats. Therefore, many service enabling activities end up in the development of proxy services for the external functionality. The use of a service proxy allows the decoupling of external services from business processes, since relevant technical adaptations (like protocol conversion or non-standardized SOAP extensions) are decoupled from the business process enactment. It is also ensured that all external services—meaning all proxy service interfaces used by the composition enactment—fulfil common demands. This becomes especially relevant with the concept of ontology-based service matchmaking (see also Sect. 3.5), which demands a mapping between interface data types and ontology concepts. Therefore, all service proxies adopt the functional interfaces to a common data type model, derived from a central ontology.

In the following sections, an example integration process based on proxy generation is explained. The example refers to the book's use case scenario described in Sect. 2.2.

Prerequisites

For the generation of the proxy services the following prerequisites are necessary:

- *Web Services Description Language (WSDL)* file of the existing service to be integrated
- Mapping information for external vs. ontology-derived data types
- Relevant information for the semantic description
- Information about non-functional properties
- Meta model

The WSDL file of the service which has to be registered is provided by the service provider itself. The file contains information about the operations and the messages of the service as well as binding information to a concrete network protocol and message format to define an endpoint. Semantic aspects of the service are preconditions, assumptions, postconditions, and effects. The *precondition* and *postcondition* explain the state of the information space before and after service execution. Hence these elements refer to input and output parameters of the service. An assumption formulates the expected state of 'the world'. If the usage of the service may result in change of the state of 'the world', then the according outcome is called effect.

This semantic service specification is based on concepts described in ontologies, as described in Sect. 3.4. A service provider or an integrator person therefore has to specify what the service does, using the concepts and relations of the given ontology. The service provider also has to associate each parameter defined in the WSDL description with concepts from the ontology.

The WSDL file does not include non-functional properties like costs or accounting information. It therefore has to be specified by the service provider. A further prerequisite of the integration process is a proxy service meta model. This meta model specifies the elements and their relationship to each other in a abstract manner.

Fig. 4.2. Parameter association using a mapping language

Example of Proxy Generation

Starting point of the registration process is the existing service provider, making available different kinds of information. This information is needed in order to create both a semantic service specification as well as proxy that wraps the available service for seamless integration. From all information which the provider has given a mapping document is created. It contains all information that is needed for the creation of the semantic service specification as well as the PIM. The intermediate stage of creating first a mapping document might seem redundant—the main idea is to decouple information from service specification and the service model. This allows an independent design of the registration interface for services on the one hand and the definition of service specification format and structure on the other hand.

Alternatively to creating a mapping document, one could think about an immediate generation of service specification and platform independent service model from the provider information. The output would be a *XML Metadata Interchange (XMI)* file. For development purposes it seems reasonable to perform an additional step because the mapping document will be much better human-readable than a XMI representation of a service model.

The service composition enactment has to be able to interact with registered services. This interaction is typically based on message exchange, for example with SOAP in the case of Web service technology. However, there is a gap which has to bridged between the explicit semantics within the platform and the implicit semantics of a service description. Therefore, a formal mapping between the operations and data types within the platform, and the methods and data types of the service is needed (see Sect. 3). Within the platform, the semantics of entities are described using ontology concepts, relations, and rules. On the other hand the existing service is functionally described by WSDL, which contains only technical interface descriptions. The therefore needed transformation has to be defined by using some conventions:

- A semantic concept is mapped on a XML element with the concepts name.
- Each semantic concept's property is mapped on a XML sub element.

Listing 4.1 shows the possible structure of such a mapping document. It contains a grounding for every data type in the WSDL file, a grounding for every operation of the WSDL file and information about non-functional properties as specified by the service provider.

Main information source for the creation of the mapping document is the WSDL file provided by the service provider. The abstract part of a WSDL description consists of message types and the operations of the service interface (see also Sect. 7.4). In the mapping document the information regarding data types is gathered in the <DataTypes> section. A WSDL type is referenced using a <WSDLElement> element as child node of <DataTypeGrounding>. The operations of a service are described in the <Operation> section. The information for a particular operation (embraced by a <Op> tag) that can be collected automatically is the referenced operation in the WSDL description (<WSDLOperation>) and the parameters it is

Listing 4.1. General structure of the mapping document

```
<RegDoc>
   <DataTypes>
      <DataTypeGrounding id="...">
         ...
      </DataTypeGrounding>
   </DataTypes>
   <Operations>
      <Op id="...">
         <Grounding>...</Grounding>
         ...
      </Op>
   </Operations>
   <NonFunctionalProperties>
      ...
   </NonFunctionalProperties>
</RegDoc>
```

comprised of (`<Parameter>`). This mapping file syntax is one possible example—the particular design mainly depends on the amount of available information.

As aforementioned, data types defined in a WSDL file have to be mapped to an ontology concept within one of the developed domain ontologies. Within the `<DataTypes>` section, a single data type is grounded using a `<DataTypeGrounding>` element. Such an element contains an `id` attribute so that it can be identified when an operation refers to it as one of its input or output parameters.

Besides the reference to a WSDL data type, a description document also has to state the corresponding ontology concept (`<OntoConcept>`) for a complete grounding. The linkage between these two elements can only be performed manually by the service provider during the registration process because the semantics of the existing service that have been implicit up to this point are only known to the provider.

It cannot be assumed that for every data type an exactly fitting ontology concept can be identified. In most of the cases, a transformation (`<Transformation>`) will be necessary to map the structure of the WSDL data type to the structure of the according ontology concept. Parts of this transformation can be generated automatically. After data type and concept have been specified by the provider it can be inferred that these elements represent source and target of the transformation. Yet the actual mapping between structures has to be specified by the provider. To express this transformation a transformation language is needed. Because this transformation is of pure syntactical nature, the *eXtensible Stylesheet Language (XSL)* transformation language is an obvious candidate. Listing 4.2 shows the `<DataTypes>` section of an exemplified description document, related to the *Web Services Modeling Ontology (WSMO)* ontology standards (see also Sect. 3.4.1).

After collecting all required provider information the mapping document can be created automatically. In order to support automated generation an XML-Schema for the mapping document is necessary. Listing 4.3 shows an example.

Listing 4.2. Data type grounding in the mapping document

```
<DataTypes>
  <DataTypeGrounding id="dtg01">
    <WSDLElement>
      "path to WSDL file" #phoneNumber
    </WSDLElement>
    <Transformation>
      PhoneNumberTransformation.xsl
    </Transformation>
    <OntoConcept>
      "path to communication-ontology WSML file" #phoneNumber
    </OntoConcept>
  </DataTypeGrounding>
  <DataTypeGrounding id="dtg02">
    <WSDLElement>
      "path to WSDL file" #Name
    </WSDLElement>
    <Transformation>
      "ProviderTransformation.xsl" #provider
    </Transformation>
    <OntoConcept>
      "path to participant-ontology WSML file" #provider
    </OntoConcept>
  </DataTypeGrounding>
</DataTypes>
```

Listing 4.3. XML Schema of the registration document

```
<?xml version='1.0' encoding='UTF-8'?>
<xsd:schema xmlns:xsd="http://www.w3.org/2001/XMLSchema">
  <xsd:element name="Accounting" type="xsd:string"/>
  <xsd:element name="Assumption" type="xsd:string"/>
  <xsd:element name="Effect" type="xsd:string"/>
  <xsd:element name="OntoConcept" type="xsd:string"/>
  <xsd:element name="Parameter" type="xsd:string"/>
  <xsd:element name="Security" type="xsd:string"/>
  <xsd:element name="Transformation" type="xsd:string"/>
  <xsd:element name="WSDLElement" type="xsd:string"/>
  <xsd:element name="WSDLOperation" type="xsd:string"/>
  <xsd:complexType name="DataTypeGroundingType">
    <xsd:sequence>
    <xsd:element ref="WSDLElement" />
    <xsd:element ref="Transformation" />
```

```
    <xsd:element ref="OntoConcept" />
   </xsd:sequence>
   <xsd:attribute name="id" type="xsd:string" use="required" />
  </xsd:complexType>
  <xsd:complexType name="DataTypesType">
   <xsd:sequence>
    <xsd:element name="DataTypeGrounding"
                 type="DataTypeGroundingType"
                 maxOccurs="unbounded"/>
   </xsd:sequence>
  </xsd:complexType>
  <xsd:complexType name="GroundingType">
   <xsd:sequence>
    <xsd:element ref="WSDLOperation"/>
    <xsd:element ref="Assumption"/>
    <xsd:element ref="Effect"/>
   </xsd:sequence>
  </xsd:complexType>
  <xsd:complexType name="OpType" maxOccurs="unbounded">
   <xsd:sequence>
    <xsd:element name="Grounding" type="GroundingType"/>
    <xsd:element ref="Parameter" maxOccurs="unbounded"/>
   </xsd:sequence>
   <xsd:attribute name="id" use="required" type="xsd:string" />
  </xsd:complexType>
  <xsd:complexType name="OperationsType">
   <xsd:sequence>
    <xsd:element name="Op" type="OpType"/>
   </xsd:sequence>
  </xsd:complexType>
  <xsd:complexType name="NonFunctionalPropertiesType">
   <xsd:sequence>
    <xsd:element ref="Accounting"/>
    <xsd:element ref="Security"/>
   </xsd:sequence>
  </xsd:complexType>
  <xsd:element name="RegDoc">
   <xsd:complexType>
    <xsd:sequence>
     <xsd:element name="DataTypes" type="DataTypesType"/>
     <xsd:element name="Operations" type="OperationsType"/>
     <xsd:element name="NonFunctionalProperties"
                  type="NonFunctionalPropertiesType"/>
    </xsd:sequence>
   </xsd:complexType>
  </xsd:element>
</xsd:schema>
```

Listing 4.4. PIM fragment for a proxy service

```
<?xml version="1.0" encoding="UTF-8" ?>
 <ServiceMetaModelInstanceProxyServicePIM >
  <metadata dc_title="GetProviderService" dc_creator="" />
   <interface>
     <operation signature="getProvider" visibility="public">
        <parameter parameterName="country" domain="Telecommunication"
                   ontology="communication" concept="telephoneNumber"
                   attribute="countryCode" ofType="string" />
        <block precondition="'P:userCode, P:nwCode':string"
              postcondition="'N:string, N:parameter,
                            QueryX:getProvider[name->N],
                            providerOf(QueryX, P)':string" />
     </operation>
   </interface>
 </ServiceMetaModelInstance:ProxyServicePIM>
```

The mapping document forms the basis for the automated generation of a proxy service. Based on the ontology, the semantic service specification will be generated, using the information from the mapping document. The generated service specification has to be registered in a service registry, which contains all available service specifications.

The next step in the registration process is the creation of the proxy service model. It is derived from the proxy service meta model and contains the information which the service provider handed in. Additionally, the service model contains data from the WSDL file. Since the service model is completely independent of any platform, it can be termed PIM. Listing 4.4 shows a partial example.

According to the OMG MDA approach, the PIM has to be transformed to a PSM. This happens by enriching the PIM information with details regarding the middleware technology utilized in the service infrastructure (see Chap. 7). One example is the *Enterprise Java Bean (EJB)* component model as the target platform, which demands the consideration of several packaging and deployment rules. Furthermore, the PSM is enriched with information from the WSDL file such as the endpoint and protocol binding information. Listing 4.5 shows a small part of such a PSM in XMI format, explaining the difference to a PIM.

The PSM than can be easily transformed into code. Listing 4.6 shows a generated wrapper for an existing service, which could be deployed to a *Java Platform Enterprise Edition (Java EE)* service architecture (see also Fig. 4.3).

The result of the integration process is a proxy service that represents an ontology-compliant wrapper for the existing service within the platform. The proxy service in the example is realized as a stateless session bean component, which is deployable as Java EE application. Figure 4.4 shows the proxy service session bean in an according service infrastructure.

Listing 4.5. PSM fragment for a proxy service

```xml
<?xml version="1.0" encoding="UTF-8"?>
<ProxyServicePSM:ServiceEJB
     xmlns:ProxyServicePSM="http://example-platform.org/metamodel/psm/"
     xmlns:xmi="http://www.omg.org/XMI" xmi:version="2.0"
     className="GetProviderService">
  <businessMethod methodName="getProvider"
                  BusinessLogic="boolean success = false;
                                 string country= phone.getCountryCode();
                                 ...">
  </businessMethod>
  <descriptor>
    <serviceRef serviceRefName="services/getProviderService"
                serviceInterface="javax.xml.rpc.Service"
                wsdlFile="META-INF/wsdl/getProvider.wsdl"
                jaxrpcMappingFile="META-INF/mapping.xml"
                serviceQname="external:GetProviderService"/>
  </descriptor>
  <wsdl serviceName="GetProviderService" portName="ProviderPort"
        wsdlURI="..."/>
</ProxyServicePSM:ServiceEJB>
```

Listing 4.6. Example for a generated proxy implementation [96]

```java
import javax.ejb.SessionBean;
import javax.ejb.SessionContext;

public class GetProviderServiceProxyBean implements SessionBean {
  public TelephoneProvider getProvider(int countryCode,
                                       int networkCode,
                                       int userCode) {

  ... // The business logic code

  return telephoneProvider;
  }
  public void ejbCreate(){}
  public void setSessionContext(SessionContext ctx) {}
  public void ejbRemove() {}
  public void ejbActivate() {}
  public void ejbPassivate() {}
  public void ejbLoad() {}
  public void ejbStore() {}
}
```

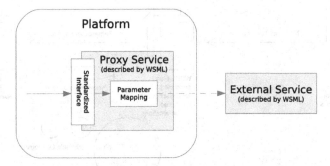

Fig. 4.3. Example for a proxy service architecture

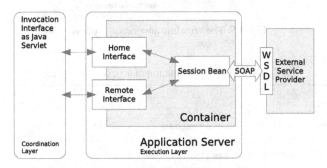

Fig. 4.4. Deployed proxy in service infrastructure [96]

4.3 Semantic Specification of Existing Services

Integrating existing services into a semantic service provisioning platform requires that the services are enriched with semantic descriptions. The semantic specification should include the mapping of the used data types from input and output messages to ontology concepts, the specification of the service functionality through preconditions and effects, and the specification of the non-functional properties of service operations.

Specifications for service functionalities are typically developed by the engineers that integrate existing services into the provisioning platform. In most cases, the internals of the service functionality (like functional behaviour, error conditions, demanded input data) are unknown to the engineer who does the integration. This is reasoned by a lack of behavioural description in typical interface languages, but also by the fact that the integration engineer is typically not a domain expert for the particular utilized service. Figure 4.5 depicts the process of specification [161] for the integration engineer.

The first integration step is the standardized description of the non-semantic characteristics of an external functionality. This is a typical development task, which is meanwhile supported by tools and development environments. In interface-driven

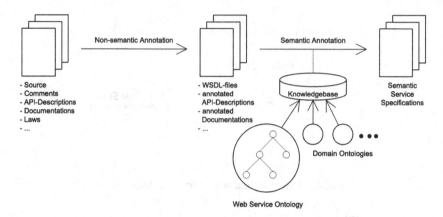

Fig. 4.5. The semantic annotation process

Listing 4.7. WSDL information of an example service

```
...
<service name="PaymentService">
  <documentation> This Web services ... </documentation>
  <port name=" PaymentServicePort"
        binding="tns: PaymentServiceBinding">
    <soap:address location="http://example.org/payment"/>
  </port>
...
```

middleware systems, like Web services and CORBA, it can be expected that accessible functionalities provide also an according functional interface description. For the typical usage of Web service technology, the interface description is realized by a WSDL file (see Listing 4.7). In many cases, such a file was already created by the service provider and can simply be accessed via the same URL as the Web service.

The WSDL file mainly provides technical information for the SOAP middleware (see also Sect. 7.4), like message encoding, defined data types and relevant access policies. However, to gain the required information about the functionality of a Web service—which forms the base for the semantic description—the engineer needs to mine different information sources. The most efficient sources are the source code, the interface descriptions of the operations of the service (as in Listing 4.8), and the documentation (as in Listing 4.9).

The different sources vary in quality, detail level, and preciseness. In addition, not all of those sources contain information about all service properties. The following list gives a short overview about some sources and analyses the contained information:

Listing 4.8. API description of the example service

```
Direct Payment Request Format
The following table lists all allowed name-value pairs that
must or can be used in a direct payment request:
Name            Description
payerName       The name of the payer. The format is:
                "LastName, FirstName"
payerAccountID  If credit card payment is chosen, this must
                be the payer credit card number. If money
                order payment is chosen this parameter must
                be empty or skipped.
...
```

Listing 4.9. Documentation of the example service

```
Direct Payment requests submit all payment information to the
Payment Service and receive in return a payment identifica-
tion number. The Payment is executed by the payment
service provider.
A list of all needed and optional parameters of direct pay-
ment requests are listed in the Direct Payment Request Format
description.
```

Source code: From the source code of an service implementation, most information about its operations could be derived. Especially information about its functionality, its preconditions, and its effects is extractable from source code.

Documentation: The documentation of a service is one of the most common information sources. However the quality of the contained information highly depends on the preciseness of the documentation. This is because of the circumstance that documentations are generally written in natural language and thus not formalized in a machine-understandable manner. Hence the information mining must be done manually.

API description: An *API* description contains explanations of the interfaces or functionality of the service operations. The explanation contains a signature, which is written by means of a concrete or pseudo programming language, and a natural language explanation. An *API* description is typically more detailed than the full-text documentation, but the natural language parts share the same interpretation problem.

Software specifications: During the software engineering process of the Web service several kinds of software specifications are created, e.g. UML-diagrams. Most of these sources provide the same kind of information as the *API* descriptions.

Source code comments: In the source code, the contained comments are another source of information. Similar to *API* descriptions, these comments often describe the interface or functionality of single operations. Because comments are generally written in natural language, they also share the interpretation problem.

In addition, like the source code itself they are often not accessible by service requesters.

Contracts: A further information source are contracts, like service level agreements, but also general contracts like end-user level agreements. They may contain information about legal usage conditions, usage costs, etc. Because they are also written in natural language, gaining information from contracts has the same problems as using documentations.

Background knowledge: Many different kinds of technical background knowledge regarding utilized services might exist. Examples are knowledge about the technical realization of utilized standards, knowledge about the application domain, or important judicial aspects. All such knowledge is useful to specify resulting service properties and to reduce initial specification efforts.

Based on such different information sources, the purely technical interface description can be extended by semantically relevant information, collected from different and only human-readable resources. The challenging next step is now to move these informal descriptions into a formal semantic specification.

4.3.1 Semantic Service Classification

The second step after the relevant information gathering is the semantic annotation of the service, based on the functional interface description. The result of this step is called a semantic service specification. As for the non-semantic description, various pieces of information are required to annotate the service. The mainly relevant information source are the service ontology and various relevant domain ontologies.

The semantic specification itself can be divided into two major steps: the semantic grounding specification and the semantic service specification.

Fundamental for the semantic specification is the classification of the service. The classification is reached by assigning the service to a specific domain (e.g. Payment, Logistic, etc.). For the Web service technology, tools like ASSAM [86] support the classification task by proposing categories basing on WSDL descriptions. The domain of the service identifies the associated domain ontology, which is required for the semantic annotation. If no suitable domain ontology exists, the engineer has to define a new one (see Sect. 3.3). Once the domain ontology is chosen, the engineer is able to connect the description of the Web service with concepts defined in the domain ontology. Specifically, the interface description is connected with ontology to specify the semantics of data types and parameters.

This task can be partly supported by tools. For instance, the names, parameters, and parameter types of the operations can be extracted automatically from the WSDL description. However the mapping to the related concepts has to be done manually, with tools like the OntoMat-Service-Browser [7]. They support the engineer by providing a graphical user interface for connecting ontology concepts with the metadata describing the Web service. The result of this step is the semantic grounding specification, the parts of preconditions and effects that specify input and output parameters (see also Sect. 3.4.1).

After the specification of the semantic grounding the functionality and the protocol needs to be specified. Parts of these are already specified implicitly as part of the grounding specification, like the input parameters. In sum, "all parts of the protocol and the functionality that can be derived from the data flow can be specified implicitly" [161]. The rest of the semantics need to be specified by means of pre- and post-conditions, assumptions and effects. The specification of those is a very complex task and must be done by the engineer manually.

The last step is to semantically specify the non-functional properties of the service. Depending on the complexity, non-functional properties can be specified automatically (e.g. name of the service) or need to be specified manually (e.g. *Quality of Service (QoS)* properties). Information about the non-functional properties can be extracted from all the information sources introduced earlier.

5

Service Composition and Binding

Marek Kowalkiewicz, Andre Ludwig, Harald Meyer, Jan Schaffner,
Christian Stamber, and Sebastian Stein

5.1 Overview and Motivation

Service composition enables the creation of services previously unavailable through the aggregation of existing services. The result is called a service composition. Exposing a service composition as a service, the result is called a composed service. It can be distinguished from atomic services. Service composition approaches can be differentiated along two axes: point in time of composition and degree of automation. With *design-time* and *run-time* we can identify two different points in time for doing a composition. Additionally we can distinguish between three different degrees of automation: *manual*, *assisted*, and *automated* service composition.

Using design-time composition, the composition is created before the system goes productive. This often happens during the development phase of an application or system. Furthermore, design-time compositions are usually indented to be re-used many times, which means that they have to be designed in such a way that they are able to handle differences in the various requests they are used for. In contrast, run-time created compositions are usually intended to be throw-away compositions. Which means that they are created for one request, optimised for this request, and later thrown away after the enactment of the request.

Distinguishing different degrees of automation is not as simple, since the borders between manual, assisted, and automated compositions are blurred. In manual composition, a human process designer creates the composition. In assisted composition, an advanced modelling tool supports him in doing this activity. Finally, in automated composition the tool creates the composition automatically. The distinction between these three categories is blurred at some points, because the following questions arise: If a human checks the correctness of the composition afterwards, are we still talking about an automated composition or is this only an assisted composition? On the other hand, how many features must a modelling tool support in order to still be characterised as supporting assisted compositions?

While giving a detailed and well elaborated answer to these questions may be interesting for academia, we will use a pragmatic criterion to distinguish the compositions. If typically no human being sees a created composition, it is automated, if a non-automated approach supports the three mixed-initiative features (which will be presented in Sect. 5.3) it is an assisted composition. Otherwise it is a manual composition.

The upcoming sections will discuss the various possibilities of constructing service compositions. Starting with Sect. 5.2, we will give a brief overview on how manual service composition works and what the resulting artefacts of such a composition usually are. Approaches to assist the manual service composition task will be discussed and presented in Sect. 5.3. Basing on this, we will then discuss in Sect. 5.4 the challenges of dynamic service environments and how these challenges can be addressed with automated service composition. Finally, we will discuss in Sect. 5.5 different service binding strategies based on service selection and negotiation regarding non-functional properties of services. These last two sections, namely Sects. 5.4 and 5.5, explain in detail how the Planning Sub-Cycle and the Binding Sub-Cycle of our proposed service delivery life-cycle, as shown in Fig. 2.6 on page 32, can be implemented in an adaptive service provision platform. To provide a broad perspective on current research in the area of service composition and binding, Sect. 5.6 introduces service composition and binding as developed in the Integrated Project SUPER, supported by the EU in the Sixth Framework Programme.

5.2 Manual Composition

Manual, design time composition is currently the prevalent approach to perform service composition in industry. A composition is created by a process designer containing all the necessary activities to reach the goal, their ordering, the data flow between them, and organisational information, if the composition contains human activities. Most of the time, the process created by the process designer is not already executable. It will lack the necessary information about which services to invoke to achieve which activity, and the data flow is not detailed enough to deal with the required transformations to map the output of one service into the input of another one. Performing these tasks and so mapping of the business process to the actual IT infrastructure is the job of the process engineer. His role is to find suitable services for the activities. To do so, it might be necessary to change the process structure. For example one activity can only be achieved by several services, or one service can achieve multiple activities.

In the following, we will show which approaches the process designer and respectively the process engineer can use today. Before we go into details of these approaches, we will elaborate the above mentioned methodology in more details.

5.2.1 Methodology

Calling the following steps a *methodology* is quite ambitious. A much more sophisticated methodology for developing service based applications is shown in Sect. 8.1.

The main idea behind showing this methodology is to make the separation between process designer and process engineer clearer and hence explain why one approach will later be characterised as a graphical notation and hence of importance for the process designer and why another approach is characterised as a composition language and hence of primary interest for the process engineer. Another reason why we present this methodology here is because it helps us later to motivate assisted and automated composition by showing which tasks can be automated. Creating a service composition includes the following steps:

1. identifying the goal of the composition,
2. selecting services,
3. ordering services correctly (control and data flow), and
4. checking whether the composition is correct.

Let us have a look at an example from the use case scenario in Sect. 2.2, to demonstrate what happens in each of these steps. We want to register a domain including web space and a hosted e-mail server. The first step is quite simple. Of course, the goal of the composition is to register a domain and to set up web space and the hosted e-mail server. As we also want to get paid, another part of the goal of the composition is that the user has to pay for the provided services.

The next step is to select the required services: a domain registration service, services to set up the web space and the e-mail server, and a payment service. A first version of the resulting process might look like Fig. 5.1.

To model the data flow of this process, we need to identify the input and output of each service. The domain registration service expects a domain name and name and address of a person to whom the domain should be registered. Its output indicates whether domain registration was successful or not. The payment service expects the payment details (credit card number, credit card validity date and owner) and outputs a receipt. Finally, the web space and mail server creation services expect the user account as well as the domain name for which they should be set up. They output details about the created web space and mail server. Looking at these inputs and outputs of the used services, we can deduce that in order to invoke the composition we need to provide:

• a domain name,
• the name and address of the person registering the domain,

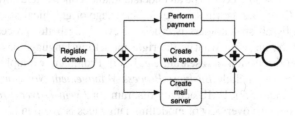

Fig. 5.1. First version of the modelled process

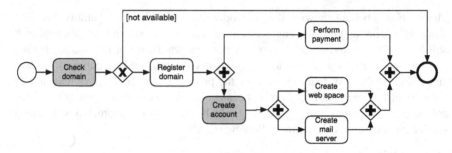

Fig. 5.2. Second version of the modelled process

- the payment details,
- a user account.

Where should the user account come from? A new customer will normally not have an user account. Hence, the composition is incomplete. Another issue is what happens if the domain has already been registered. Depending on the implementation details of the enactment engine and the domain registration service, the composition will either be aborted with a cryptic error message or will continue to reach an undesired state (customer has paid but the domain has not been registered). The second version of the composition depicted in Fig. 5.2 is an attempt to solve these problems. Before creating web space and mail server, the account is created and in the beginning we check whether the domain is available or not.

The problem of an already registered domain is not solved completely. Somebody could register the domain after we checked its availability. To prevent this, we would need to run the whole composition as one transaction. But as at least some of the services are external, distributed transaction management is required. While standardisation approaches for distributed transactions of Web services exist, this is outside the scope of this book.

5.2.2 Graphical Notations for the Process Designer

The main job of the process designer is to identify the processes of a company and model them. It is his task to foster discussion about them, to make process optimisation or outsourcing possible, and to enable their automation. Hence, the result of the process designer's work needs to be an understandable, concise, and correct model of the processes. Choosing the right modelling language or graphical notation that can be understood by all stakeholders is crucial. Developing better process modelling languages and the question what is the right modelling language has been an important point of discussion in research, e.g. [159]. Prominent examples for process modelling languages include *Business Process Management Notation (BPMN)* (as seen in Figs. 5.1 and 5.2), UML activity diagrams or *Event-Driven Process Chains (EPC)*'s. An extensive overview of modelling languages is given in [204].

5.2.3 Composition Languages for the Process Engineer

A composition language describes the actually executable processes. Hence, they are used by process engineers to create the executable process out of the modelled processes by the process designer.

Today, the predominant composition language in service oriented systems is *Web Services Business Process Execution Language (WS-BPEL)* [149]. Recently, the version 2.0 of the language has been released providing extensions and clarifications to version 1.1. The development of WS-BPEL 2.0 was triggered by the transfer of the specification to the *Organization for the Advancement of Structured Information Standards (OASIS)*. Previously, WS-BPEL (at that time also known as BPEL4WS) was developed by several vendors including IBM, Microsoft, and SAP. This effort originated from two previous efforts: XLang by Microsoft and the *Web Services Flow Language (WSFL)* by IBM.

These origins explain some of the specifics of the WS-BPEL control flow model. As XLang supports composition in a block-structured way and WSFL in a graph-structured way, it was decided that WS-BPEL should support both. In the following, we will give a brief overview of WS-BPEL constructs. For a more detailed description we refer you to the WS-BPEL language specification [149] and the WS-BPEL primer [150]. To describe the control flow in a block-structured way, WS-BPEL supports structured activities:

- *sequence*: execute contained activities sequentially;
- *if-else*: execute either one or the other activity;
- *while, repeatUntil*: loop based on a condition, with *while* the condition is checked before and with *repeatUntil* afterwards;
- *forEach*: loop a fixed number of times; a sequential and a parallel variant exist;
- *flow*: execute contained activities in parallel.

All these structured activities can themselves contain structured or atomic activities. To support graph-structured compositions a flow activity may contain links. A link provides an ordering between a source and a target activity. The most important atomic activities in WS-BPEL are of course the Web service activities to send and receive messages:

- *receive* a message from an external partner;
- *invoke* a service provided by an external partner;
- *reply* to a message received previously.

A receive activity is always the first activity in a WS-BPEL process creating the process instance and receiving the input data. Typically a service ends with a reply activity, returning the process result to the partner who initiated the process. Figure 5.3 shows a summary of atomic and structured WS-BPEL activities.

One important aspect of an executable composition is the data flow. Services can only work correctly if invoked with the correct data. Getting the correct data is not trivial. The output data (or part of it) of a service is typically the input data (or part of it) of another service. This means that data needs to be extracted and recombined.

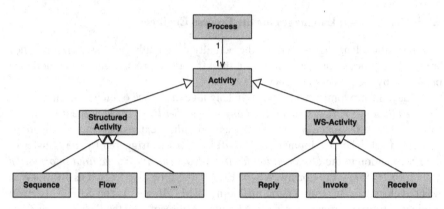

Fig. 5.3. Structured and atomic WS-BPEL activities

As WS-BPEL composes Web services, all the data are XML artefacts. Accordingly, XPath is used to extract data from service output to be inserted into the input data of another service.

As the services invoked and provided by a WS-BPEL process are Web services, the integration with *Web Services Description Language (WSDL)* is crucial. The key point for the integration is the WS-BPEL concept of partner links and part link types. A Web service activity in a WS-BPEL process references a partner link and a Web service operation name. The partner link is an instance of a partner link type and a partner link type has two roles referencing the port type publishing the operation. The link to a concrete service is typically done using a WS-Addressing endpoint reference in the partner link. All these relations are displayed in Fig. 5.4.

WS-BPEL itself is limited as it only allows for the composition of Web service interactions. Hence, several extensions were proposed to enhance its use cases:

- BPELJ [20] allows for in-lined Java constructs in a WS-BPEL process for e.g. loop and branching conditions or variable assignment;
- BPEL4People [6] together with WS-HumanTask [5] extends WS-BPEL by human tasks;
- BPEL-SPE [93] enables the invocation of WS-BPEL processes as sub processes of another WS-BPEL process;
- BPEL4Chor [55] uses WS-BPEL to model choreographies;
- *BPEL^{Light}* [143] is a light-weight version of WS-BPEL without the dependency on WSDL.

None of the above mentioned extensions is currently standardised or in the process of being standardised by any independent standardisation body. BPEL4People and correspondingly WS-HumanTask currently have the broadest industry support, while BPEL-SPE is a joint white paper between IBM and SAP, BPELJ is a joint white paper between BEA and IBM, and BPEL4Chor and *BPEL^{Light}* are currently academic efforts.

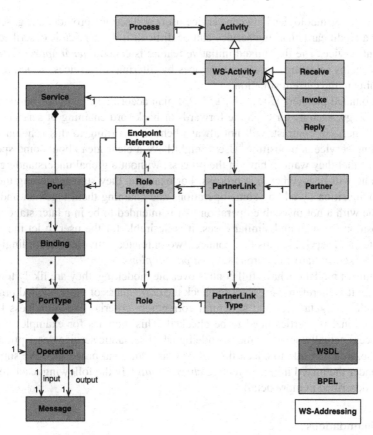

Fig. 5.4. Integration of BPEL and WSDL

5.3 Assisted Composition

Given large service landscapes, creating compositions is a time-consuming and error-prone task. As we have seen in the short methodology above, you have to find the correct services, order them and their data flow correctly, and verify that the resulting composition does indeed achieve the intended goal. Assisted composition tries to simplify these steps. Different degrees of assistance exist. Even the most simple composition tool provides some assistance (e.g. searching for services). To classify them, three distinct features, called *mixed-initiative features* can be identified [168, 169].

Finding correct services is a crucial yet complicated task in large service based systems. First of all, such systems tend to be large incorporating hundreds or thousands of services. Second, these service landscapes are at best described by accurate service names and textual documentation. Finding a service is possible only through free text search. If service names are inaccurate or incorrect and documentation non-existent, this task becomes even more complicated. Issues also arise from different mindsets or terminologies between service users and service providers. E.g. searching for a credit card charging service can be difficult if the service is described as a payment service. The first mixed initiative feature is called *filter inappropriate services*. It helps selecting the correct services by filtering all services, which are not applicable in the current situation.

Automated planners [213, 154, 177, 23] plan according to an algorithmic planning strategy, such as for example forward- or backward chaining of services. Human planners, in contrast, will not always behave according to this schema when modelling service composition. Users might have a clear idea about some specific activities that they want to have in the process, without a global understanding how the whole will fit together as a process. For example, they start modelling the service composition by adding some operations and chaining them together, and then continue with a not invocable operation that is intended to be in a later stage of the composition. In such and similar cases, it is desirable for the user to let the editor generate valid service chains that connect two unrelated activities. Accordingly, the second mixed-initiative feature is *suggest partial plan*.

If human modellers have full control over the modelling, they are likely to make mistakes. It is therefore necessary to check the correctness of the modelled process. This includes syntactical and structural correctness criteria, like soundness [198]. But additional properties need to be checked. This includes for example whether the process actually achieves the intended goal. If semantic service descriptions are available, it is possible to check this, as well as additional properties. We subsume them under the mixed initiative feature *check validity*. In the following, each feature will be described in more detail.

5.3.1 Foundations

In this section, we provide the necessary formal foundations. We begin with introducing the notion of *service operations*. They are the basic building blocks from which service compositions are built. Each service operation has a semantic specification of its functionality.

Definition 1 (Service operation). *A service operation is a tuple* $op = (I, O, pre, eff)$ *consisting of:*

- *I: List of input parameters consisting of variables.*
- *O: List of output parameters consisting of variables.*
- *pre: The precondition of the service is a logical expression and must be satisfied in order to invoke the service.*
- *eff: The effect of the service is a logical expression. It describes the changes to the current state resulting from the invocation of the service.*

A service invocation $i = (s, Z)$ *is a pair consisting of a service operation* $s = (I, O, pre, eff)$ *and a variable assignment* $Z : V \rightarrow T_{ground}$ *that assigns every variable a ground term. Formally speaking, this is a Herbrand interpretation and* T_{ground} *is the Herbrand universe* [109]. *Variables* $v \in V$ *are all the elements from* I

and $\mathcal{O}$ plus the variables from pre and eff. pre^Z and eff^Z are the precondition and effect with all variables bound according to the variable assignment Z.

The syntactic interface consists of the input and output parameters. The semantic interface specifies the precondition that must hold true in order to invoke the operation and the effect specifying the state changes resulting from invoking the operation. Both precondition and effect are logical expressions. The logical expressions are sets of literals defined over the relations, functions, constants, and variables. The input and output parameters are typed variables used also in these logical expressions. Formally, this is defined as:

Definition 2 (Logical expression). *A logical expression $e \in E$ defined over a alphabet (R, F, C, V) with the set of relations R, the set of functions F, the set of constants C, and the set of variables V is:*

- *T is the set of terms. T_{ground} is a subset of T containing only ground terms. A term $t \in T$ is a logical expression:*
  - *A variable $v \in V$ is an atom ($v \in T$, $v \notin T_{ground}$).*
  - *A constant $c \in C$ is an atom ($c \in T_{ground} \subset T$).*
  - *If $f \in F$ is a function and $t_1, \ldots, t_n \in T$ then $f(t_1, \ldots, t_n) \in T$. If $t_1, \ldots, t_n \in T_{ground}$ then $f(t_1, \ldots, t_n) \in T_{ground}$.*
- *If $r \in R$ is a relation and $t_1, \ldots, t_n \in T$ are terms then $r(t_1, \ldots, t_n) \in E$.*
- *If e is a logical expression, so is $\neg e$ ($e \in E \Rightarrow \neg e \in E$).*
- *If e_1 and e_2 are logical expressions so is their disjunction $e_1 \vee e_2$ and conjunction $e_1 \wedge e_2$ ($e_1, e_2 \in E \Rightarrow e_1 \vee e_2 \in E$ and $e_1 \wedge e_2 \in E$).*

A logical expression is disjunction-free if it does not contain disjunctions. A disjunction-free logical expression a can be divided into the two logical expression a^+ and a^- where a^+ contains all positive literals and a^- contains all negated literals. If $a^+ = a$ then a is negation-free.

A state is a disjunction-free and negation-free logical expression without variables. All states form the set $E_{state} \subset E$.

A logical expression a satisfies another logical expression a' (written as: $a \models a'$) if every positive literal of a' is in a and no negative literal of a' is in a.

With these basic definitions of what a service is, how service functionality can be expressed, and how services can be composed, we can start describing the mixed initiative features.

5.3.2 Filter Inappropriate Services

Filter inappropriate services filters those services that are not invocable in the current state. For example, in the current state shown in Fig. 5.5 only few service are actually invocable (e.g. perform payment and create account) and others are not (e.g. create web space and create mail server). The invocable ones should be the only ones available after all inappropriate services have been filtered. To realise this feature, we

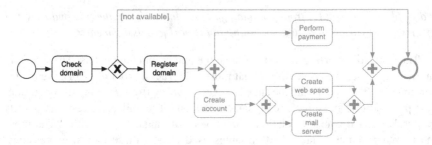

Fig. 5.5. One intermediate modelling step

need to know what service invocability means. A service is invocable if all its input parameters are available and its precondition is satisfied. Formally, invocability is defined as follows.

Definition 3 (Invocability). *A service invocation* $i = (s, Z)$ *with* $s = (\mathcal{I}, \mathcal{O}, p, e)$ *is invocable in state* a *if* $a \models p$. *Invoking service an invocable* s *with variable assignment* Z *in state* a *leads to a state transition. This can be defined by the state transition function* $\gamma(a, i) = a \cup e^+ \setminus \{x | \neg x \in e^-\}$. γ *is a partial function only defined if* $a \models p$.

As defined above, states contain only positive literals. This means that we only add the positive literals from the effect to the state. The negated literals are then used to remove all literals from this state for which a negated literal exists in the effect. During our experiments, we learned that filtering all services which are not invocable is too restrictive. For fully automated composition, such restrictive filtering is appropriate, because the algorithm should not create invalid service compositions. In the mixed initiative environment we target at, it might be the case that human modellers want to add services to the composition although they are currently not invocable. Therefore, we introduce the notion of nearly invocable services. A service is nearly invocable to the degree k if at most k input parameters are missing. Formally:

Definition 4 (Nearly invocable). *Given a state* S *and a service operation* $op = (I, O, Pre, Eff)$, *op is nearly invocable to the degree* k *if* $(I = \{i_0, \ldots, i_m, \ldots, i_{m+k}, \ldots, i_n\}$ *with* $n = |I|)$:

- $\forall i_i \in I, i < m, i_i \in facts(S)$,
- $\forall i_i \in I, i > k + m, i_i \in facts(S)$,
- $\forall l \in Pre^+$ *with* $l = r(x_0, \ldots, x_i), r \in R$ *and* $\forall x_i \notin \{i_m, \ldots, i_{m+k}\}$: $l \in S$, *and*
- $\forall \neg l \in Pre^-$ *with* $l = r(x_0, \ldots, x_i), r \in R$ *and* $\forall x_i \notin \{i_m, \ldots, i_{m+k}\}$: $l \notin S$.

If an operation is invocable to a degree k, *then it is also invocable to all degrees* j, *with* $1 \leq j \leq k$.

The first two conditions specify exactly what was described above: it might be the case that k inputs are not satisfied in order for the operation to be invocable. The last two conditions are necessary to relax the satisfaction requirement for the precondition. Only those literals in the precondition not containing one of the missing inputs need to be satisfied in the state.

Using the notions of invocable and nearly invocable services, the modeller is now able to retrieve more service suggestions through the filtering mechanism. E.g. in Fig. 5.5 now the services to create web space and mail server are selectable.

5.3.3 Suggest Partial Plan

Suggesting a partial plan can be reduced to solving a planning problem:

Definition 5 (Planning problem). *A planning problem* $P = (s_0, s_g, SD)$ *is a triple consisting of the initial state* a_0 *in* E_{state}, *the goal* $g \in E$ *and a service domain SD. A service domain* $SD = (OP, O)$ *consists of a set of service operations OP and ontology describing the concepts used to specify services.*

In order to suggest a partial plan, it is therefore necessary to determine the initial state and the goal state for the planning problem. The initial state can be determined by adding up all the effects of the services leading to the gap. The initial state then contains all the available information. The goal state can be determined from the pre-conditions of the services succeeding the gap. But of course, the information already known in the initial state can be removed from the goal state. These are preconditions already satisfied by preceding operations. Additionally, preconditions of services after the gap can be satisfied by other services also succeeding the gap but preceding this service. These preconditions can also be removed from the goal state. Using the generated planning problem an automated planner can be used to fill the gap.

5.3.4 Check Validity

Checking the validity of a modelled process actually consists of two distinct tasks: checking whether the process itself is correct and checking whether it achieves the intended goal. We call the first one *semantic correctness* and the second one *semantic conformance*. We define semantic correctness as:

Definition 6 (Semantic correctness). *A service composition is semantically correct if*

- *it does not contain activities with unsatisfied inputs or preconditions,*
- *all activities in the composition are relevant, and*
- *it does not contain potentially redundant activities that have not been flagged as explicitly not redundant.*

Let us have a look at each criterion individually. Unsatisfied inputs and preconditions of activities mean that the composition is incorrect. It cannot be invoked without producing an error. Our first modelling example (Fig. 5.1 on page 75), would have yielded several errors as the input and probably also the precondition of creating web space and mail server were not satisfied. Formally, these two properties can be defined by:

Definition 7 (Unsatisfied Input). *An input $i \in I$ is unsatisfied for a service operation $op = (I, O, Pre, Eff)$ in a state S if $i \notin facts(S)$.*

Definition 8 (Unsatisfied Precondition). *The precondition Pre of a service operation $op = (I, O, Pre, Eff)$ is unsatisfied in a state S if*

- $\exists l \in Pre: l \notin S$ *or*
- $\exists \neg \in Pre: l \in S$.

These definitions are inverse to the invocability definition from above. While a service composition violating the first criterion will also be syntactically ill-formed, a service composition violating the second criterion might very well be syntactically correct. It only affects the composition on the semantic level. This means that it is possible to technically invoke a service composition containing operations with unsatisfied preconditions while this is not possible if operations have unsatisfied inputs.

The third criterion defines the relevance of a service operation inside a composition. This is necessary because it can be difficult for human modellers to determine whether each service operation is required in a complex service composition. This property can be used to assure us that the create account service is actually needed. A service operation in a composition is relevant if one of its outputs is consumed by a successor operation in the composition. If the operation does not have no successor operation, we assume that it is relevant. Formally:

Definition 9 (Relevance). *A service operation $op' = (I', O', Pre', Eff') \in OP$ in a service composition is relevant if*

- $\exists op'' = (I'', O'', Pre'', Eff'')$ *and* $op' \xrightarrow{e^*} op''$ *with* $\exists x, x \in O' \wedge x \in I''$ *or*
- $\nexists op'' = (I'', O'', Pre'', Eff'')$ *and* $op' \xrightarrow{e^*} op''$ *(final activity).*[1]

It might be the case that several operations in a service composition produce the same output. Such activities are potentially redundant. Detecting redundancy in a fully automated fashion is very complex: not only the outputs of the redundant operations, but also the effects must exactly match. This is rarely the case. Instead, operations without matching outputs and precondition are often redundant. We therefore define potential redundancy as a week criterion: An operation is redundant if another operation produces the same output. Formally:

Definition 10 (Potential redundancy). *A service operation op' with $op' = (I', O', Pre', Eff') \in OP$ is potentially redundant if another operation $op'' = (I'', O'', Pre'', Eff'')$ exists with $o' \in O', o'' \in O'', type(o') = type(o'')$.*

This potential redundancy needs to be addressed by the human modellers. They can either resolve the potential redundancy or flag it as not redundant. This mechanism leads to many potential redundancies. A potential extension could include the ranking of possible redundancies based on the overlapping of operation outputs and to only alarm the user if the match is higher than a predefined threshold.

---

[1] $op' \xrightarrow{e^*} op''$ denotes that that there is a path in the composition connecting op' and op''.

With the second property, *semantic conformance*, the process is checked against a specification. It can be used to check whether a process achieves the intended functionality. This can be defined as:

Definition 11 (Semantic Conformance). *A process n is semantically conform to a process specification* $R = (I, O, pre, eff)$ *if:*

1. $pre_R \models pre_n$ *with* pre_n *the precondition of the process,*
2. $eff_n \models eff_R$ *with* eff_n *the effect of the process, and*
3. $(pre_R \cup s) \models pre_i$ *for all activity instances i and for all states s of the process in which i can be invoked.*

This means that a process is conform to the specification, if every possible precondition of the modelled process is valid according to the precondition of the specification, if it always reaches the goal (effect) of the specification, and if every contained activity instance is invocable whenever it can be invoked. To test these properties we need to be able to calculate three things: pre_n, the precondition of the process, eff_n, the effect of the process, and all states s in which an activity instance can possibly be invoked. In [128] we showed how they can be calculated using a Petri net based model of the process.

Using the approach for calculating semantic conformance will actually enable us to detect more *semantic correctness* violations. For example we could use it to test whether parallel activities are in conflict or not. It also will make checking for unsatisfied preconditions easier. But these extensions of semantic correctness are still in research.

5.3.5 Case Study

Together with SAP Labs in Palo Alto we realised the three above-mentioned mixed-initiative features as an extension of the SAP Netweaver Visual Composer. How the architecture looks like is shown in Fig. 5.6. Crucial components of the back end were actually the reasoner and the composer from the Adaptive Services Grid project that were used to implement the mixed-initiative features. The composer will be presented in the next section on run-time composition.

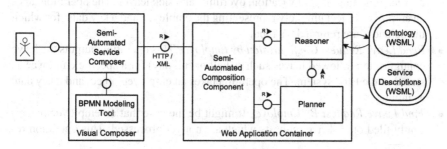

Fig. 5.6. Assisted composition with SAP Netweaver Visual Composer

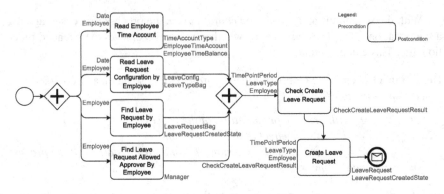

Fig. 5.7. Leave request scenario

As a show case a small process from Duet,[2] a recent software product by SAP and Microsoft. Duet extends the reach of SAP's business processes to a large number of users by embedding them into Microsoft's Office environment. We extracted the process flow among the ERP Web services Duet is built upon. The leave request scenario consists of two parts. First, an employee files a leave request. Second, his manager approves or denies this request. Therefore, the two roles *employee* and *manager* participate in the leave request process. Due to length constraints, we limit ourselves to the part of the process in the role of the employee. The scenario is depicted in Fig. 5.7 using the BPMN [159]. The activities in the diagram correspond to Web service operations. To describe the semantics of the operations, we extended the BPMN syntax so that we can depict *Web Services Modeling Ontology (WSMO)* service capabilities: The inputs that a service consumes and the conditions over these inputs make up the precondition. The outputs of a service and the relation between input and output make up the postcondition.

Before the employee files a leave request, he will typically try to get an overview of his time balance and suitable dates for the leave. Duet will collect this information when the leave request application pane is opened. Therefore, Duet will call the following four Web service operations.

- *Read Employee Time Account* This operation returns the time balance of an employee consisting of paid vacation, overtime, and sick leaves. The operation takes an employee object uniquely representing the employee and a key date, for which the balances are returned, as input.
- *Read Leave Request Configuration by Employee* This operation outputs the leave configuration (allowed leaves such as half or full day) for a specific employee as stored in the ERP system. The operation takes an employee object and a key date as input.
- *Find Leave Request By Employee* It might be the case that an employee has recently filed other leave requests which are not yet processed. This operation re-

---

[2] http://www.duet.com.

turns an employee's pending leave requests, so that he or she can consider them together with the time balance. The operation takes an employee object as input.

- *Find Leave Request Allowed Approver by Employee* A leave request is approved by the line manager of the employee filing it. In some cases, a different approver or no approval at all is necessary. This operation returns the employee object corresponding to the allowed approver for the leave request. It takes an employee object as input.

The information retrieved by the four service operation described above is visualised in Duet and the employee can decide on a day or a period browsing his Outlook calendar. This yields the sequential invocation of the two following operations:

- *Check Create Leave Request* Before a leave request is created in the ERP system, it must be checked for plausibility. This operation takes the same inputs as the operation that creates the leave request, which are an employee object, the leave period and the leave type. If the check is successful, the operation returns a positive result.
- *Create Leave Request* After the plausibility check has been successful, this operation finally creates the leave request in the ERP system. As a result, a leave request is created.

Now let us have a look at how the three mixed initiative features can support modelling this process.

Filter Inappropriate Services

When the leave request is to be created from scratch, the tool will first retrieve all available Web services. The modeller starts out with adding the role *employee* to the composition by selecting this role from a list of all available roles (e.g., *supplier*, *customer*, *manager*). Our tool then assumes the implicit availability of a variable of the complex type *employee*, representing the person who takes part in the business process in this role. The tool is now able to filter the list of available service operations to those that require an employee object as an input. Our experiments have shown that filtering all service operations that are not be invocable in the current step of the composition is too strict. The tool therefore also presents service operations that are nearly invocable in the sense that only one input is missing. Using this technique, we are able to retrieve very reasonable suggestions from the service repository. The operations in this repository are grouped around so-called enterprise services. In our example, the modeller would therefore now expand the *Time and Leave Management* enterprise service and select the first four operations depicted in Fig. 5.7. As there are no dependencies between the activities, the user connects the operations using a parallel control flow. This is shown in Fig. 5.8.

At this point, the modeller is able to retrieve more service suggestions through the filtering mechanism by clicking on the merge node of the parallel split. Our tool will then present a list of service operations that are invocable or nearly invocable based on the union all postconditions of the services which are in the composition so

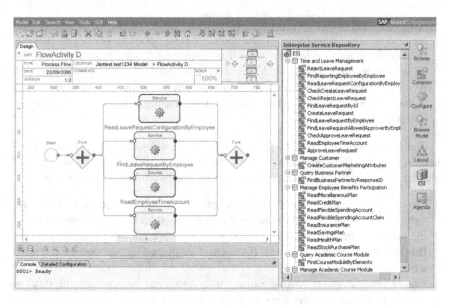

Fig. 5.8. Screenshot of the modelling tool

far. The postconditions (i.e., the output data types) of the operations are also depicted in Fig. 5.7. Amongst others, our tool will suggest the operation *Check Create Leave Request* as a nearly invocable service. The modeller adds it to the composition and creates a link between the merge node and the operation.

Suggest Partial Plan

In the last step, the modeller resolved a problem with the *Check Create Leave Request* operation. If the user clicks on the operation to refresh the filtered list of available services, the tool will suggest the *Create Leave Request* operation. From the perspective of the user, this is the final operation. However, the modeller might not be familiar with the fact that a specific check operation needs to be invoked in order to create a leave request in the system. He then directly selected the *Create Leave Request* operation after the merge node depicted in Fig. 5.8. The modeller also creates the human activity producing the *TimePointPeriod* and links it to the *Create Leave Request* operation. Now, the modeller tries to create a link between the merge node of the parallel flow and *Create Leave Request*. The tool will detect that the set of postconditions up to the merge node does not satisfy the preconditions of *Create Leave Request* (the type *CheckCreateLeaveRequestResult* is missing). The tool instantly queries the semi-automated composition engine which detects that the insertion of the *Check Create Leave Request* operation would satisfy this open information requirement. The user is prompted whether or not the *Check Create Leave Request* should be inserted. The modeller approves this suggestion and the composition is complete.

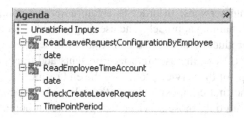

Fig. 5.9. Agenda summarising the problems with the composition

Check Validity

As the last step, the modeller added the nearly invocable operation *Check Create Leave Request*. The tool highlights operations for which problems are tracked. As the added operation is not invocable, but nearly invocable, one input type is missing. The tool therefore marks the operation with a red border. This can also be seen in Fig. 5.8, where two out of four activities are highlighted. By clicking on the *Check Create Leave Request* operation, the user can open a panel showing its input and output types as inferred from the pre- and postconditions. The user sees that all input types of the operation are currently available in the composition, except *TimePointPeriod*, which is also highlighted using red colour in this drill-down view. The user can also get an overview of all current problems with the composition by looking at the agenda, depicted in Fig. 5.9.

The missing parameter *TimePointPeriod* represents the date or period for which the employee intends to request a leave. As our scenario has been taken from Duet, this data is provided by Microsoft Outlook after a the user selects a date from the calendar. In our example, the modeller therefore creates a human activity (modelling a task such as marking a period in the calendar) that produces a *TimePointPeriod* output. The modeller connects the human activity with the *Check Create Leave Request* operation. The colouring of the operation and the *TimePointPeriod* input type in the parameter view disappear and the issue is removed from the agenda.

5.3.6 Other Assisted Composition Approaches

Web Service Composer

Sirin, Parsia and Hendler [176] present a prototypical implementation of a composer for Web services. Their tool allows creating compositions of Web services that are semantically specified with OWL-S [125] and their execution. The created service compositions can in turn be stored as OWL-S process models. Process models are a part of OWL-S ontologies which is normally used to encode the choreography for a described service. Well-known control constructs from the area of Workflow Management can be used within OWL-S process models. It is therefore a suitable format for representing service compositions. The focus of their work is on filtering the list of available services at each composition step and thus helping the user to select the appropriate services. In order to create a service composition, the user follows a backward chaining approach. The user begins with selecting a Web service that has an output producing the desired end result of the composition from a list of all available services. Next, the user interface presents additional lists connected to each OWL input type of the service producing the end result.

In contrast to the first composition step, these lists do not contain all available services: They contain only those services that generate an output compliant to the particular input type they are connected to. An output of a service A is compliant to an input of a service B, if their types are exactly the same or if the output of A subsumes the input of B (i.e., the input of B is a specialisation of the output of A). If a service is selected from the list of compliant services, this service's inputs must again be produced by selecting services producing compliant outputs. This is repeated until the user decides at one point to provide the inputs that are not connected to a compliant service by entering them as input values (or connecting them to compliant services that have no input parameters).

Creating the service composition by forward chaining (i.e., starting with the first activity in the process instead of the last one) is planned but not implemented in their prototype. In addition to filtering on the compliance of the services in terms of their inputs and outputs, the user can apply further filtering based on the non-functional properties of the services. This only works for services that adhere to a specific OWL-S service profile (i.e., they implement the service profile). Once the user has selected a service profile, the system renders an UI element which allows him or her to provide values for the non-functional properties that are specified for the selected service profile. The user can then apply the filter, thereby further restricting the set of services that are presented for the current composition step.

The Web Service Composer filters the list of services that can be included in the composition at each composition step. This realises the *filter inappropriate services* feature. However, the realisation of this use case in Web Service Composer is restricted in two ways: First, the tool only considers inputs and outputs, i.e., the mere data transformation that services realise. The preconditions that must be satisfied before the execution of the services and the effects that the executions of the services have on the state of the world are not taken into account. Second, the selection of appropriate services is done per input of a downstream service that must be satisfied, which is due to the strict backward chaining approach imposed by the tool. This means in consequence that the plans constructed with the tool are not always optimal. For example, when one service operation delivers two outputs each of which satisfies a different input of a downstream service, this services operation has to occur twice in the composed service. Web Service Composer supports two extensions of the *filter inappropriate services* feature: First, the tool can further restrict the set of filtered services according to user-specified values of non-functional properties that are common to that set. Second, the list of filtered services which is presented to the user is ordered according to the goodness of match: Services that exactly produce a necessary input for a downstream service (such as an exact match) are ranked higher than services that produce outputs that subsume the necessary inputs.

PASSAT

Myers et al. present PASSAT (Plan-Authoring System based on Sketches, Advice, and Templates) [137], an interactive tool for constructing plans. PASSAT is not directly concerned with the creation of service compositions, but its concepts can be mapped into the context of service composition.

PASSAT is based on hierarchical task networks (HTN) [187], while the model has been extended to realise some concepts that are outlined below. In HTN planning, a task network is a set of tasks (or service calls) that have to be carried out as well as constraints on the ordering of these tasks. Moreover, it consists of a set of constraints that must be valid before the execution of the tasks and information about how the tasks instantiate variables. Because the variables (partly) describe the state of the world before and after the execution of a specific task, the constraints on these variables can be used to express preconditions and effects.

The HTN based approach naturally imposes top-down plan refinement as the planning strategy the user must adhere to: The user can start by adding tasks to a plan and refine them by applying matching HTN templates. A template consists of a set of sub tasks that replace the task being refined, as well as the preconditions and effects of applying individual tasks and the entire template. It is noteworthy that the user has the possibility to override unmatched constraints when applying a template. This is especially desirable when comprehensive domain knowledge (i.e., a collection of templates) cannot be provided. Task refinement is repeated until the plan contains no activities that can be further expanded. A core feature of PASSAT is its automated planning mode, which allows the user to have the system expand all remaining tasks, applying the templates that are currently available to the system. PASSAT also features an advice mechanism that allows the user to specify high-level policies for the overall plan being created. These policies are global constraints that restrict the set of actions that the user can undertake when developing a plan. However, they can be relaxed and overridden and need not to be necessarily satisfied to reach the overall goal. The automated planning mode also takes these policies into account when it selects the templates for refining the open tasks. Opposing the strict top-down refinement approach implied by the use of HTN networks, PASSAT provides a plan sketch facility: This allows the user to freely arrange tasks that need not to be necessarily fully specified and that can reside on different layers of abstraction (regarding the template hierarchy). After the user has outlined a plan sketch, the system tries to find possible expansions by applying matching templates. The user can then choose one of these expansions to be included in the plan and return to the normal planning mode. PASSAT also informs the user about open tasks and outstanding information requirements in order for the plan to be completed. Therefore, it presents the user with an agenda of actions such as expand task, instantiate variable and resolve constraint. The system helps the user to choose from the applicable templates at a given composition step by keeping track of past user experience: A statistic about how often a template has been applied in plan refinement is encoded in the templates.

PASSAT is the only tool of those included in this survey that partially supports the *suggest partial plan* feature. PASSAT is a tool for interactive plan authoring based on HTN networks. The user can invoke an automated planning mode to expand open tasks in the plan. This can be seen as a specialisation of the *suggest partial plan* feature in the sense that partial plans can only be generated from the current state to a state in which the composition is finished, i.e. all tasks can be executed. However, this realisation of the feature is restricted in the way that the user must have completed the plan on a high level of modelling—otherwise the task network cannot be expanded. PASSAT also supports the *check validity* feature, as it interleaves a checking mechanism with the actual planning process: After each user action the system updates an agenda showing open information requirements that must be satisfied in order to have an executable plan. As an extension to this mechanism, PASSAT orders the agenda according to user-specified criteria.

CAT

Kim, Spraragen and Gil introduce CAT (Composition Analysis Tool) [107], a tool which illustrates their approach to interactive workflow composition. The focus of their work is to assist the user in the creation of computational work flows. The authors' work is not directly related to service composition. However, we can conceive a computational workflow as a service composition. The activities of the workflow are represented by services that realise data transformations.

The authors have developed their own knowledge base format, which they use to semantically describe the components that can be used in a workflow and their input and output parameters: Component ontologies describe hierarchies of components, from abstract-level components to executable components. An abstract component represents a common set of features that applies to all components of that type. Domain ontologies semantically specify the data types which can serve as inputs and outputs of the components described in the component ontologies. In CAT, the user can add components to the composition at any time. There is no need for the user to follow a strict backward or forward chaining composition. The end result of the composition can be specified by declaring outputs produced by components as the end result (or as a part of it). Control flow in CAT is described by explicitly linking inputs and outputs of different services together. Values of input parameters can also be default values from the respective ontologies or values entered by the user. Instead of filtering the set of services that can be included in a composition, CAT provides a list of suggestions about what to do next. These suggestions resolve errors and warnings, which are also displayed. The idea is that consequently applying suggestions will produce a well-formed workflow as a result. The authors therefore introduce a set of properties that must be satisfied by the composition in order to be well-formed. These properties ensure that

- the composition has an end result,
- all components' inputs are satisfied,
- all components have been specialised to executable components,
- all components produce outputs relevant for producing the end result,

- for all links between components there is a *subsumes*-relation between the output of one component and the input of the other component,
- the composition does not contain redundant links or components.

Depending on whether these properties are satisfied or not, the ErrorScan algorithm (which is also provided in [107]) determines which suggestions are presented to the user. CAT uses heuristics to determine the ordering of the suggestions, so that more recent and more severe errors are displayed before warnings that do not necessarily have to be resolved in order that the workflow is well-formed. It is noteworthy that the suggestions in CAT have the property of being corrective or additive: Applying a suggestion never causes more errors than it resolves.

CAT checks at each composition step if the composition complies with a set of properties that describe the well-formedness of the composition. In case these properties are violated, the system consequently presents a list of warnings and errors. As an extension of this use case, the authors present an algorithm that presents the user with suitable suggestions for next steps based on the evaluation of the well-formedness criteria. The applicability of CAT has been shown in the domain of seismic hazard analysis; however, it remains unclear why the authors opted for developing their own correctness criteria for computational work flows rather than building upon more established approaches to verify workflow correctness, such as the soundness criteria introduced by van der Aalst [198]. Also, the authors do not describe how their notion of well-formedness relates to the soundness criteria for work flows.

5.4 Run-time Composition

In the previous section we presented approaches for the creation of service composition, where the focus was on manual modelling of the composition during design-time. Often these are viable approaches. However in dynamic domains with large service landscapes, this leads to a lot of work because changes in the landscape have to be manually and regularly transcribed into the composition models. In this section, we will first elaborate the problems of design-time composition and motivate run-time composition (5.4.1). Then we will present the requirements for doing automated service composition (5.4.2). In Sect. 5.4.3 an approach for run-time composition is given that uses heuristic search.

5.4.1 Motivation

Dynamic domains are characterised by two possible types of dynamics:

- service landscape changes: constantly new services are published, old ones change or are removed,
- business requirement changes: new, changing, or obsolete business requirements.

As already discussed in Sect. 2.3 traditional approaches for *service oriented architecture (SOA)* suffer from drawbacks when applied to dynamic service landscapes. If a service landscape changes, existing service compositions might become inadequate or even incorrect. A newly published service might be more suitable then previously used services because it is cheaper, faster, or aggregates the work of several existing services. If a service changes it might no longer be suitable for the compositions in which it was used previously. Of course, if a service is removed all service compositions using this service will fail. If service types exist and some form of dynamic binding (without semantics) is in place some of these problems can be solved. However this rarely works with existing Web services based on simple WSDL descriptions because the probability for a full overlapping of functionality and data structures is rather low.

Business requirement changes can have a variety of reasons. If the business expands into new markets (e.g. selling in new countries), new services are required. Business requirement changes can also be yielded by changing corporate policies or legal requirements. In both cases, if the service landscape or business requirements change, manual adjustments or the creation of new compositions is required.

Another problem with the manual composition of service compositions, is that it is an error-prone, complex tasks. Highly qualified specialists are required, who not only can model service compositions but also understand the business requirements and know what the services do. These specialists are likely to create incorrect compositions that do not work for some special case or in-optimal compositions because of the usage of in-optimal services or their incorrect chaining (e.g. sequence although parallel invocation is possible).

In-optimality can also yield from other problems. Compositions are not tailored to the individual service request. Instead they need to work for all requests including also very rare requests. This leads to more complex service compositions including decisions (xor-splits) for handling different requests. Such compositions are harder to understand and maintain by humans. Sometimes it can also be the case that a for some requests a specific service can be used but all the other requests require the more generic, probably more expensive or slower service. This service will then be used for all requests, leading to in-optimality for some requests. Changes to the service landscape can render existing service compositions in-optimal.

Shifting the service composition creation from design-time to run-time promises to solve these problems. In this case, no human modeller is involved in creating the compositions. Instead, the compositions are created automatically, on-demand based on a semantic request specification and semantic service specifications for the services in the service landscape. As compositions are not modelled up-front but created on-demand, they reflect the current status of the service landscape. Changes to the service landscape are therefore unproblematic. As there is still a time interval between creation of the composition and its actual enactment, service landscape changes happening between creation and enactment still affect the composition. But as this time interval is reduced, such problems are unlikely. Business requirements are specified in form of semantic request specifications. If they change only these specifications need to be adjusted. The resulting compositions change automatically.

As no human modeller is involved, errors and in-optimality yielding from manual modelling can only happen if semantic service specifications are incorrect. Finally, the specific tailoring to the request and the current service landscape prevent further in-optimality.

5.4.2 Requirements

Requirements analysis incorporates the collection and categorisation of requirements. The categorisation includes three main categories: general, functional and non-functional. While the general requirements can (and will) also be justified through the usage scenarios they precess the other requirements temporarily and logically. The requirements are ordered according to the following categorisation:

- elements of composition defines the building blocks of composition.
- control flow defines the order of the elements of composition inside a composition.
- data flow defines how data is exchanged between the elements of composition.
- data model defines how data elements are described.
- *Quality of Service (QoS)* defines how optimisations for compositions are described.

Following this model the requirements are described in the following.

General Composition Requirements

Service Composition Is Automated

Service composition can be performed manually, assisted, or automatically. Systems following the paradigm of service orientation, are open: Service requesters appear and disappear, and service providers register new services, change or delete existing services. Handling these demands with manually modelled compositions can be inadequate or impossible. On top of that, a company might provide a lot of very similar products. Our use case scenario might be very complicated in the real world. The company can offer just domain registration, domain registration plus e-mail addresses, or full-fledged packages. Manually modelled service compositions that handle all this different cases are complex. Complexity increases, if dependencies between services exist (e.g.: domain registration is only possible if web space is ordered, too) or if providers register or remove services.

Service providers register their services (e.g. domain registration) and offer them to customers. This can also include new types of services. A provider of e-mail accounts may want to offer its services in the Dynamic Supply Chain Management. With manual or assisted service composition the service provider asks the end service provider to adjust its service composition in order to allow customers to include an e-mail account in their package. If the end service provider uses automated service composition, new services will be used automatically. A service provider may also change or de-register its services. Again this will result in manual modelling if no automated service composition is used. Finally, the end service provider can change its application. Using automated service composition, the end service provider only needs to change the service requests. The service composition component automatically adjusts the service compositions.

Each situation presented above involves some change in the service compositions. For manual or assisted service composition this means that a person has to change the compositions manually. This is time-consuming and costly. With automated service composition no service compositions to change exist. Adaptation to changes resulting from the above mentioned openness of service oriented architectures is therefore easier.

Service Request Describes the Goal of Composition

A semantic service request is the input for automated service composition. If service enactment executes the resulting service composition, its effect should be in line with the service request.

To allow automated service composition a service request includes initial state, goal state and request data. The initial state describes the current situation before enacting the service composition. The goal state describes the state of the world that should be reached. Request data includes concrete data elements that are available in the initial state.

Service Composition According to Service Request

A service composition component creates compositions, that accord the service request: The service composition is enactable in the initial state with the given request data and enacting the service composition leads to a state that fulfils the criteria defined for the goal state.

Requirements on the Elements of Composition

The elements of composition are the building blocks from which service compositions are composed. The service specification language defines their concrete format.

Elements of Composition Are Service Interactions

The elements of a composition are activities that perform a task. The only activities are service interactions. Besides invoking services, a composition can itself be invoked as a service. The resulting composition includes service interactions only on the specification level without a binding to a concrete implementation. During the binding sub-cycle the specification is later bound to a concrete implementation. For the scenarios this means that every activity must be invocable as a service. This restriction includes all internal activities. For example, the activities to create an account and to reserve disk space on a web server are services, too.

Services Have Input and Output Parameters

Services perform a specified functionality. Often this functionality is parameterised with data provided in the service request. The registration of the domain name requires at least the domain name to register as an input parameter. Services also return a result. To allow the input and output of data, parameters are needed. A service has zero or more input and output parameters.

Service Functionality Is Described Semantically

Service functionality is described semantically to allow automated service composition. Besides input and output parameters, specifications of services include preconditions and effects. Preconditions and effects describe the state of the world and the state of available information. To do so, it is possible to define logical relations between input parameters, between output parameters and between input and output parameters. To describe functionality often additional variables that are not parameters are necessary.

Services Can Have More than One Precondition or Effect

It is common that a service has more than one precondition or effect. For example, the service to provide web space has the preconditions that enough disk space is available and that the load on the machine is acceptable. It has the effects, that web space is reserved and that an account for the user is created. All of the preconditions must hold in order to execute the service and all effects of the service happen if the service is executed.

Expressions are defined in first-order logic. Therefore expressions can be conjunctions or disjunctions of other expressions (Fig. 5.10). Conceptually services have only one precondition and one effect. If more than one precondition or effect is needed, both can be conjunctions of other expressions.

Services Can Have Disjunctive Preconditions

Besides having multiple preconditions that all must be true in order to invoke the service, a service can have disjunctive preconditions. The service is invocable, if just one of the preconditions is true. Again, we can use just one expression from first-order logic to express disjunction. It is therefore sufficient that we still limit services to just one precondition. If disjunctive preconditions are not available, they can be simulated using several distinct services.

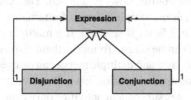

Fig. 5.10. Composition of logical expressions

Services Can Have Disjunctive Effects

Disjunctive effects are necessary to express services that can have several different effects. The web space provisioning service that is responsible for multiple web servers is an example for such a service. Depending on the selected web server, the web space will be provided on just one of the managed web servers. Implementation-wise disjunctive effects are more complicated. While missing disjunctive preconditions can be simulated, this is not possible for disjunctive effects. Disjunctive effects also increase the complexity of automated service composition [61, 73].

Control Flow Requirements

The control flow of a process or service compositions defines the order in which the elements of composition are enacted. This includes simple sequential ordering but also complex parallel or alternative control flows. Figure 5.2 on page 76 included sequential, parallel, and alternative control flows.

Requirements regarding control flow can be separated into two types of requirements: Requirements regarding the composition functionality and requirements regarding features of the composition language. With workflow patterns [197] a categorisation for different control flow constructs exists in workflow management. Requirements analysis regarding control flow will be performed according to these patterns.

Composition of Sequential Control Flow

In a sequence of activities the activities are enacted one after another in a well-defined order.

Composition of Parallel Control Flow

Parallel control flow allows the parallel invocation of activities. Parallel control flow is realised by two different patterns: parallel split and synchronization. A Parallel Split splits a single thread of control into multiple threads. A Synchronization merges them later.

Composition of Alternative Control Flow

Alternative control flows are parts in a process where—depending on some condition—one out of many possible control flows is selected. The patterns exclusive choice and simple merge constitute the simplest form of alternative control flow: Exactly one of the alternative control flows is selected. If a multiple choice is used instead, multiple alternative flows can be taken. To merge them three different patterns synchronizing merge, discriminator and multiple merge can be used. Only synchronizing merge performs synchronisation of control flows. In contrast to multiple merge, the discriminator pattern executes subsequent activities only once.

In general, a service composition component should support at least multiple choice as a splitting pattern. It can simulate parallel split and exclusive choice as special cases. Merging patterns are more complex. Of the synchronising pattern— Synchronization, simple merge and synchronizing merge—only the last one is necessary. Non-synchronising patterns are currently not possible with automated service composition algorithms.

Composition Language Supports Workflow Patterns

So far all control flow requirements were requirements regarding the functionality of the composition component. The actual output as an instance of the composition language is important as well.

The basic requirement on the composition language regarding control flow is the support of the above-mentioned required workflow pattern. This can be achieved through a graph-structured or a block-structured approach. In a graph-structured approach activities are vertices that are connected through edges that symbolise ordering constraints. In a block-structured approach structured activities exist that contain other activities and determine their enactment order. While a graph-structured approach is more generic, is a block-structured approach easier to visualise and reason about. Reasoning on process structures is for example necessary during negotiation to adhere to quality of service properties. In general it is best to support both approaches like WS-BPEL [149] does. The composition language should also support the patterns that cannot be composed automatically. This makes sense as automated composition can reuse manually modelled process fragments.

Data Flow Requirements

The data flow of composition defines how data is exchanged between the service. Services have input and output parameters. Output parameters of one service can be the input for other services. Data flow requirements include for example the ability to exchange data and the usage of process input data. The following four requirements regarding data flow are all defined over activities instead of services. This is valid as the activities represent invocations of services and the actual data exchange is done between the activities.

Activities Exchange Data

The fundamental data flow requirement is the ability to exchange data. Exchanging data between activities and therefore data flow is supported in nearly all process meta models [51, 119]. Activities have formal parameters that are replaced by actual data when invoked. This data can either be process input data or output from other activities.

Figure 5.11 illustrates data flow for our example. The *notes* are the data elements that are exchanged between the activities. An arrow leading to a data element means that it is created or modified by the originating activity. The account (*ACC*) is for example created by the create account activity. An arrow leading from a data element

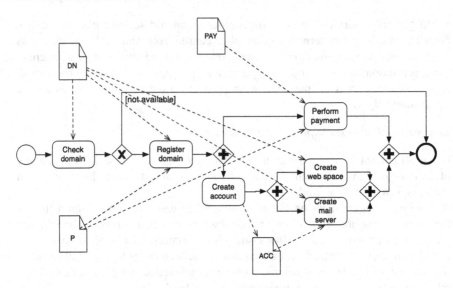

Fig. 5.11. A data flow example

to an activity symbolises that this data element is an input parameter for the activity. For example, the account is input to the create web space and create mail server activities.

In workflow management, two different approaches to model data flow are in use. With the first approach all data is stored on the process level. Input parameters of activities are read from this central storage. Output parameters are stored in this central storage or—as it is called—*blackboard*. With the second approach, data actually flows between activities. Explicit data flow connectors connect the outputs of one activity with the input of another one. So the main difference is that in the first approach all data exchange must be done through the central storage. If the output of one activity is used by two other activities, it is still written only once to the storage and read twice. In the second approach two distinct data connectors exist. WS-BPEL uses the blackboard approach through process variables [149]. In contrast, Leymann and Roller [119] propose a meta model, used in IBM MQSeries Workflow, that facilitates explicit data connectors. The flexibility gained by the blackboard approach, stands in contrast to its harder to follow—implicit—data flow. This requirement and service composition in general are agnostic to the actual approach selected.

Activities Use Process Input Data

Figure 5.11 shows the data flow for an example composition. Certain data elements, like *DN* (the domain name) and *P* (the personal details), are not produced by any activity. These data elements are part of the process data and are inputs for the process. Processes must have such data, and activities must be able to use them.

Data Exchange Implies Control Flow

Control flow embeds an ordering constraint between two activities if one activity depends on another one. Dependencies are for example causal links (e.g.: an activities creates the precondition of another one) or the protection of causal links. Causal links do not only exist on the level of semantic service descriptions, but also for input and output parameters. If one activity uses the output of another activity as an input a causal link between the two activities exist. Therefore an ordering constraint between the two activities must be included.

Activities Create New Variables

While this requirement sounds trivial and self-evident, it actually is not for automated planning. Activities create new variables, means that activities do not just write data into already defined variables, but they create variables on the fly. With automated planning this is usually not possible. All the variables that are used during composition must be defined in advance. This includes also intermediate variables that are neither used in the input nor in the output. When creating the web space, an account variable must be available. This variable is never used in the input or the output. It is also not obvious why such a variable could be necessary. Hence, by adding this variable we are encoding assumptions about automatically created service composition into the service request. This is bad as it hampers flexibility. Other service compositions are possible that do not need this variable.

Defining all necessary variables requires a lot of information about the available services and at least a rough idea on how the composition could look like. Therefore it is required here that activities can create new variables and that the service composer takes these into account.

Data Model Requirements

The data model defines how data elements are described. The data model is of importance for the service composition component, as it has to use data elements to replace the formal parameters with actual parameters.

Data Elements Are Typed

Data elements are exchanged between services as parameters. To ensure that only valid data elements are passed as parameters it makes sense to type them. Besides predefined types, user-defined types are necessary as well. By typing parameters we know for example what the payment service requires as an input: Neither a string nor a number, but a credit card number. But type-safety not only prevents service enactment from invoking services with wrong parameters, it also eases planning. With typed data elements and parameters the service composer knows that it can only use the services for which all necessary inputs are available.

Data Element Types Are Defined in an Ontology

Service specifications are annotated semantically to allow automated service composition. Service specifications therefore include preconditions and effects. Both are modelled as logical expressions. To use input parameters, output parameters and variables in these logical expressions, the types of data elements are described in an ontology.

An ontology defines concepts and their relations. A concept can be a sub-concept of another concept (inheritance). Aggregation and composition relations can also exist between concepts. As the example shows all these different relations are necessary. As no mediation is supported, all concepts used in one scenario have to be defined in one ontology. A service provide is therefore required to use only these concepts to describe his services.

Composer Is Aware of Data Element Structure

Besides having data elements with ontology based types it is also necessary that the composer is aware of the internal structure of data elements described using an ontology. To do so the composer has to not only understand function-free first-order logic but also Frame Logic [105]. Frame logic is an enhancement of first-order logic as it adds object oriented concepts like object identity, inheritance and complex objects.

Data Elements Can Be Used to Evaluate Control Flow Conditions

Above, we stated the requirement to compose alternative control flow. An alternative control flow can be the result of an exclusive choice or a multiple choice. Both have one incoming and multiple outgoing control threads. To decide which control threads are actually executed, conditions are assigned to the individual threads. Based on the result of the check domain activity, the process is either continued to register the domain or finished with an error message. Conditions are necessary to express which path in the process should be taken.

5.4.3 Heuristic Search as a Composition Algorithm

Heuristic search algorithms are currently not used for automated service composition. Our work is based upon previous research by Hoffmann and Nebel who developed the planners FF [89] and Metric-FF [87]. They introduced enforced hill-climbing and relaxed graphplan as a heuristic. Metric-FF also supports numerical properties and the optimisation for them. This functionality can be used to optimise for QoS properties. As demonstrated earlier their algorithm does not support uncertainty about the initial state or service invocation effects, is not able to compose parallel or alternative control flows, and does not create intermediate variables.

Above we presented an elaborated requirements analysis for automated service composition algorithms. Most of these requirements are fulfilled by existing heuristic search algorithms. The following ones are not supported:

1. Parallel control flow
2. Uncertainty in initial state and service effects
3. Alternative control flow
4. Creation of new variables

The first requirement is parallel control flow. Compositions consist of service invocations and their ordering. This ordering is the control flow. The straight forward approach is to assume a total ordering between service invocations and perform them sequentially. But in reality service invocations are often only partially ordered. If services do not depend on each other's results and do not conflict with each other, they can be invoked non-sequentially or in parallel. This saves execution time. Therefore a composition algorithm must be able to create compositions with control flows that only contain the necessary orderings.

The second requirement is to support *uncertainty in the initial state and service effects*. Executing a service with uncertain effects leads to several new states. This is necessary to represent a service that determines the issuing credit card company based on a credit card number. The exact outcome can only be determined after actually invoking the service for a given credit card number. After invoking a service with uncertain effects we are in more than one possible state. Hence, we might as well start with multiple possible states. Uncertainty in the initial state is necessary to express that for a certain fact only the possible values but not the exact value are known. For compositions containing service invocations with uncertain effects starting in an uncertain initial state it must be ensured that they work correctly in all possible situations.

The third requirement—*alternative control flow*—yields from the support of uncertainty in the initial state and in service effects. Invoking the service to determine the issuing credit card company based on the credit card number leads to several possible states. Based on the actual state, different service must be invoked to perform the payment. But determining the actual state can only be done when enacting the composition and invoking the services. To create compositions that work in all possible states it is necessary to support XOR-splits that lead to alternative control flows.

The fourth requirement—*creation of new variables*—results from the fact that in the data flow of a composition new data is created on the fly. Variables hold the output of service invocations. E.g. the service to determine the issuing credit card company for a given credit card requires a variable to hold the new credit card company. As one does not know prior to composition which variables are necessary (this depends on the actually selected services), variables need to be created on the fly during composition. This is complicated and often not possible in automated planning. This limitation of the planning model, already criticised in [28], simplifies planning. As all the variables are known, all possible service invocations can be calculated in advance. Services that are not invocable because the necessary variables for input or output parameters are missing, can be pruned.

Hence, in this planning model all variables used during composition must be defined in advance. This includes also intermediate variables that are neither used in the input nor in the output. Defining all necessary variables requires a lot of information about the service landscape and at least a rough idea of how the composition could look like (e.g. which services might be used). For a realistic composition approach it is therefore required that activities can create new variables and that the service composer takes these into account.

Recently, several extensions to heuristic search algorithms were proposed to support some of the required features [72, 58, 34, 88]. But all of them are based on the restricted planning model imposed by the Planning Domain Description Language (PDDL) and thus are not able to created intermediate variables [28]. LPG [72] performs heuristic search in plan space instead of state space. The nodes of the search space are (partial) plans and transitions between them are plan refinement operations (e.g.: adding an additional service invocation). LPG is a temporal planner and hence supports parallel control flow. Compositions are partially ordered and durations are assigned to service invocations. LPG supports optimisation for duration and other numerical properties. It can not deal with uncertainty and it cannot create alternative control flows. Sapa [58] is also a temporal planner and supports optimisation for duration and numerical properties. But unlike LPG it does perform search in state space. In that regard it is very similar to FF and Metric-FF. Sapa uses A* as the search strategy. In contrast to Enforced Hill-Climbing is A* complete and optimal if an admissible heuristic is used. We did not use A* because you have to trade in performance for completeness and optimality. Sapa does not support uncertainty and the creation of alternative control flows. Conformant-FF [34] and Contingent-FF [88] are both extension of the original FF planner. They extend it by functionality for conformant planning and contingent planning. Both work with uncertainty through the notion of belief states. A belief state is equivalent to our extended state definition and incorporates a set disjunction-free states. It represents the possible states. For Conformant-FF the main difference to FF is the handling of the belief states: Planning starts in a set of possible states and is finished if all the possible current states satisfy the goal. It creates conformant plans without alternative control flows and is therefore not usable for automated service composition. Contingent-FF on the other hand creates contingent plans that include alternative control flows. It is quite similar to out approach. Through its more efficient representation of possible states and further optimisations it has some advantages over our approach. But it does currently not support parallel control flow and alternative control flows are not merged resulting in tree-shaped compositions.

In the following, a composition algorithm that overcomes all these limitations will be presented. Before starting with the description of the algorithm, the notions service composition, and service request are introduced.

Definition 12 (Service request). *A service request* $R = (a_0, g, SD)$ *is a triple consisting of the initial state* a_0 *in* E_{state}, *the goal* $g \in E$ *and a service domain* SD. *A state is a logical expression. This concept is refined later. A service domain* $SD = (S, o)$ *consists of a set of service operations* S *and ontology describing the concepts used to specify services.*

Definition 13 (Service composition). *A service composition c is a list of service invocations $c = \langle i_1, \ldots, i_k \rangle$. A service request is fulfilled by a service composition that starting from the initial state reaches a state that satisfies the goal state by subsequently invoking the services from the composition.*

Enforced Hill-Climbing

Our algorithm is based on enforced hill-climbing [89]. It is a forward heuristic search in state space. State space is the search space that is spanned by the states and the transitions in between them.

Definition 14 (Direct successor). *A state a has a direct successor a', written as $a \to a'$, if a service invocation i exists and $\gamma(a, i) = a'$. The successor relation can be inductively extended to indirect successors $\to^+ = \to \bigcup \{(a, a'') | (a, a') \in \to \land (a', a'') \in \to^+\}$.*

Enforced Hill-Climbing is an extension of Hill-Climbing. Hill-Climbing uses a heuristic function $h : E_{state} \times E \to \mathbb{R}_0^+$ to select states until the goal is reached. The heuristics $h(a, g)$ delivers an approximation of the distance (measured in numbers of services to invoke) of the state a to the goal g. Starting with the initial state, a new state is selected from the direct successors. The first successor that is, according to the heuristic, better than the current state is selected and assigned as the new current state. This process is continued until the current state satisfies the goal state or search fails. Given an admissible heuristics and a mechanism to prevent visiting states multiple times, the algorithm always terminates. It terminates successfully if it reaches a state that satisfies the goal state. It fails if a state a, which is unequal to g, is reached so that no direct successor a' with $h(a', g) < h(a, g)$ exists. This means that the heuristics estimates every direct successor to be farther away from the goal state than the current state.

Hill-Climbing does not create optimal compositions and it is incomplete. Figure 5.12a illustrates the reason for the in-optimality. Displayed are states, their heuristic values, and possible state transitions. If the state with heuristic value 2 is evaluated first, it is selected even though a shorter path exists. Another problem is the greediness of Hill-Climbing. Greediness means that optimisation is done locally

(a)   (b)

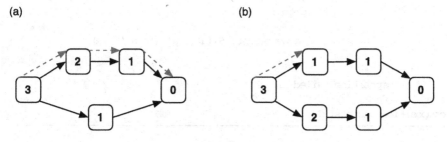

Fig. 5.12. Hill Climbing is not optimal (**a**) and incomplete (**b**)

without taking the path to the current state into account. This is only of importance if a cost function is associated with state transitions. Otherwise the admissible heuristics guarantees that greediness does not affect the composition result. Figure 5.12b demonstrates why Hill-Climbing is incomplete: If the upper path is taken, composition fails after the first state with heuristic value 1 as no direct successor with a better heuristic value can be found. Such a state is called a local maximum.

Enforced Hill-Climbing solves the problem of local maxima by switching to breadth-first search if it gets trapped in a local maximum. This works as depicted in Fig. 5.1. If the evaluation of a state shows that it is not better than the current states all its direct successor are added to the end of A'. Hence when all direct successors are evaluated and none was better than the current state, Enforced Hill-Climbing starts evaluating the successors of the successors. This is continued until either a better state is found or no reachable states are unevaluated and composition fails. In the situation from Fig. 5.12b Enforced Hill-Climbing switches to breadth-first search in the state with no better direct successors. Through breadth-first search the state with heuristic value 0 (the goal) is found and it can finish successfully. Regardless of this extension is Enforced Hill-Climbing still incomplete but termination is still guaranteed as breadth-first search always terminates. Figure 5.13 shows that composition fails if the upper path is taken. The upper path is a dead end and the algorithm is not able to turn around and leave it. As termination is always guaranteed, one approach to deal with incompleteness, as proposed by [89], is to switch to another complete but slower search algorithm (e.g. A*) if Enforced Hill-Climbing fails. The enforcement extension of Hill-Climbing does not affect the in-optimality of the algorithm.

Listing 5.1. Enforced Hill-Climbing

```
$a = initial state$
$c := $ empty composition
while $\lnot (a \models g)$
        $A''$ = new Queue
        enqueue($A'$, $\{a' | a \to a' \}$)
        for $a' \in A'$
                if $h(a', g) < h(a, g)$
                        add(c,i) with $\gamma(a,i) = a'$
                        $a = a'$
                        goto 3
                else
                        enqueue($A'$, $\{a'' | a' \to a'' \}$)
                end
        end
        composition failed
end
composition successful
```

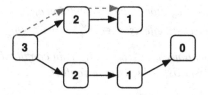

Fig. 5.13. Enforced Hill Climbing is incomplete

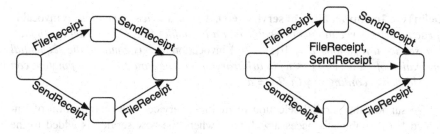

Fig. 5.14. State space without and with parallel selection

5.4.4 Extending Enforced Hill-Climbing

Enforced Hill-Climbing does not support any of the aforementioned requirements. Uncertain effects or initial states cannot be handled by creating alternative control flows. Compositions are strictly sequential and no variables can be created during the composition. In the following we present how each requirement can be addressed.

Implementing Requirement 1: Parallel Control Flow

The first step towards parallel control flow is to support the parallel selection of multiple services. Figure 5.14 illustrates that this leads to a denser search space as more state transitions are possible. But at the same time paths become shorter.

To invoke services in parallel it must be ensured that they can actually work in parallel. First this means that services where one service depends on the outcome of another service cannot be invoked in parallel. This can be ensured by extending the invocability definition to sets of services: a set of services is invocable in a given state if every service is invocable in the state. But this definition is not sufficient as two invocable services may be in conflict. Before we can define invocability for sets of services we need to define what it means if two service invocations are in conflict:

Definition 15 (Conflict). *Two service invocations* $i_1 = (s_1, Z_1)$ *with* $o_1 = (\mathcal{I}_1, \mathcal{O}_1, pre_1, eff_1)$ *and* $i_2 = (s_2, Z_2)$ *with* $o_2 = (\mathcal{I}_2, \mathcal{O}_2, pre_2, eff_2)$ *are in* conflict *if*[3]:

- o_1 *deletes the precondition of* o_2: $\neg x \in eff_1^{Z_1} \wedge x \in pre_2^{Z_2}$

---

[3] $x \in p$ denotes in the following the atom x that is part of formula p.

- o_1 creates a fact whose negation is the precondition of o_2: $x \in eff_1^{Z_1} \wedge \neg x \in pre_2^{Z_2}$
- o_1 and o_2 have inconsistent effects: $x \in eff_1^{Z_1} \wedge \neg x \in eff_2^{Z_2}$

A set of service invocations $\mathcal{I} = \{i_1, \ldots, i_n\}$ is in conflict if two services i_i ($1 \leq i \leq n$) and i_j ($1 \leq j \leq n$) exists which are in conflict.

Based on this notion we can define invocability and invocation for service invocation sets:

Definition 16 (Invocability of service sets). *A set of service invocations is invocable if each service invocation is invocable and it is conflict-free. Given a set of conflict-free service invocations $\mathcal{I} = \{i_1, \ldots, i_n\}$ invocation of $\mathcal{I}$ is equal to the sequential invocation of all i_i ($1 \leq i \leq n$) in arbitrary order. The state transition function can be extended accordingly: $\gamma(a, \mathcal{I}) = a'$.*

To support the parallel selection of multiple services one modification of Enforced Hill-Climbing is necessary: Line 8 where the new service is added to the composition must deal with the extended state transition function $\gamma(a, S)$. More than one service can be added to a composition at the same time. As the parallel selection should be reflected in the resulting composition, we need to modify our composition definition. The easiest way to do that would be to extend the previous list of services to a list of service sets. But with respect to further additions we choose another definition:

Definition 17 (Extended composition). *A composition $C = (S, \overset{cond}{\prec})$ consists of a set of service invocations S and a partial order $\overset{cond}{\prec}$ between them. For two service operation $o_i, o_j \in S$ an ordering $o_i \overset{cond}{\prec} o_j$ is defined if o_i was added to the composition before o_j. Here cond is that part of the effect of o_i that is necessary to invoke o_j. Likewise, $o_i \overset{cond}{\not\prec} o_j$ if both were added in the same step.*

Implementing Requirement 2: Uncertainty in Initial State and Service Effects

States, preconditions, and effects must include disjunction to support uncertainty. Disjunction in states is not only used to express uncertainty about the initial state. It also used to express several distinct goal states. Disjunction in the precondition of a service allows to express that the service is invocable in different situations. This does not increase the expressiveness as this can be simulated by multiple services. Disjunction in service effects can be used to express uncertainty about the service's outcome. To work with these richer expressions, we introduce a set-based representation of logical expressions with disjunctions:

Definition 18 (Set-based representation of logical expression). *Given a logical expression a its disjunctive normal form can be expressed as a set $a_{set} = \{a_1, \ldots, a_n\}$ of disjunction-free logical expressions. Here each a_i represents one conjunction of the disjunctive normal form.*

A logical expression and its set-based representation can be used interchangeably. When a distinction is necessary we will name the set-based notation a_{set}. When speaking about a state and its set-based representation it is helpful to think of the set-based representation as a set of possible states. The definition for state satisfaction needs to be extended accordingly:

Definition 19 (Satisfaction). *A state a satisfies another state g if* $\forall a_i \in a_{set}\ \exists g_j \in g_{set} a_i \models g_j$.

Hence, a set of possible current states satisfies a set of allowed goal state if every possible current state satisfies at least one allowed goal states. Now we have developed the foundation to represent uncertainty. Yet it is unclear how we can actually deal with uncertainty during planning. In automated planning two approaches have been developed: conformant planning and contingent planning. Using conformant planning, additional service invocations are added that ensure the correct working of the composition, without actually determining the current state or the actual effects of service invocations. While this is a simple model, it is often not practicable. For example instead of first determining the correct credit card company and then charging the credit card only with the correct payment service, it is tried to charge the credit card using each payment service. While, hopefully, the credit card is only charged once, the other services may charge a fee making the payment process very expensive. Conformant planning makes most sense when controlling robots that lack sensors. In business scenarios another approach is more practicable. Contingent planning introduces the ability to sense the actual value of fact during run-time and then continue accordingly. This means after determining the credit card company for a credit card, the actual value is sensed during run-time and then the correct service is invoked. This is a viable approach. Hence, contingent planning is required to handle uncertainty in the initial state and service effects.

Implementing Requirement 3: Alternative Control Flow

In the previous section, we extended the notion of states to include uncertainty. Service effects can now include disjunction as well. This means that we can actually reach several alternative states by invoking a service. To support contingent planning it must also be possible to invoke a service if it is only invocable in some of the current states. Let us look at the payment part of the book's use case scenario.

After registering the domain, the provider wants to charge the customers. To do this, it relies on the help of services provided by payment processing companies. To allow different payment options (various credit cards, charging from a bank account, etc.) services from several companies are used. Depending on the selection by the customer, the correct one is selected. This can only be done after planning during the enactment of the composition, as only then the necessary information is available. Hence, during planning we need to deal with the inherent uncertainty.

Figure 5.15 illustrates this situation. Invoking the service to determine the credit card company leads here to two possible states.[4] In the first state, the Pay1 authen-

---

[4] In reality this might be more, but two is sufficient for a presentation of the idea.

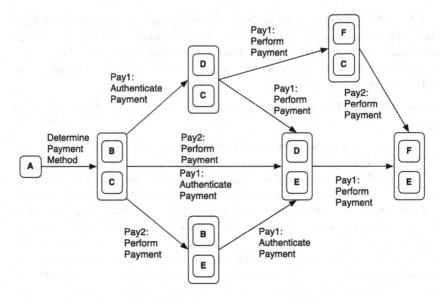

Fig. 5.15. An extended state transition

tication service is invocable and in the second state the Pay2 payment service is
invocable. Invoking them only changes the state in which they were invocable. As
multiple services may be selected (see Sect. 5.4.4) both services can be selected in
parallel changing both states at once. To support this notion, invocation and invocability need to be extended:

Definition 20 (Invocability). *A service invocation* $i = (s, Z)$ *with* $o = (\mathcal{I}, \mathcal{O},$
$pre, \mathit{eff})$ *is* invocable *in a state* a *if* $\exists a_i \in a_{set} \exists pre_j \in pre_{set} a_i \models pre_j$. *Invoking*
a service s *with a variable assignment* Z *in a state* a *leads to a state transition.*
This can be defined by a state transition function $\gamma(a, i) = \{a_i | a_i \in a_{set}, \forall pre_j \in$
$pre_{set}, a_i \not\models pre_j\} \cup \{a_i \circ \mathit{eff} | a_i \in a_{set}, \exists pre_j \in pre_{set}, a_i \models pre_j\}$. *The operation*
$a_i \circ \mathit{eff} = \{a_i \cup \mathit{eff}_j^+ \setminus \{x | \neg x \in \mathit{eff}_j^-\} | \mathit{eff}_j \in \mathit{eff}_{set}\}$ *applies the effect to one logical*
expression.

Invoking a service with uncertain effects results in several possible states. If subsequent services cannot be invoked in all states, an XOR-split is added to the composition. In our example this is the case after determining the credit card company.

For our composition algorithm it is irrelevant which path from Fig. 5.15 is actually taken, because only necessary orderings between service invocations are added.
This is done by linking two service invocations only if one produces the precondition
of the other or if they are in conflict. Formally:

Definition 21 (Causal links). *For two service operations* $p_1 = (\mathcal{I}_1, \mathcal{O}_1, pre_1, \mathit{eff}_1)$
and $o_2 = (\mathcal{I}_2, \mathcal{O}_2, pre_2, \mathit{eff}_2)$ *a link* $o_1 \overset{cond}{\prec} o_2$ *exists if:*

- $cond \in pre_2 \wedge producer(o_1, a, x) \wedge x \in cond$ where $producer(o, a, x)$ is the relation of term x from state a produced by service operation o,
- or o_1 and o_2 are in conflict.

For a link cond defines the logical condition that must hold in order to follow this link.

Often it is not only necessary to create alternative branches but to also merge them later. In our example this is necessary after payment has been performed. A first approach to merging might be to detect equivalent states and unify them to one state. In Fig. 5.15 states E and F seem to be merge-able be merged because they represent the same fact: payment has been performed. In reality, things are not that easy and calculating state equivalence is hard and may be impossible. We can only merge states which are exactly identical. This is unproblematic as in the end we are not interested in merging states but merging control flows. This is a lot easier: Control flows can be merged if a service that is selected is invocable in all control flows. As we still need to keep even equivalent states, this affects performance and space consumption. But it does not prevent merging control flows.

The interesting point about introducing only necessary links is that it renders the parallel selection of service unnecessary. As only necessary links are added, two service that can be invoked in parallel will be composed as running in parallel even if they are selected subsequently. We are still using the parallel selection as it is currently unclear whether its denser search space is a disadvantage or its shorter search paths are an advantage.

Implementing Requirement 4: Creation of New Variables

Creating new variables is currently not supported by most planners. This results not only from limitations of the language used to describe requests [28] but it also greatly simplifies creating the composition. If all variables are known in advance it is easy to determine which services can be invoked. To solve this problem we need to allow the creation of new variables, if a matching variable for the output of a service does not exist. But the unrestricted addition is problematic as this yields a possibly infinite set of states and makes planning semi-decidable [41, 62]. Thus we are introducing a very restricted form of variable creation. A variable may only be created if no variable of the same type already exists. While this keeps the problem decidable it may be too restrictive as it fails if two variables of the same type need to be created. We are currently not allowing the deletion of variables, as we have not encountered any practical use for it.

5.4.5 A Heuristic for Extended Enforced Hill-Climbing

As the heuristics guides the search it is crucial for the performance of the composer. An approach to find a heuristics for a problem is relaxation. The original problem is relaxed (made simpler) and the size of the relaxed solution is used as the heuristics for

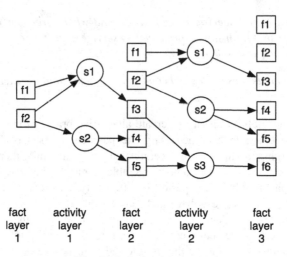

Fig. 5.16. A planning graph

the original problem. This approach was also used for enforced hill-climbing. The planning problem is relaxed by ignoring negative effects. Then the graphplan [27] algorithm is used to find a solution for the relaxed problem. In the following we will first detail this algorithm, then we will show how we adjusted it and finally we will look at the complexity of this heuristic.

Original Heuristics Used in Enforced Hill Climbing

graphplan is a planning algorithm, which separates planning into to phases: graph building and solution extraction. In the graph building phase a planning graph is built. It is a bipartite, directed graph. Figure 5.16 illustrates such a graph. The two different kinds of nodes are fact and activity nodes. Fact nodes (rectangular) represent atoms and activity nodes (circular) represent service invocations. The planning graph can be separated into different layers according to the order in which services are invoked and facts added to the different layers. A fact layer represents a state. Hence, fact layer 1 is the initial state.

Enforced Hill-Climbing was originally developed together with the relaxed graphplan heuristic [89]. Essentially it solves a simplified version of the composition request using the graphplan planning algorithm [27]. We take the length of the generated composition as the heuristic. graphplan works by first creating a planning graph and then extracting the solution from it. The relaxation or simplification of the problem results from ignoring the negative effects of service invocations. In the presence of negative effects back tracking is necessary during solution extraction. As negative effects are ignored, the heuristics can be calculated in polynomial time [89]. Starting from the initial state all invocable services (in this case $s1$ and $s2$) are added to the first activity layer. This activity layer *produces* a new fact layer including all the effects of $s1$ and $s2$. Now a new service $s3$ is invocable. The resulting fact layer now includes our goal (e.g. $f6$) and we are finished with building the graph. The original planning graph from graphplan additionally contains mutual exclusion relations between two activities or two facts if the activities are in conflict or if the facts only result from conflicting activities. If negative effects are ignored no mutual exclusion relations will be added as all conflicts emerge from negative effects.

After building the planning graph a solution needs to be extracted. For this purpose backward search is performed. Starting from the goal state, all service invocations in the previous layer are selected that contribute to goal. In the next step producing service invocations are selected for the facts required by the previously selected service invocations. This is continued until the initial state is reached. The total number of service invocations selected is then taken as the heuristic value for distance from the initial state to the goal.

Advanced Heuristics

The heuristics used here is not an extension but rather a simplification of the original heuristic. FF is a total-order planner, hence to get a sensible heuristic estimation for the distance from a given state to a goal state, it makes sense to use the length of a sequential solution for the relaxed problem. Because of this, it is necessary to perform the solution extraction phase.

As the presented composition algorithm generates partially ordered compositions, the length of a sequential solution for the relaxed problem is not a good idea. Actually it can lead to wrong results, as this heuristics is not admissible. A sequential solution for the relaxed problem can be significantly longer than a partial ordered solution of the real problem. This over-estimation is forbidden for an admissible heuristic. But by skipping the solution extraction phase and using the number of activity layer as the heuristic, we find a heuristics for our extended version of enforced hill-climbing:

Proposition 1. *The number of activity layers in a planning graph for a relaxed planning problem is an admissible heuristics $h : E_{state} \times E \to \mathbb{R}_0^+$ for the real distance*

$$d : E_{state} \times E \to \mathbb{R}_0^+$$

of the initial state to the goal of the original problem.

Proof: *We need to show that for every two states a_1 and a_2: $h(a_1, a_2) \leq d(a_1, a_2)$. We can distinguish three cases:*

1. *Two service invocations are necessary, but they are in conflict. In this case, they need to be sequentialised in the original problem. In the relaxed problem no conflicts arise and the service invocations can happen in parallel. Therefore in this case the number of activity layers can only be smaller than the length of the optimal solution for the original problem ($h(a_1, a_2) \leq d(a_1, a_2)$).*
2. *Two service invocations are necessary, but one depends on the effect of the other. In this case, they need to be sequentialised in the optimal solution to the original problem and in the planning graph ($h(a_1, a_2) = d(a_1, a_2)$).*

3. *The planning graph contains unnecessary activities. If an activity layer contains only unnecessary activities, the number of activity layers could be larger than the length of the optimal solution. But this can not happen. Given an activity layer $A_i = \{u_1, \ldots, u_n\}$ containing only unnecessary service invocations u_j and the following activity layer $A_{i+1} = \{n_1, \ldots, n_m, u_{n+1}, \ldots, u_p\}$ containing unnecessary and necessary service invocations u_k and n_l. Then for each n_k at least one fact f_m in the previous fact layer exists that must be produced by one $u_j \in A_i$. Then u_j is not unnecessary and A_i does not only contain unnecessary service invocations $(h(a_1, a_2) = d(a_1, a_2))$.*

To summarise, the only case where the number of activity layers in the planning graph for the relaxed problem differs from the length of the optimal solution for the original problem is if two necessary service invocations are in conflict. They can be selected in parallel in the relaxed problem but need to be sequentialised in the original problem. Hence, the number of activity layers is smaller or equal to the length of the optimal solution.

5.4.6 Reasoning & Matchmaking for Service Composition

In Sect. 3.5 we introduced two different forms of matchmaking called matchmaking on capabilities and matchmaking on preconditions that are useful for an automated service composition approach like the one we presented above. Using run-time composition, two additional reasoning tasks are required. We will present them in the following.

Virtual Invocation of a Service

When creating a service composition at run-time, it is necessary to know what happens if a service is invoked. Of course, we cannot actually invoke the service. We need to simulate the invocation by only applying the service effects to the current state. The method computes a new state as a result of applying the effects and post-conditions of the given service to the state given as parameter. The state is given as input parameter. The variable binding must be given as input, to distinguish between the (possibly many) different substitutions.

Check if a State Is a Goal State for a User Request

During composition we must be able to check whether the current state is a goal state. If this is the case we have found a service composition that fulfils the user's request. The method checks if a goal is resolved in a certain state. The state and goal id are provided as parameters.

5.5 Service Binding

5.5.1 Binding by Selection

The open architecture of SOA environments enable the utilization of a multiplicity of services with an unlimited number of characteristics, frequently denoted as the service landscape. Due to different organisational goals and application requirements, participants in decentralised SOA environments have diverse perspectives, possibly oppositional objectives, and possibly competing interests. Therefore, service quality requirements are varying depending on the individual service request.

A service provisioning platform should be able to select and integrate the most suitable service implementations into an end-to-end service composition. It therefore needs to compare alternative implementations for the same kind of service, which only differ by their non-functional properties. Finding the most suitable service implementation essentially means to match service requirements and offered service capabilities. Since capabilities are varying, just like service requirements, it is not sufficient to decide on the data provided during registration only.

Because of this, SOA environments with a multiplicity of services from different origins and with changing characteristics demand an automation support for service selection. How can this service selection be performed?

5.5.2 Binding by Agent Based Negotiation

One of the solutions in this area, adopted from humans when faced with the need to reach agreement on a variety of issues, is to make use of negotiation. Negotiation is a process, by which a joint decision is made by two or more parties. The parties first verbalise contradictory demands and then move toward agreement by a process of concession making or search for new alternatives. In this process, a party tries to convince another party to act in a particular way by making proposals, trading options, and offering concession [122]. Automation support for intelligent negotiation, by which participants come to a mutually acceptable agreement on some matter, can be provided by software agents.

Software agents are computer systems capable of independent, autonomous action on behalf of their users or owners. They are able to figure out what needs to be done to satisfy design objectives, rather than constantly being told what to do [207]. Agents are characterised by autonomy, communication, and collaboration capabilities. This means that agents can act independently without user interventions based on intelligent behaviour models in pursuance of a goal. For this reason, agents have the ability to communicate with other agents. Such interactions can vary from simple information exchanges to cooperation and coordination and is the base for managing inter-agent dependencies at run-time.

Software agents are a promising technology and their autonomous behaviour is a key capability to support automated negotiation. It can significantly reduce the time that is necessary to select a suitable service implementation since it allows making a large number of transactions within a small amount of time, as opposed to

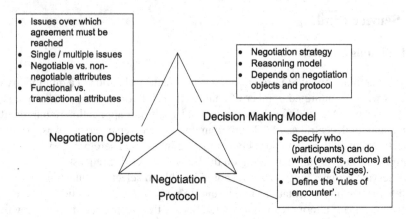

Fig. 5.17. Aspects of automated negotiations

direct communication between humans (manual negotiation), which takes considerably more time.

Agent based negotiation facilitates dynamic choice of negotiation commitments and enables adjustment of negotiation behaviours at runtime [122]. Similar to manual negotiations, for automated negotiations a broad range of issues has to be considered. This includes issues about the necessary negotiation interactions, characteristics of the negotiated services, and issues about the behaviour when decisions have to be made. A commonly recognised approach (presented by [98]) to logically structure this area is to decompose automated negotiation into three broad topics: negotiation protocols, negotiation objects, and decision making models (Fig. 5.17). To each of these topics a deeper insight will be given below.

Negotiation Objects

Negotiation objects are described by the range of issues over which participants must agree. The object may either contain a single issue, such as price, or may cover hundreds of issues related to price, quality, timings, penalties and so forth. Negotiation objects in SOA environments are the provided services itself. A number of classification schemes exist to characterise and structure services features for negotiation. For example, services can be characterised by a number of attributes that can be classified as follows:

- service-specific attributes, such as functional and non-functional parameters, quality of service parameters, or other technical specifications;
- transaction-specific attributes that are generic for the service and encompass business-related parameters, such as price, penalties and so on.

Moreover, attributes may be:

- non-negotiable having a fixed value, or
- negotiable having multiple characteristic values.

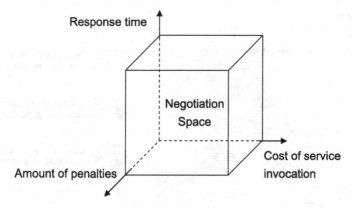

Fig. 5.18. Three dimensional negotiation space of a service negotiation object

In most scenarios, parties that have to find an agreement about a service do not just focus on one attribute of an object (i.e. price) but are rather interested in multiple aspects of a service. In order to represent this complexity, each attribute can be associated with a dimension. The entire number of dimensions spans a vector space that formally characterises an object and represents the negotiation space (also called negotiation domain) for the negotiating participants [122]. Figure 5.18 shows an example of a three dimensional negotiation space that describes a service by three attributes, namely: service response time, price per service invocation, and amount of penalties that applies if the service response time is higher than agreed.

Decision Making Models

The decision making model embodies the decision making apparatus, which is employed by the participating software agents to achieve their objectives. It governs the agent's general behaviour and best course of actions and policies to achieve a goal. For this reason a sequence of actions, e.g. making offers and react on responses, must be followed. This is called a negotiation strategy. The sophistication of the decision making model and the decisions that have to be made, are influenced by the negotiation protocol in place, by the nature of the negotiation object, and by the range of operations that can be performed on it [115].

With the model of negotiation space (in Fig. 5.18), the question remains how software agents find a mutually acceptable combination of service attributes, whereas each of the unlimited number of coordinates of the negotiation space represents a possible service configuration. Participants are only willing to make agreements in limited areas of the negotiation space. In order to find acceptable attribute combinations, participants' agents suggest specific points in the negotiation space and terminate when a mutually acceptable configuration is found. This formalism abstracts automated negotiation to 'moving from one point of the negotiation space to another one in order to find mutual acceptance' [98]. In the field of software agents this moving process is called the negotiation strategy or decision making model of an agent.

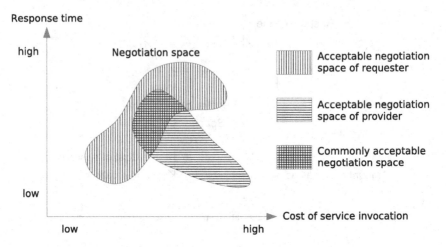

Fig. 5.19. An example of a two-dimensional negotiation space

In the simplest case the negotiation strategy is rather static and the software agent can either accept or reject exchanged configuration proposals.

In order to evaluate individual configurations, distinct ratings for certain areas in the negotiation space are defined. Figure 5.19 illustrates a possible negotiation space, where the attributes *service response time* and *price per service invocation* are open for negotiation. The vertical striped area represents the service requester's and the horizontal striped area the provider's acceptable negotiation space. Only response time-price combinations that are within the acceptable negotiation space of both participants lead to a commonly acceptable agreement (overlapping area in the negotiation space).

The process of automated decision making becomes even more complex, if the negotiation space is extended or decreased by launching or removing attributes during the negotiation. However, random proposal making and evaluation is very time consuming and inefficient as no feedback, whether the proposal is close to the acceptable negotiation space or why the proposal is unacceptable, is made [174]. Instead of random negotiation space movement and 'picking points', the negotiation process can be improved by granting participants the flexibility to change the values of the negotiation object attributes. This can either be made by critiques that explain which part of the proposal is unacceptable or by counter proposals—e.g. as alternative proposals generated in response to previous proposals. Proposals, critiques, and counter proposals express what a participant wants, based on the negotiation object. This advanced object based negotiation model can even be extended by giving agents the capability to provide arguments that support their stance (argumentation based negotiation). The agent can thereby justify its attitude toward a particular issue or persuade the opponent by constructive arguments that make a deal possible. As a result, the agent can modify the recipient's region of acceptability (negotiation space). These arguments can include threads, rewards, or appeals. Examples of decision making models used for automated negotiation are game theory based models [140, 167], heuristic approaches [157, 158], and argumentation based approaches [175, 152]).

A few considerations have to be made when using software agents. Firstly, agents negotiating services are characterised by autonomy. Hence, the conditions and rules that influence the agent's behaviour are private knowledge and not available to other parties. Agents do not know the reasoning model or the placed utilities of the opponent's agent. It is in fact not sure whether a mutual agreement is possible at all and whether a common acceptable negotiation space exists. Autonomy also presumes that an agent only knows the agents it communicates with but not whether or not the opponent agent initiates subcontract negotiations with other agents for that service. Such parallel negotiation threads are invisible to the initiating agent and can be done either concurrently or after the negotiations are finished. Moreover, they are independent from the initial conversation and can be based on different protocols, decision making rules or other conditions. Secondly, a critical factor in service negotiations is the question of how long it takes to reach an agreement and by what time the negotiated service must be executed. It is assumed that both the provider and the requester have an interest that the time should be reasonable with respect to the value of the service agreement. Time constraints can be integrated with the negotiating agent or using the lifetime management facilities of transient services itself.

Negotiation Protocols

Negotiation Protocols define a set of rules that prescribe the circumstances under which the interaction between agents takes place. [122] calls this the 'rules of encounter'. These rules cover the permissible types of participants, e.g. the negotiators and any relevant third parties, the negotiation states, e.g. accepting bids, negotiation closed, the events that cause negotiation states to change, e.g. no more bidders, bid accepted, and the valid actions of the participants in particular states, e.g. which messages can be sent by whom, to whom, at what stage. Since negotiating agents have the goal to find a mutual accepted agreement, each negotiation may involve interactions that are based on a sequence of events. As it is difficult and computationally expensive to design agents that are able to reason about a message's meaning, a pragmatic solution to support agent interaction are pre-defined protocols. A negotiation protocol contains the basic rules for the negotiation process and communication. Formally, a protocol is 'a set of norms that constrain the proposals that the negotiation participants are able to make' [98]. Protocols include rules about the temporal validity of messages, at what times proposals can be made, which values can be set, and which procedures are necessary to place a bid. Proposals can be private messages passed between service requesters and providers or they may be broadcast among all participants. While negotiation protocols are quite different for different categories of negotiation, they have one thing in common: interaction protocols expand the scope from single messages to complete transactions, also called conversations or dialogues. A significant role in defining such protocols and providing interoperability between heterogeneous software agents is played by the *Foundation for Intelli-*

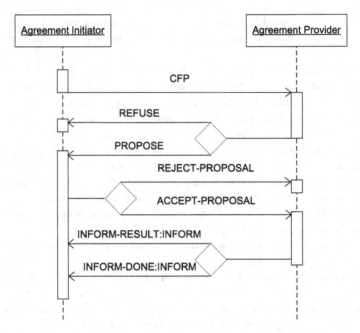

Fig. 5.20. UML sequence diagram of the FIPA Contract Net Protocol

gent Physical Agents (FIPA). The organisation specifies several negotiation protocols and defines an agent communication language that provides mechanisms for adding context to message contents. In FIPA protocols communications make use of communicative acts that tell a receiving agent in which context to interpret the contents of a message. Below, two of these FIPA protocols are presented as examples. More information on FIPA negotiation protocols can be found on the FIPA website.[5]

Contract Net Protocol

Simple and very static ways of coming to an service configuration agreement are negotiations where the participants can either accept or reject. This class of dialogues are called contract net approaches and are discussed below. The *Contract Net Protocol (CNP)* is an interaction protocol that is specified by FIPA and illustrated by the UML sequence diagram in Fig. 5.20.

The negotiation initiator (Agreement Initiator) addresses a *call for proposal (CFP)* to a number of providers (Agreement Providers) in order to get a quote for a service that solves a problem or performs a task, i.e. an application service. The *call for proposal (CFP)* has a globally unique conversation id and contains a specification of the task and possible conditions the initiator is placing upon the execution of it. The Agreement Providers have the chance to respond on the CFP by making a proposal or refusing to make a bid. They can also deny reacting at all. The Agreement

---

[5] http://www.fipa.org.

Initiator receives the proposals from possible Agreement Providers. It can, either immediately after receiving a proposal or after a certain deadline runs off, evaluate the proposals and select a provider to perform the task. For that reason the Agreement Initiator sends an 'accept-proposal act' to the chosen provider and reject-proposal acts to the remaining providers.

In FIPA, the messages including proposals are binding to the participant and require the performance of the task. After completing the task the provider sends an inform-result respectively an inform-done message to the Agreement Initiator. It may also send a failure message if the performance of the task was not successful. The CNP is limited to bidirectional information exchanges and does not involve explicit negotiations between the Agreement Initiator and the Agreement Provider. It has no centralised control of the awarding and execution of tasks and evaluations of proposals are based on personal views. It can be used for simple tasks that can easily be divided and evaluated and follows a fix accept-or-refuse protocol workflow.

Iterated Contract Net Protocol

The CNP can be extended by integrating recursive negotiations and allowing multi-round iterative bidding to find a compromise. For this reason, FIPA defines the *Iterated Contract Net Protocol (ICNP)*. Using a CNP the Agreement Initiator can either accept or reject a proposal after sending a CFP to the provider agents. In the ICNP the Agreement Initiator alternatively may decide to iterate the process by issuing a revised CFP to particular Agreement Providers and rejecting the remaining proposals. By exchanging modified proposals and counter-proposals, a real negotiation is possible and a trade-off is more likely. The process terminates when the Agreement Initiator refuses all proposals and does not issue a new CFP, the Agreement Initiator accepts one or more of the bids, or the provider agents refuse to bid. The *Unified Modeling Language (UML)* sequence diagram in Fig. 5.21 illustrates this.

5.5.3 Service Level Contracting

Beside binding services by agent based negotiation, an instrument that defines the relationship between service providers and consumers is needed. The key concept in addressing this issue is *Service Level Agreement (SLA)*. SLA is not a new concept: the approach emerged in the 1960s as a way of ensuring service quality in engineering and production and is now the norm for both internally and externally provided services. The goal of this section is to provide basic background information about service level agreements and their relationship with service selection and binding.

A service level agreement is a formal, written, concluded for a certain duration agreement between a service consumer and a service provider, in which the service provider guarantees the provision of a defined (as regards quality and contents) service to the service consumer and in which the service consumer guarantees the return of a defined financial consideration (mostly compensatory payment). The definition of the service quality provided by the service provider is regulated by service levels which are mutually defined, quantifiable and relevant for the service consumer. The

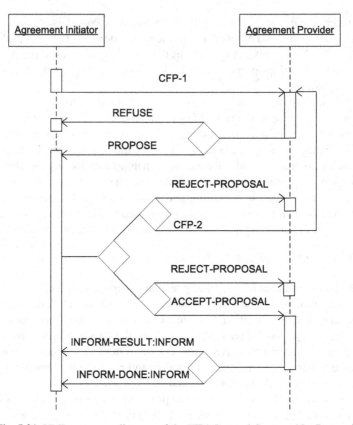

Fig. 5.21. UML sequence diagram of the FIPA Iterated Contract Net Protocol

SLA defines procedures that regulate the monitoring and evaluation process as well as that consequence that applies in case of service level violations.

Classification of SLAs

Several basic types of SLAs can be differentiated. A first basic differentiation of SLAs can be made based on the legal relationship that exists between the contracting parties. It can be divided into the case that both provider and requester belong to the same legal body (internal parts of an organisation or system such as different departments), and the case that both provider and consumer belong to different legal bodies (independent from each other such as two independent companies). In literature this differentiation results in separating between internal service and external service. In consequence, SLAs can be divided into external agreements (cross-organisational) and internal agreements (intra-organisational).

The characteristics of an SLA are different depending on whether it is internal or external. An internal SLA is defined between units and departments of one corporation, thus problems and violations that may occur during service provision are treated differently from those occurring with external partners. Even though sanctions and penalties are less relevant for internal SLAs. The agreed relation between internal providers and requesters can be externally used as a marketing instrument, by claiming validated and formal processes in the company as quality property.

In contrast, external SLAs are a stricter type of an agreement. They are realized as legal contract between different companies, which makes the definition of sanctions, monitoring and reporting mechanisms, and escalation scenarios much more important.

Another basic differentiation of SLAs can be made based on the content (nature of resource and its degree of abstraction) of the service and the roles of the SLA participants (function, position, industry). Malu et al. [124] distinguish between business SLAs and IT SLAs. Business SLAs refer to the semantics of the service rather than to system- or application-level metrics. Business SLAs are usually created between IT service providers and IT service users that use the provided service for fulfilling non-IT business functions. For example, a business SLA could state that product orders over 1000 pieces should be received within 15 days of the order, or within 10 days from payment. Business SLAs need to be formulated in a way that is understandable by the (non-IT) service user and abstracts IT service metrics to the specific needs of that user.

In contrast, IT SLAs are related to system or application-level metrics (such as response time of an individual operation or availability) that are applicable to the specific services. For example, an IT SLA could state that 90 percent of the operations executed with a service should complete within 3 seconds. IT SLAs are usually created between IT service providers and IT service consumers that use the service either directly in IT systems or (usually after processing, refinement or composition with other services) resell/re-provide the service to other service users.

Elements, Contents and Structure of SLAs

From the definition and classification of SLAs it can already be assumed that SLAs are documents that have a consistent structure with recurring elements. SLA models proposed in literature reveal more or less the same overall structural components (i.e. [192, 13, 12]). In some models contents and structure vary in detail, some authors emphasise different elements than others, and often elements are differently named. A consistent catalogue of elements, vocabularies and their meaning has not established itself yet. Since the numerous elements of a SLA need to be differentiated from each other and brought into a context, the logical structure of a SLA will be provided before defining the elements themselves. [100] structures SLAs into 'two sets of elements: service elements and management elements'. Service elements define issues such as the provided service, conditions of service availability, responsibilities of the parties, costs, and escalation procedures whereas management elements focus on tracking service effectiveness, solving service-related disagreements and reviewing and revising the SLA. [101] states that

> a large part of the current contracts deals with legal (non-IT related) terms
> and conditions, such as the scope of work, the legal responsibilities and

proprietary rights of the parties, or the modes of invoicing and payment. [...] Another observation is that every analysed contract contains (in a more or less straightforward way) the involved parties, the QoS parameters, the raw metrics used as input to compute the QoS parameters, the algorithm for computing the QoS parameters, the service guarantees and the appropriate actions to be taken if a violation of these guarantees has been detected.

Overall the following elements of a SLA can be identified: organisational elements, service-related elements, and management-related elements.

- *Organisational elements* of a SLA are elements that define the contextual aspects of an agreement. By this means a SLA is scoped by its associated organisational elements. Organisational elements include the subject-matter of the SLA, involved parties and their roles, associated duration during which a SLA is valid, and all legal information.
- *Service-related elements* of a SLA are elements that characterise the different aspects of the service a SLA is concluded for. This includes the definition of the service, service parameters, and service levels that are used in the context of service-related elements of a SLA. If a SLA comprises multiple services these elements need to be defined for each of the involved services. Service-related elements include the description of the provided service as regards contents and interfaces by a domain-specific semantic description (i.e. [54]), the target quality of the provided service including associated metrics, and the charges and billing and payment procedures associated with a service.
- *Management-related elements* of a SLA are elements that address the management aspects of the SLA. They comprise of information about reporting, SLA monitoring and evaluation procedures, a formal consequence of SLA non-conformance, and directives for dealing with such situations.

SLA Lifecycle Management

In order to successfully manage this relationship, the service provider and consumer need to adopt an organised approach to managing SLA documents during their entire validity. This task is called SLA lifecycle management. Different authors classify the SLA lifecycle differently into phases. This is a result of different usage and business areas. The lifecycle of a SLA can be divided into the following five phases: SLA creation and negotiation, SLA deployment and fulfilment, SLA monitoring and evaluation, SLA termination, and finally, SLA explanation and prediction. There are sub-phases within each phase, i.e. for negotiation or monitoring. Also parties in a service relationship use advertising and search functions to find suitable agreement partners, either directly or using intermediaries and repositories. These activities may precede the first phase of the lifecycle.

In each phase of the SLA lifecycle, different tasks need to be performed. The first phase, SLA creation and negotiation, addresses the definition and creation of the SLA document. The provided service has to be outlined and described precisely and service parameters such as quality of service have to be defined by means of service levels. Also financial regulations such as terms and conditions of payment, penalties and bonuses have to be agreed on, i.e. by using agent based negotiation. The result of the SLA creation and negotiation phase is a concluded SLA between a service provider and a service consumer. Following the creation and negotiation phase the deployment and fulfilment phase addresses the set up of a service provisioning and monitoring system and the deployment of the provided service in accordance with defined service levels. Fulfilment of the SLA has to be assured by the service provider during usage of the service and the SLA. It is essential that service providers are able to meet the SLAs stipulated with their consumers, as SLAs are one of the main metrics by which requesters judge the quality of the service offered by service providers. Therefore, SLA monitoring and evaluation are executed in order to control the service provision and its accordance to the SLA. SLA monitoring and evaluation is a phase that takes place in parallel to service fulfilment. Service levels defined in a SLA are measured and compared with actual service levels during service provision. Consequential actions of service level variations have to be triggered as defined in the SLA document. Finally, SLA termination describes the phase in the SLA life cycle in which the service provisions finishes and the SLA is no longer valid. SLA explanation and prediction examines the SLA and controls usefulness of the regulation defined in the SLA. The objective of this phase is to gather valuable experiences whether implications in the first phase were appropriate and which improvements can be implemented in the future.

5.5.4 Example for Negotiation Based Service Binding

To show potential benefits of service binding by negotiation, we demonstrate the negotiation aspect of the book's use case scenario. Service composition is offered here by the service provider (Hostit) in a B2B context. Extending the use case scenario, we introduce a list of provided services. We also assume that there may be more than one service consumer and each of them may have different quality requirements. Our focus her is to aim on the integration of QoS aspects. At the same time, we do not consider some details such as the dynamic creation of new service compositions.

Individual service requests may differ in terms of quality requirements. Therefore, the platform provided by Hostit needs to dynamically decide which composition of services is most valuable to a requester. A sample request sent to Hostit may be as follows:

> Provide a service for domain name registration, web space, e-mail account set-up, and payment facilities, whereas the service needs to be available in less than 60 time units (TU) and costs for setting up the services must be below 16 monetary units (MU). Based on that request, the Hostit platform should create a service composition that can fulfil the request.

Services such as CheckDomain can be provided by several candidate service providers (e.g. Denic, UnitedDomains, or domainPro), while other services can only be provided by one service provider (e.g. `CreateWebhostingAccount`). Beside that, some service providers may be able to adjust QoS values, like duration of execution of their services, while others are not. In some cases, duration of services may be dependent on various external factors, and therefore not fixed. By analogy, some of the service providers can be able to quote different prices/costs, while others only accept fixed prices/costs. Hence, QoS parameters and costs are variable or fixed and negotiable or non-negotiable. The `CheckDomain` service can be delivered at different QoS levels, i.e. different duration (`DurationX`, `DurationY`, etc.) and costs (`CostX`, `CostY`, etc.), and various combinations of them, while the `CreateWebhostingAccount` service has a fixed duration of less than 5 TU and costs of 0.50 MU.

In case a service composition includes neither conditional nor alternative branches, the service provisioning platform decides to apply the *first-contract-all-then-enact* enactment strategy. The different kinds of enactment strategies are discussed in Sect. 6.2 in the next chapter.

Since the service composition is abstract, it does not reference specific services. Therefore, the platform needs to select executable service implementations from a potentially high number of service providers in the second step. In order to fulfil this complex task of end-to-end QoS management and service selection, the platform makes use of negotiation for finding the most suitable configuration of QoS parameter values for all included services.

One of the main problems in this area is the decomposition of QoS parameters onto the services involved in the service composition and their optimisation to fulfil the reseller's business requirements. In the example the overall maximum duration is less then 60 TU, the `CreateWebhostingAccount` service takes up to 5 TU, the `CreateDomain` service takes up to 30 TU and so forth. Negotiation must find service implementations for `CheckDomain`, `RegisterDomain`, and `Credit-cardPayment` that take as little time that the maximum duration threshold of 60 TU holds. Figure 5.22 presents a possible solution found by negotiation to meet the above described constraints.

As stated above, the services involved in the scenario are from external providers. Hence, the possibility to maintain the quality of service provision is outside the influence of the `Hostit` service composition provider. In consequence it may happen that services are not satisfying in means of agreed quality, for example, duration of the `denic:CheckDomain` service is higher than 1 TU.

While individual compensation mechanisms such as payment of penalties are an important instrument to deal with such violations with external providers, the contractual obligations with the service requester demand urgent exception handling, for example a dynamic replacement of the faulty service. Since end-to-end QoS requirements are still valid for the service composition, dynamic re-selection mechanisms must be applied to find an alternative candidate for the service to be replaced. As an example, the `CheckDomain` services can be provided by different service providers as well, i.e. `UnitedDomains` and `domainPro`. `Denic` was initially chosen to be the involved service provider with service duration of 1 TU and costs of 0.5 MU.

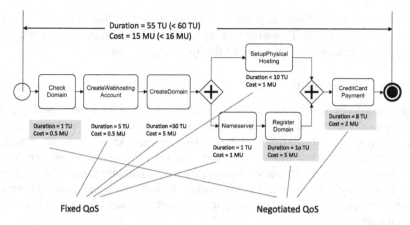

Fig. 5.22. A duration configuration that meets an overall duration threshold

The replacement service of the CheckDomain service provided by United-Domains or domainPro may not have the same service qualities, but it must be ensured that the end-to-end QoS requirements of the service composition are still fulfilled. The process of dynamic re-selection is driven by re-negotiation, essentially a negotiation with the goal of fulfilling overall QoS requirements. Re-negotiation may have chosen UnitedDomains as replacement provider for the CheckDomain service, which leads to a duration of 3 TU and costs of 1 MU for the service, and therefore to 57 TU and 14.5 MU for the overall service composition. The resulting loss in benefits of the service composition provider may at least partially be compensated by penalties claimed from the service provider Denic of the faulty service.

With a general understanding of how services can be composed on a logical level and bound to existing service implementations, the next chapter will discuss the issues of composition enactment.

5.6 Semantic Business Process Management

5.6.1 Introduction

The previous sections discussed different strategies to enable individual functionalities as services for a semantic service provisioning architecture. This section shows another possible service enabling strategy, where semantic descriptions are managed in context of *Business Process Management (BPM)* [178]. In general, Web services in combination with business processes are said to be the basis for future software applications [118]. Hepp et al. [84] were one of the first extending this approach by combining business processes with semantic descriptions to create a new discipline—semantic business process management. This section gives a short overview of semantic business process management and outlines a transition strategy to implement it. The following subsection introduces the basic idea of business process management, as foundation for the upcoming sections.

Business Process Management

In general system theory [201] a system is defined by its border, by its goal or purpose, by its elements, and by the relationships between those elements. An enterprise is such a system, because it fulfils all those characteristics. An enterprise has a border to the environment (customers, competitors, market). It also has a goal like creating a high return on investment or maximizing the shareholder value. An enterprise consists of many elements and the relationships between those elements. During its lifetime, the enterprise is restructuring itself in order to adapt itself to a changing environment.

An enterprise model captures all relevant aspects of the enterprise. It is created to document the structural and dynamic aspects of the enterprise, but also to plan and communicate possible changes internally and externally. The structural elements of the enterprise model are grouped according to their nature into different dimensions like organisational elements, functional elements, data elements, etc. Different diagram types are used to model the static relationships between elements of the same dimension. For example, an organisational chart is used to model the formal hierarchy of power within the enterprise. In contrast, dynamic models define how the different system elements of the enterprise are working together to achieve the enterprise's goals (or sub-goals). Those dynamic models are called business processes, workflow processes or executable processes depending on their purpose and level of abstraction. The enterprise model is usually structured according to an enterprise architecture framework like Zachman,[6] ArchiMate [53, 196] or ARIS [170, 171]. Such an enterprise architecture framework defines the dimensions, abstraction levels, possible element types and relationship types.

Figure 5.23 shows the ARIS framework as one possible example. It distinguishes 5 dimensions, each having 3 abstraction levels. The process dimension in the centre of the figure links the elements of the other dimensions together. For example, a process like a business process consists of functions from the functional dimension, which are executed either by organisational elements from the organisational dimension or by IT systems from the functional dimension. Each function in the business process consumes and produces data elements defined in the data dimension. A business process also produces products, which are defined in the product dimension.

As mentioned before, the enterprise as a system changes during its lifetime to adapt continuously to the ever-changing business environment. Changes are initiated unconsciously or consciously. In the first case, system elements like employees react spontaneously like providing a discount on a partly damaged product. In the second case, changes are carefully planned, implemented, evaluated, and adjusted in a change program. This cyclic approach of process improvement is known as Deming cycle [57].

---

[6] http://www.zifa.com and http://www.zachmaninternational.com.

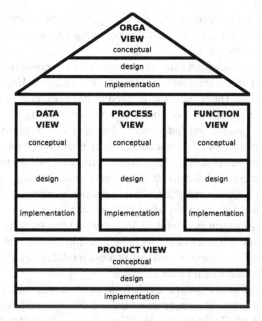

Fig. 5.23. The ARIS enterprise architecture framework

Business process management compromises all tasks related to the elements and models in the process dimension. For example, existing as-is processes are documented, future to-be processes are planned, executable processes are derived from more abstract business processes, executed processes are monitored and measured, etc. Business process management is a complex task requiring very different skills. For example, a business expert is documenting the as-is processes by interviewing the process owners and making their knowledge explicit. An integration expert derives executable processes from the business processes modelled by the business expert. A software engineer implements missing functionality or customises an existing software package. An executive is reviewing the business processes on a very abstract level to judge how much effort is needed to cooperate with another enterprise or how much money can be gained by outsourcing certain business processes.

Taking a more abstract view on business process management shows that there is a top-down as well as a bottom-up approach. For example, planning a new business process and deriving an implementation is top-down, whereas extracting process models from execution log files is bottom-up. The following sub-section explains the different technologies involved in a top-down approach to business process automation. This helps to identify the benefits of semantically described business services.

Business Process Automation

The field of business process automation generally aims to reduce cost of business processes by raising the efficiency of certain tasks through automation. With respect to the introduced topic of business process management, the desired area of automation described here is to reduce the effort for creating an implementation out of the abstract business process model.

In order to better understand the exact procedure of transforming the business process model in an executable implementation, the concept of *Model-Driven Architecture (MDA)* is used. The model is structured in three levels of abstraction, which can be adopted based on the area of business process modelling.

Models in the *Computation Independent Model (CIM)* level provide a very abstract view on the process. It is independent of any kind of technology. It represents the business view on the process. This model is produced by business experts. That means that the process model consists of business functions supported by abstract services, but it is not further specified, if these abstract service are later provided by a human or implemented using any kind of software. The CIM is the basis for the other two models (*Platform Independent Model (PIM)* and *Platform Specific Model (PSM)*) and therefore the foundation for a later technical implementation. Typical modelling languages in context of business process modeling are EPC (see next section), BPMN, and value-added chain diagrams.

The PIM is a refinement of the CIM. It is enriched with general technical details and the model provides already an awareness of software in general. The PIM is typically created by IT experts but is still abstract enough, that business experts can cope with it. The added details are necessary for a technical implementation but on a very generic level, so that the model itself is in no way dependent on any specific technology. For example, the business process model on the PIM level consists of business functions, which are supported by software service. However, the model does not contain any details on the implementation technology to use, so it is not said that the software services must be implemented using Web service technology. This platform independence allows using the same business process model as a base for different implementation. This is important in enterprise computing, because usually a big company has heterogeneous technology in the service infrastructure. In such a case having a platform independent model is an advantage, because different implementations can be derived from this single source of truth. Therefore, the PIM model is the base for implementation.

The PSM is the most concrete model. Compared to the PIM, it is refined in terms of a specific technology platform. For example, the introduced software services of the PIM are mapped to specific Web services, defined by WSDL descriptions. The usage of a particular communication protocol like *SOAP* therefore includes the clear definition of messages exchanged between the services. The control flow is represented with languages like *Business Process Execution Language (BPEL)* or *XML Process Definition Language (XPDL)*, since EPC or BPMN are not suitable for these technical descriptions. Although there is tool support for the transformation from PIM to PSM (e.g. Stein and Ivanov [183] describe a semi-automated EPC to BPEL transformation) there is still manual work necessary to create an executable BPEL process. For example, the mentioned data transformations between the different message types has to be done manually and also some parts of the control flow have to be further detailed like adding conditions to split and join statements.

As discussed above, the pure functional CIM is firstly transformed to PIM and then into PSM. Business process automation here aims at lowering manual effort when creating the PSM out of the PIM. Despite the fact that partial automatic transformations are available, eliminating manual work is the goal. As mentioned in the previous section, the business process models are permanently subject to change. Business experts constantly change the CIM and PIM models to adapt to the business environment. The underlying implementation (PSM models) must be regenerated each time the CIM or PIM is changed. In reality, the PIM is the starting point for modifications, as it is abstract enough to be handled by business experts. Nevertheless, as of today the transformation from PIM to PSM has still to be done partially manually, which is slow and may harm the consistency of the models.

Different modelling languages are used on the different modelling levels. EPC [102] is a language for business process modelling, which was developed under supervision of Prof. August-Wilhelm Scheer at Saarland University, Germany in 1992. The EPC language is an accepted industry standard in business process modelling. EPCs are business oriented. They are not suitable for modelling of executable processes, because of missing implementation specific details like exception handling. As mentioned before, EPCs reside in the CIM and PIM levels of the MDA paradigm.

An EPC is an ordered graph consisting of six types of elements:

- *Events* describe the state of the process. Events activate business functions. Each EPC starts and ends with an event.
- *Functions* symbolise a certain business activity, which leads to a change of state and therefore to a certain event. In general, a function is preceded by an event and followed by an event.
- *Relations* connect functions and events specifying the actual process.
- *Operators* are used to split or join the control flow. Different operators like *AND*, *XOR*, and *OR* are available. Operators, relations, events, and functions together form the control flow of the process model. The EPC language allows modelling of the most important workflow patterns [197]. A detailed discussion of the workflow patterns supported by the EPC language can be found in [127].
- *Organizational Units* can be assigned to a function to specify that the given function is executed by the organizational element. This is known as human task in other modelling languages.
- *Information Objects* can be assigned to a function to specify the input and output data of the given function. The information objects represent parts of a logical (conceptual) enterprise data model. Typical elements of such an enterprise data model are customer, contract, and invoice.

Figure 5.24 shows an example EPC defining the business process of placing a domain order. The modelled process is based on the book's use case scenario. The process is started, if the event *Place Domain Order* is triggered. As a first business function the login and password are verified. This business function is repeated as long as login or password is incorrect. Afterwards, the business process continues with other business functions. It can be seen that various information objects are

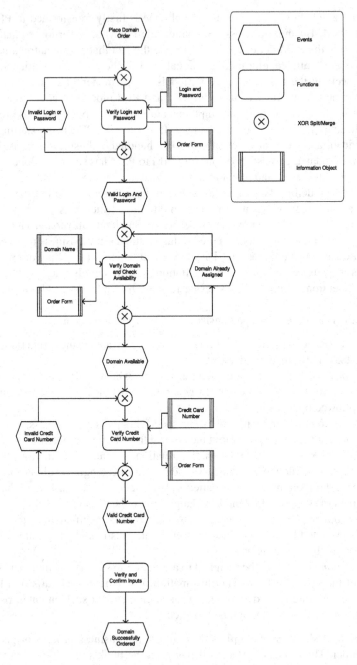

Fig. 5.24. Example EPC: place domain order

consumed and produced by the business functions. At the end, the business process is terminated with an event.

BPEL [11] is used to model executable business processes. Contrary to EPC, BPEL provides a more concrete and very detailed technical representation of a business process. In BPEL implemented processes can be executed by orchestration engines like Oracle SOA Suite or IBM Websphere. BPEL process models reside in the PSM level. Section 5.2.3 describes BPEL in more details.

WSDL [44] is used to describe the syntactic interface of Web services. Web services, more precisely their operations, are the activities described in the BPEL process. A WSDL file describes the operations and its input and output variables of a specific Web Service and the binding to its concrete implementation. The BPEL process references to such WSDL definitions and particularly to its operations to realize the single activities of the process. More details about WSDL and the connection to BPEL can be found in Sect. 5.2.3. WSDL is described in Sect. 7.4.1.

5.6.2 Motivation for Semantic Business Process Management

The previous section motivated a particular problem in business process management. Process models on a more abstract modelling level must always be refined to create executable models. As outlined before, different people with different skills are creating the models on the different levels. The more abstract business processes are created by business experts, who usually have a strong background in business administration, but less computer science knowledge. In contrast, executable business process models are implemented by integration experts or software engineers, who usually have a computer science or mathematical education. Therefore, it is not just a pure technical problem, but it also involves mediating between the two very different user groups. This phenomenon is well known as the business IT gap. Smith and Fingar [178] envision in their work to not just bridge this gap, but to instead obliterate it. That means, business experts are enabled to create the executable models on their own without any IT expert support.

A business expert must be able to select appropriate services for its processes. The business expert must be able to validate, if the business service fulfils the business requirements and supports a given business function. Today, service description approaches miss this semantic information. The gap between business and IT therefore remains, even though preliminary work exists on supporting business experts to select ordinary services [182]. By introducing semantic descriptions in the enterprise computing technology stack, this problem can be solved completely.

Besides using semantic descriptions for discovering appropriate services for business requirements, there are other possibilities to leverage semantic technologies in enterprise computing. One example is the enterprise model itself, which should be based on clear semantics. All model types should be grounded in ontologies, so that intelligent queries can be computed against those models. Another important application of semantic technologies is possible during the execution of processes. It can help to overcome compatibility issues, by using semantic mediation and late service binding.

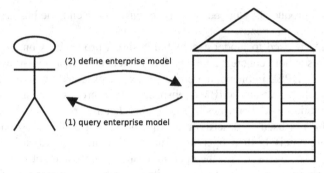

Fig. 5.25. Semantic business process management use cases

A comprehensive usage of semantic technologies was outline by Hepp et al. [84]. They propose a stack of ontologies to cover all aspects of an enterprise model. This includes a high level ontology for business processes and a technical oriented ontology for executable ones. A detailed discussion of the proposed ontology stack is presented in [85].

Figure 5.25 illustrates the general problem to be solved by applying semantic technologies. From an abstract point of view, there are two main use-cases of semantic technologies within business process management. First, an existing enterprise model needs to be analysed using semantic queries. The enterprise model or parts of it might be defined explicitly or implicitly. In case of extracting information from execution log files, the model is only implicitly defined whereas an organisational chart representing the hierarchy of power is an explicit definition. The semantic querying of the enterprise model can be used to identify all business processes affected by a new governmental regulation. Another example is to check the enterprise model semantically for compliance to a given rule set like *Sarbanes-Oxley Act* [49]. The second application of semantic technologies is in the definition or creation of full or partial enterprise models. As outlined before, a business expert can be supported by semantic technologies to select a matching service while designing an executable process.

Using a semantically grounded enterprise model would be perfect approach if a company is starting from scratch. As a matter of fact, companies already invested in business process and enterprise modelling for more than 10 years. Existing models must be reused to secure the investments made so far. In addition, existing standards for modelling and process execution must be reused and extended. It is therefore impossible to introduce a completely new technology stack, for example by replacing orchestration engines based on BPEL and XPDL with semantic ones. Instead, existing engines must be extended to also support semantic models. The model types must be extended instead of introducing completely new model types, which also ensures that only delta training is needed. Such an approach could increase the chance that semantic technologies will be accepted and actually applied in industry.

The following section describes how semantic technologies could be used in business process automation. The presented approach takes into account the discussed constraints by extending model types, instead of replacing the technological stack.

5.6.3 Semantic Technologies for Business Process Automation

For business process automation, it is of utmost importance to preserve existing investments and to reuse existing models and employees' competences. The following section shows how business processes modelled as EPC are semantically annotated. Such semantically annotated models allow the automated discovery of services for a particular business function, but it also allows semantically querying the process space. All examples are described by the EPC notation, since the authors already implemented the described approach as a prototypical extension of the ARIS SOA Architect[7] product.

In our approach, the business process model is automatically transformed into an executable process described in BPEL. The BPEL model can be generated by using and adapting existing approaches [183]. The semantic information needed for discovering and invoking semantic Web services is then hidden in variables. The consideration of semantic information is done during run-time by the *Semantic Invocation Service (SISi)*, which is a small web application using a semantic execution environment or a reasoner to discover and invoke a matching Web service. SISi provides a standard Web service interface described in WSDL so that it can be easily invoked from another BPEL process. This ensures that the approach outlined here can be used directly without changing or extending existing business process frameworks. A reference implementation of SISi is provided on SISi's homepage.[8]

SISi's software architecture is shown in Fig. 5.26. The architecture is a classical 3-tier design [38]. The top layer *External Interface Component* provides different external interfaces to SISi's functionality. At the current point there is only a Web service interface implemented by the *Web Service Interface Module*. By reusing existing Web service frameworks like Axis2 or CXF, it is possible to almost completely generate this implementation. The interface component receives external calls and forwards them to the second layer called *Core Component*. The core component consists of a *Controller Module*, which calls the *Semantic Discovery Module* for semantic Web service discovery. Discovered Web services are called through the *Web Service Invocation Module*. The usage of the controller module allows easily extending SISi with additional functionality like semantic data mediation. For invoking Web services described by WSDL, again existing frameworks like Axis2 or CXF can be used.

As of today, there are no frameworks available which provide abstraction from the actual semantic environment used. Therefore, the core component calls the *Semantic Abstraction Interface Module* belonging to the *Semantic Abstraction Component*. This module provides a unified interface so that the core component is not bound to any specific semantic environment or reasoner. Instead, different adapter modules are provided as part of the semantic abstraction component implementing

---

[7] http://www.aris.com/soa.

[8] http://code.google.com/p/semanticinvocationservice/.

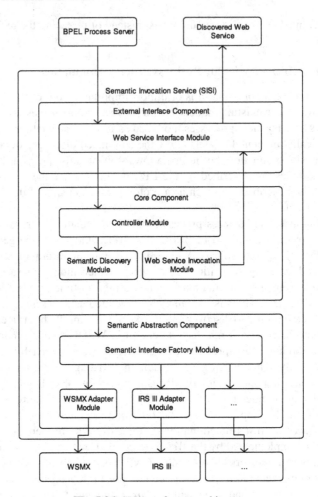

Fig. 5.26. SISi's software architecture

this interface for semantic environments which must be supported. The reference implementation of SISi contains an example implementation for *Web Service Modeling Execution Environment (WSMX)*.

Figure 5.27 illustrates the overall approach as a simplified EPC process model, which can be applied not only to SISi but to all scenarios for semantically enriched business processes. Steps that can be automated are marked in the figure with the letters *SYS*.

It can be seen that different roles are involved. A business expert defines and models the business process. This also includes semantic annotations of the process model. Experts for semantic technologies like ontology engineers annotate existing services so that they can be discovered through semantic service matching. The final preparation and execution of the executable process is supported by integration engineers.

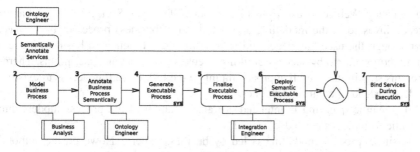

Fig. 5.27. Approach for semantically enriched business processes

Step 1—Semantically Annotate Services

A core element of semantic provisioning is the semantic service description. This book already presented different formalisms and approaches to capture semantic descriptions of Web services (see Sect. 3.4).

The approach presented here works with any kind of semantic formalism, if a reasoner exists which can compute the service match later on. Therefore, it is highly recommended to use the ontology family the company is most familiar with. Another important question to solve is how to relate the semantic annotation to the Web services they describe.

There are different possibilities, like the SAWSDL [66] (see Sect. 3.4.2). The standard is independent of the semantic formalism used, because it only provides a way to reference the semantic description. On a first glance it seems like a perfect fit, but there are also some drawbacks connected to this solution. SAWSDL introduces new elements and attributes to the WSDL standard and not all tools handling WSDL files are aware of those extensions. This is no problem as long as the tools do not touch or even change the unknown extensions. Before a company decides to use the SAWSDL standard to reference semantic annotations, all tools in the tool chain should be checked if they can deal with the extended WSDL files.

In case the tool chain is not able to support SAWSDL, another solution must be found. In such a case it makes sense to decouple syntactic and semantic descriptions by not mixing them in one file. A central service registry can be used to provide a pointer to the syntactic as well as the semantic description of the Web service. Many tools also allow using attributes to attach additional information to a Web service.

Semantic annotation of existing Web services can be done parallel to the other activities. However, the semantic descriptions must be ready before the business process is executed. Creating semantic descriptions is mainly led by ontology engineers, who may consult business experts or service owners to correctly capture the functionality.

Step 2—Model Business Process

As core assets of every company, business processes are constantly documented, managed, and communicated. Before a business process can be implemented using semantic Web services, it must be modelled first (see Sect. 5.6.1). Companies already invested in the modelling and definition of business processes in the past, even though the used languages and formalisms vary. If semantic business process automation wants to be successful, it must reuse those existing descriptions. Therefore, this step in the overall approach might be the task of getting access to existing models, instead of creating new ones.

If semantic querying is intended, a transformation of the process models into semantic formalisms is needed as well.

Business process modelling is led by business experts. However, the authors' experience shows that support from modelling experts might be needed to define a correct process model, which can later be transformed in an executable process. For example, in case of the EPC notation, the usage of the *OR* operator must be avoided, because it has no clear operational semantics [127] and it is hard to transform to an executable language like BPEL.

Step 3—Annotate Business Process Semantically

In a world without semantics, services must be added directly to the process model. Such a service selection during design-time can be also be supported by discovery algorithms as shown in [182], but it does not allow a flexible service provisioning during run-time. Therefore, instead of selecting a service directly in the process model only a semantic description of the expected functionality is added. The actual service selection and binding happens during execution of the process. This approach slightly differs from the one presented in Chap. , since here the business process is enriched with semantic information, instead of deriving it from the composition description.

In order to annotate a business process model with semantics, the same problems must be solved as for annotating Web services semantically. The first decision to be taken is selecting the ontological formalism. In order to make the overall solution not too complex, it is recommended to select the same ontological formalism also used for semantic Web service description. Otherwise, transformations between the different formalisms must be added to the solution stack, for example as ontology to ontology mediators.

It must also be investigated if the tools already have functionality for semantic business process modelling. Usually, modelling tools provide attributes for each modelling element (like business functions, operators, etc.). Such attributes can be used to either store the semantic description or a reference to an external file containing the semantic description.

If business process modelling was not done in the company, it might be a good idea to directly start with a semantic modelling tool. However, this scenario is very unlikely and there are only prototypical implementations of such semantic modelling tools available. Therefore, using an existing modelling tool with a well understood modelling language like EPC and BPMN is a much more realistic approach.

Semantic annotation should be led by business experts, because they know the requirements they have for each business function. As semantic annotation requires profound knowledge of the semantic formalism used, so ontology engineers will have to support the business experts in correctly expressing the requirements they have.

Step 4—Generate Executable Process

In the next step, the semantic business process model is transformed into an executable one. Depending on the process middleware available in the company, different languages like BPEL or XPDL might be generated. As of today, no major BPEL engine or middleware product understands semantic extensions. There is also no common standard for embedding semantic annotations in BPEL beside some initial initiatives. Therefore, one should either find a way to execute a semantic process model on an unmodified engine, or to extend an existing engine.

A pragmatic solution is the usage of the described SISi framework. For each service call, which should result in dynamic service discovery and binding during runtime, SISi is invoked with the semantic description as an input parameter. Invoking a service requires an input and an output message. The message type of the discovered Web service may vary. Therefore, it is impossible that SISi provides an operation with the correct signature for each combination of possible input and output message types. Instead, a generic interface must be provided, which can consume any input message type and return any output message type. This can be done by dumping the content of the input and output message in an own message part. The input message type of SISi also contains another message part to transfer the semantic description. Again, as the used formalism might vary, no specialised interface can be provided. Instead, the content of this message part is forwarded directly to the semantic execution engine. To make this work, not only the BPEL invoke activities for calling SISi must be generated, but also BPEL assign statements to define the input and consume the output of SISi.

Even though the BPEL process with injected semantics is not trivial, it is possible to automatically generate it. This might be surprising on a first glance, but manually modelling such a BPEL process shows that certain modelling tasks are repeated all the time. Therefore, this step is marked as an automated one in the SISi architecture figure.

Listing 5.2 shows the syntactical description of the SISi's Web service interface defined using WSDL. There is exactly one operation to invoke a semantic Web service. The message definitions of the operation's parameters are shown in Listing 5.3 as XML Schema definitions.

Listing 5.2. Syntactical description of the SISi interface (WSDL)

```
<?xml version="1.0" encoding="utf-8"?>
<wsdl:definitions name="WebServiceInterfaceWS"
 targetNamespace="http://sisi.externalInterface/"
 xmlns:wsdl="http://schemas.xmlsoap.org/wsdl/"
 xmlns:tns="http://sisi.externalInterface/"
 xmlns:dataNs="http://sisi.externalInterface/dataTypes"
```

```
xmlns:xsd="http://www.w3.org/2001/XMLSchema">
 <wsdl:types>
  <schema xmlns="http://www.w3.org/2001/XMLSchema">
   <import namespace="http://sisi.externalInterface/dataTypes"
    schemaLocation="SISi_WebServiceInterface_dataTypes.xsd"/>
  </schema>
 </wsdl:types>
 <wsdl:message name="invokeSemanticWebServiceRequest">
  <wsdl:part name="semanticDescription" element="xsd:string"/>
  <wsdl:part name="parameters" element="dataNs:hashMap"/>
 </wsdl:message>
 <wsdl:message name="invokeSemanticWebServiceResponse">
  <wsdl:part name="parameters" element="dataNs:hashMap"/>
 </wsdl:message>
 <wsdl:portType name="WebServiceInterfaceWS">
  <wsdl:operation name="invokeSemanticWebService">
   <wsdl:input message="invokeSemanticWebServiceRequest"/>
   <wsdl:output message="invokeSemanticWebServiceResponse"/>
  </wsdl:operation>
 </wsdl:portType>
</wsdl:definitions>
```

Listing 5.3. SISi datatypes (WSDL)

```
<xsd:schema xmlns:xsd="http://www.w3.org/2001/XMLSchema"
 xmlns:tns="http://sisi.externalInterface/dataTypes">
 <xsd:complexType name="hashMap">
  <xsd:complexContent>
   <xsd:extension base="map">
    <xsd:sequence/>
   </xsd:extension>
  </xsd:complexContent>
 </xsd:complexType>
 <xsd:complexType name="map">
  <xsd:sequence>
   <xsd:element name="mapEntry" type="mapEntry" minOccurs="0"
    maxOccurs="unbounded"/>
  </xsd:sequence>
 </xsd:complexType>
 <xsd:complexType name="mapEntry">
  <xsd:sequence>
   <xsd:element name="key" type="xsd:anyType"/>
   <xsd:element name="value" type="xsd:anyType"/>
  </xsd:sequence>
 </xsd:complexType>
</xsd:schema>
```

Step 5—Finalise Executable Process

If everything goes fine, a generated BPEL process can be deployed and executed directly. According to the authors' experience, this is usually not the case. For example, each execution environments has some specifics requiring a manual adaptation of the generated BPEL process. Also, some information is not available in the platform independent model and can therefore also not be generated or transformed. A typical example is technical exception handling. Business experts can only define business exceptions like a customer cancelling an order during the order process, but it is not their task to define technical exception handling like if a Web service is not available or messages are corrupted. Adding such information to business oriented process models makes those models unreadable and lowers them to a platform specific level. This step is usually led by integration experts of the used execution environment.

Step 6—Deploy Semantic Executable Process

Deploying an executable process on a process execution engine is usually straightforward, if clustering, security aspects and other non-functional properties must not be taken into account. In case of semantic business process execution, the following tasks must be done in addition:

- Besides setting up the execution engine, the semantic execution engine or reasoner must be made productive as well.
- The semantic descriptions of all Web services must be made available to the semantic execution engine so that arriving queries can be computed against the semantic descriptions of available services.
- The semantic execution engine must be made accessible by the BPEL execution engine.

If those additional steps were done, the generated BPEL process can be deployed on the BPEL engine. This step is led by integration engineers, who are familiar with the different systems. This step is marked as an automatic one, because most tasks can be automated after enough experience was gathered.

Step 7—Bind Services During Runtime

In the final step, the BPEL process is executed. The BPEL orchestration engine navigates through the process model and executes each activity. Each time a semantic Web service should be discovered during run-time, SISi is invoked. Figure 5.28 shows the different steps performed to discover and invoke a semantic Web service using SISi. The steps are:

1. The BPEL process is executed on a standard orchestration engine like Oracle BPEL Server or IBM Websphere. In case a semantic Web service should be bound during run-time, the request is forwarded to SISi. SISi is executed on a JAVA servlet container.

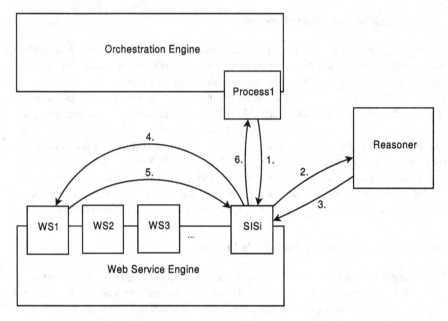

Fig. 5.28. System architecture for the SISi example

2. SISi receives the semantic discovery request and passes the semantic goal description (see Sect. 3.4.1) to a reasoner.
3. The reasoner uses semantic discovery algorithms to find matching semantic Web service descriptions (see Sect. 3.5). The best fitting Web service description is selected and passed back to SISi.
4. SISi uses this information to invoke the semantically discovered Web service with the data received from the BPEL process as input parameter.
5. The Web service is executed and the output data returned to SISi.
6. SISi forwards the output data back to the BPEL process.

Those steps are repeated for each semantic Web service to be bound during runtime of the executed BPEL process.

5.6.4 Chances of Semantic Business Process Management

Business process management as a sub-discipline of enterprise architecture deals with managing and defining a core asset of the enterprise model—the business processes. Business processes define the interaction between the different elements of the company. Today, there is a gap between the view of business and IT experts on the business processes, which is caused by no shared conceptualisation between both groups. This fact prevents any easy solution for deriving an IT implementation out of the business processes, which is a major goal of business process automation. To overcome this problem, the usage of ontologies resulting in clear semantic descriptions is suggested. Activities in a business process as well as Web services to automate them are semantically described and semantic matchmaking is used to bring them together. The presented approach is very pragmatic, because it reuses existing technologies and standards where possible instead of introducing a completely new technology stack. This general approach of re-using existing services and standards reflects the unavoidable consideration of legacy technology and existing functionalities in all service enabling scenarios.

After the discussion of service enabling in this and the presentation of proper means for semantic service description in the previous chapter, the next chapter will present details about service composition and binding.

6

Service Composition Enactment

Marek Kowalkiewicz, Mariusz Momotko, and Alexander Saar

6.1 Overview and Motivation

Enactment of manually or automatically created service compositions as the crucial part of a service oriented approach is not novel; there are several standard execution languages and there are many existing composition enactment engines.

The de-facto standard for service composition and business process description is the *Business Process Execution Language (BPEL)* [11, 26]. In BPEL, a service composition is defined as a business process in terms of control flow (i.e. order of the invoked atomic services) and data flow (input and output parameters and mappings between them). On the market, there are quite many BPEL execution engines available both as open source engines (e.g. ActiveBPEL, FiveSight PXE) as well as commercial engines (e.g. IBM WebSphere Process Server, OfficeObjects®WorkFlow, and Oracle®BPEL).

Also for service monitoring there are (at least) several well defined approaches based on service level agreements, like the *Web Service Level Agreement (WSLA)* project from IBM or WS-Agreement from the *Open Grid Forum (OGF)* standardisation body.

Most of the existing tools do quite well with adaptability at the atomic service level. For instance, they are able to replace dynamically the invoked service with another one of the same functional specification. However, their support for adaptability at the service composition level is weak. To cope with this problem several intensive research works have been carried out recently. The *eFlow* project from HP Labs [40] proposes an adaptive and dynamic approach to manage service compositions focusing on their functional aspects such as dynamic service discovery and ad hoc changes. The *QUEST framework* [79] extends the work done on *eFlow* by introducing the notion of *Quality of Service (QoS)* provisioning. The *MAIS* project [48] focused on negotiation of Web service QoS parameters with the ability to use different negotiation strategies. Also in the area of SLA-based contracting and monitoring, there are several advanced approaches and frameworks [18].

Despite all this efforts, still an open and valid question is how to manage service compositions in order to satisfy both functional and non-functional requirements properly as well as adapt to dynamic changes. So far, adaptability in the existing approaches and tools is weak or inadequate. They do not work well in case of dynamic changes related to the contracted atomic services. In case of failures they have problems with finding alternative solutions that would satisfy both functional and non-functional requirements. In particular, they are not able to re-negotiate a contract in case of QoS constraint violation, and re-select dynamically another atomic service that satisfies QoS constraints. In addition, the existing approaches do not pay much attention on service profiling and historical execution data and therefore they are not able to optimise their way of working.

The following chapter describes some recent results in adaptive service composition management and enactment. The presented concepts may be considered as one possible strategy towards a comprehensive approach for adaptive management of QoS aware service compositions. It integrates well known concepts and techniques for contracting, enacting and SLA management, monitoring, and profiling. In general, the presented approach proposes various execution strategies based on dynamic selection and negotiation. The consecutive sections are focused on the elements of these strategies: composition enactment, composition monitoring, and composition profiling.

6.2 Enactment Strategies

Composition enactment and monitoring are two tasks of adaptive service composition management. The other three tasks, namely selection, contracting and rebinding (or exception handling) have already been discussed in Sect. 5.4. The different ways of combining these five basic tasks may be used to define various execution strategies, which are independent from the according composition description and enactment technology. As usual, there is no optimal strategy. Every strategy focuses on different aspects of service executions and has both advantages and disadvantages (see also [212]). These strategies may be treated as a next step toward adaptive composition management. They therefore complement the already described adaptability approaches:

6.2.1 First-contract-all-then-enact Strategy

This strategy assumes (see Fig. 6.1) that selection and contracting of all atomic services included in the service composition is done before its execution. Execution and monitoring of the individual atomic services is done step by step according to the control flow defined for the service composition. Any failure reported during service execution is handled by exception handling mechanism described in the previous sections.

This strategy makes it possible to guarantee non-functional requirements for the whole service composition (global level). Since contracting is done before execution,

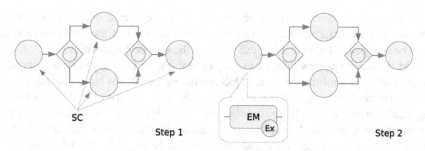

Fig. 6.1. First-contract-then-enact strategy

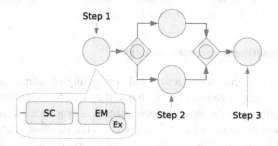

Fig. 6.2. Step-by-step-contract-and-enact strategy

concurrent selection and negotiation is allowed. As a result, it is possible to consider aggregated concession sets and preferences (e.g., if the same provider provide services for several atomic services, then some discount may be regarded), so that the service composition QoS parameters can be optimised.

On the contrary, in this strategy all the activities on conditional branches need to be selected and contracted although some of them may never be enacted. This calls for some kind of reservation mechanism. Also service implementations registered during service execution cannot be selected. Finally, the strategy requires coordinated negotiation mechanisms with a coordination agent and a set of negotiation agents (e.g. concurrent or market mechanisms).

6.2.2 Step-by-step-contract-and-enact Strategy

This strategy assumes (see Fig. 6.2) that selection, contracting, and atomic service execution is intertwined. That is, the first atomic service in the service composition can be executed and monitored when its SLA document is established. After completion of this atomic service, the selection and contracting is carried out for each subsequent atomic service and followed by its execution. Any failure occurred during service execution is handled by exception handling mechanism.

This strategy allows for on-the-fly selection and negotiation based on results and actual QoS values of services that have been executed. This will lead to more accurate and efficient negotiation since it is based on what has already been executed.

Only the invoked atomic services are contracted, not executed branches of service composition are not considered. Also it is possible to select atomic services that have been registered after starting execution of the service composition.

On the contrary, the strategy can only optimise QoS for a given atomic service (local level). As a result, the global QoS requirements can not be optimised. Local constraints need to be considered, but if a framework gets a list of providers satisfying local constraints then there is still a risk of missing their combinations. Instantiation and execution of the whole service composition can not be guaranteed. One example would be an service implementation that is executed, but which hinders other service implementations from being selected or contracted. In this case, the whole service composition would fail, and waste the resources of already executed services, or may even demand costly roll-back activities.

6.2.3 Late-contracting-then-enact Strategy

This strategy assumes that the selection and contracting of atomic services is done before their execution, as soon as it is sure that they will be executed within a given composition. If, for example, there are two alternative branches, as soon it is known which of them will be taken, all atomic services on the satisfied branch are selected and contracted. Execution of the atomic services is carried out according to the control flow definition. This strategy is similar to the first negotiation then enact strategy but minimises the risk in contracting services which will never be executed. The risk to not satisfy the global QoS requirements is less than for the mentioned strategy but still exists.

6.2.4 First-contract-plausible-then-enact Strategy

This strategy tries to select and contract first (before service composition execution) all atomic services that belong to one of composition path which is the most likely to be executed. The path is predicted on the basis of historical data from previous execution of the service composition. The services belonging to other paths are not selected and contracted. Execution of the atomic services is carried out according to the control flow definition. This strategy minimises the risk of (a) contracting services that will never be executed, (b) satisfying the global QoS requirements. However, it will work properly only for those cases which execution concern the most probable path in the composition. For the other paths it will have similar problems as the step by step contract and enact strategy.

6.2.5 First-contract-critical-then-enact Strategy

This strategy selects and contracts before execution only those atomic services which are hard to be contracted dynamically. 'Hard' in this context means that the number of service candidates for those service specifications is significantly less than the number of candidates for the other services included. This strategy is similar to the

Table 6.1. Several simple rules for selection of the execution strategy

If service composition includes ...	... then apply strategy
neither conditional nor alternative branches	first-contract-all-then-enact
a small number of conditional/alternative branches	late-contracting-then-enact
one path with high probability of execution	first-contract-plausible-then-enact
easily contracted atomic services	step-by-step-contract-and-enact
large number of hard-to-contract services	first-contract-critical-then-enact

step by step contract and enact strategy but reduces the risk of not satisfying the global QoS requirements. On the other hand, it also does not cope with branches which will never be executed.

Table 6.1 gives a possible set of rules for choosing the right execution strategy with a given service composition.

6.3 Composition Monitoring and Profiling

With a strategy for composition enactment and service contracting, the according framework still needs to supervise the ongoing enactment. This monitoring and profiling enables the reaction on service faults or performance gains, or might be simply needed because of legal regularities. We distinguish between two major issues: service monitoring is the activity of collecting performance and operational data for a service under use. service profiling describes the activity of using this data for the derivation of a condensed description reagarding the non-functional properties of a service. This service profile enables the qualitative comparison of service candidates, which is a prerequisite for dynamic service binding.

6.3.1 Service Monitoring

Service monitoring plays an important role for the negotiation and profiling of non-functional QoS characteristics, since it provides the source data for them. For this reason, it is important to investigate monitoring strategies that can be applied in heterogeneous environments.

QoS attributes and their usage for *Service Level Agreement (SLA)* documents appears in different application domains, like networking hardware, telecommunication environments, finance management, agent systems, or *service oriented architecture (SOA)*. The according researchers and engineers typically refer to different data models for their quality attributes, since the nature of service quality depends on the particular domain. It is therefore not possible to talk about an ultimate set of monitoring attributes, which can be applied across all application domains and business areas. This tends to be a problem in generic service monitoring and profiling frameworks, which may be intended to work independently from the application domain.

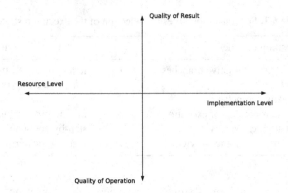

Fig. 6.3. Classification of monitoring values

Even with the positioning in one particular domain, heterogeneous technologies can still prevent a consistent gauging and retrieval of monitoring values by the service provisioning platform. Therefore, the generic monitoring of services must rely on an abstract and domain-independent approach.

One possible generic classification of monitoring attributes is shown in Fig. 6.3. The vertical dimension differs between quality-of-result and quality-of-operation, while the horizontal dimension covers *resource-level* and *implementation-level* values. In addition to the two dimensions mentioned before, we can differ between calculated and directly measurable (atomic) values.

The quality-of-result parameters provide a quantitative representation for non-functional requirements on operation results. An example could be a service that returns a map which contains a route description. The service can provide a coloured and high resolution map, or a monochrome and low resolution one. These values are specified by the particular service implementation and define the quality of the result. They are therefore specific for the particular implementation.

quality-of-operation parameters express non-functional requirements on result delivery. Typical examples are the request throughput of a service or the response time of service invocations. These parameters are similar for all service types and application domains.

The horizontal dimension considers the difference between values that can be provided by the environment, and values that must be provided by the service itself. The monitoring of *resource-level* parameters depends on the resources that execute the service, for example an application server in the service infrastructure. Examples are resource utilisation values, such as the CPU load or memory consumption of a running service implementation.

In contrast to *resource-level* values monitoring of *implementation-level* parameters relies on specific service implementation characteristics, for example the cost of a service invocation. The actual values can therefore only be obtained by the help of the service implementation itself.

In general, a SLA can be related to any kind of QoS value. Many standards for SLA definition, like WSLA [63] or *WS-Agreement* [12] provide the ability for defining own parameter types. Thus, providers and consumers of services can define various QoS values, depending on their business area and technologies used. Nevertheless, there are some widely accepted QoS values, that are ubiquitous and common to all kinds of services. In majority of the cases, these values are related to quality-of-operation, because this is the only common class of properties that all services share. Resource, implementation, and quality-of-result related values are mostly domain, or service technology specific and thus they can not be generalised. The following list provides a set of commonly accepted QoS values, taken from the *Service Level Measurement Quality* section of the *Quality Model for Web Services* [106]:

response time: Measures the time to send a request and receive the response. It is usually calculated using a mean value during a certain time.

maximum throughput: Measures the number of requests that a system can process over a certain period of time (1 unit). It is often used as a performance index, evaluating the system.

availability: Measures the ratio of time, when a Web service is ready for use or being used (uptime, as opposed to downtime). For instance, if a Web service is ready for use or being used for 54 minutes per hour, then $Availability = 54/60 = 90\%$.

successability: Measures the ratio of successfully returned messages after requested tasks are performed with no errors. In contrast to accessibility, that measure can be used to indicate how effective the service is.

accessibility: Measures the ratio of acknowledgement messages in relation to the number of request messages. In some cases services may be available, but they not operate properly. That situation is not captured by accessibility, however it is reflected in successability, that by definition can never be greater than a accessibility.

These and other parameters are typically relevant for the permanent supervision of service execution. Typically, the responsible service infrastructure controls the uniform invocation of services and monitoring of *resource-level* and quality-of-operation parameters. It decouples higher layers of the platform from heterogeneous execution environments, operating systems, application servers, and resource binding mechanisms. In most cases, this layer is part of the service infrastructure (see Chap. 7), which provides the according runtime environment for self-contained or wrapper services.

A general understanding of a service invocation in the service infrastructure is illustrated in Fig. 6.4. Every invocation—including request and response—of a service passes a set of mediators. These mediators have various responsibilities from packaging and (de)serialisation on client and server side, up to message transformation and routing at intermediaries. The realisation of the mediators depends on the particular environment and configuration.

The model shown in Fig. 6.4 can be used for definition of measurement points, marked with "MP". For example, if provider and consumer of a service define a

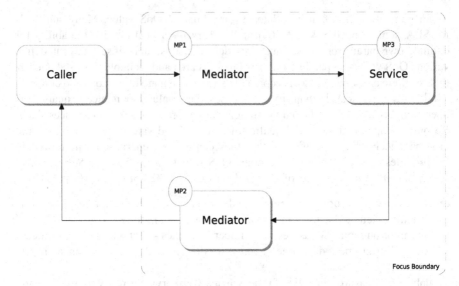

Fig. 6.4. Common service invocation model [193]

maximum end-to-end response time, the model can help in understanding the value generation and therefore the semantic of the according measurement results. It is possible to define that the request time gauging is the first operation in the first client side mediator (MP1 in Fig. 6.4), and that the corresponding measurement of request completion time is the last operation in the last mediator of the response mediator chain (MP3 in Fig. 6.4). The resulting response time is now semantically clearly described, without any technological relation:

$$Response\ Time = Completion\ Time\ (MP2) - Start\ Time\ (MP1). \qquad (6.1)$$

One of the interesting aspects in the example is that the end-to-end response time refers not only to the time for processing a service invocation (request and response), but also includes the efforts of marshalling, routing and un-marshalling. The measured time therefore nearly reflects the end-user perception, which is a crucial issue for real-world SLA monitoring. Resource metrics are typically obtained at MP3, since the measurement technology such as an operating system API is only available on the service execution host.

The definitions of implementation-level and quality-of-operation parameters are bound to the particular kind of service. These types of QoS values are part of service responsibilities and thus they must be provided by the service implementation. The service infrastructure therefore does not need to handle this class of monitoring parameters, but must offer some mechanisms for supporting the storage, accumulation, and consistent provisioning of such values.

6.3.2 Service Profiling

Based on the monitoring of single services, a composition enactment framework must maintain profiles of integrated services. A service profile is defined as an up-to-date description of a service. It allows the service comparison based on non-functional parameters. Most common service descriptions in *Web Services Description Language (WSDL)* do not provide necessary information to create a service quality profile. A service provider may include only a few of non-functional parameters in the semantic service description, like missing QoS values. That is why the other important parameters have to be determined by other means. The description provided by service providers is also rather static, whereas the values of some service characteristics change in time and depend strongly on changes in the environment (problems with network, throughput, etc.). Service properties specified by service providers also change occasionally, for example when new resources become available etc. For frequently changing values, service providers are able to provide value ranges, exact values of which are established during a negotiation process.

The main task of service profiling is to create and update service profiles of individual and composed services used within a semantic service provisioning platform. Data gathered in service profiling repositories during execution of services serves as a source of up-to-date information used by other components, such as the negotiation process or the re-planning components (see also example in Sect. 9.1.2). The latter may need the data to perform analysis and to select an appropriate part of the composition for re-planning. Service profiles for individual, as well as for composed services, are created while analysing available data (historical and current). They represent up-to-date characteristics of services. When creating a service profile, the horizon of the prognosis needs to be taken into account. For example, a SLA negotiation can request service profiles that forecast either their short time or long time behaviour (parameters). A high-level overview of actors involved in service profiling is provided in Fig. 6.5.

Additionally, service profilers can suggest tuning possibilities (for example replacing non-optimal services) that help to improve quality and performance of already designed service compositions. Moreover, in more advanced environments, service profilers have the chance to trigger early warnings in case of detected high probability for a service failure.

It is important to notice that service profiling is not directly responsible for current monitoring of actual values of composition enactment. The main goal of service profiling is to collect information from composed services executions, aggregate it and derive new information about services. The information is then provided to interested parties in order to influence planning, negotiation, and enactment. Table 6.2 shows a sample list of profiling parameters considered in many typical use cases involving Web services.

Service profiling is invisible to end service requesters and independent from their usage scenario. The service profiling is most useful if there are many service substitutes available that offer the same functionality with different service levels.

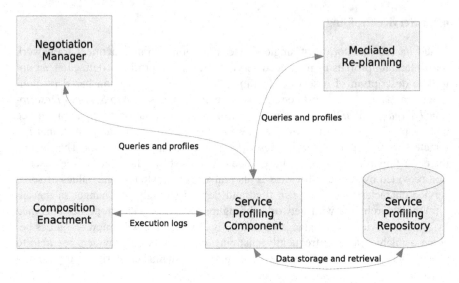

Fig. 6.5. Service profiling actors

Table 6.2. Sample list of profiling parameters

Parameter name	Value type
Response time (Avg/Min/Max)	Time (ms)
Duration of execution (Avg/Min/Max)	Time (ms)
Price (Avg/Min/Max)	Cost (MU)
Reliability	Percentage
Accessibility	Percentage
Charging method and payment method	String
Response latency or execution duration	Percentage
Provider reliability or provider accessibility	Percentage

For the clarification of basic properties, we consider an example of an end service consumer who wants to register a new domain (see use case scenario in Chap. 9.1.2). Hence, the scope of the scenario is to check whether the desired domain name is available, to create the desired Web hosting account, and finally to allow payment for all services through electronic channels. Services in this scenario are divided into three groups:

1. Domain services,
2. Web hosting services,
3. Payment services.

In the category of domain services, we distinguish between services checking the domain name, services that register domains, and services updating nameservers. Exemplary services for Web hosting services are Web hosting accounts creators, domain creators, or e-mail configurators. Payment services handle all aspects of settlement of each transaction, like credit card authorisation, payment, refunds, or currency conversion.

A starting point for the scenario can be the following user request: "Register domain lehmann.de for the customer Max Lehmann and provide him with 100 MB of webspace". Moreover, the customer needs a domain to be registered in less than 1 minute, in order to keep a reasonable response time on the front-end Web page. It should also be ensured that the participating service has a high level of accessability.

In a semantic service provisioning platform, the negotiation subsystem is used to select the most suitable atomic service implementation to be contracted by negotiation for each atomic service specification. In the sample scenario these atomic service specifications are the *CheckDomain, CreateWebhostingAccount, CreateDomain, SetupPhysicalHosting, UpdateNameserver, RegisterDomain,* and *CreditCardPayment* services. The negotiation subsystem needs to decompose the overall non-functional requirements and assign them to each atomic service. In order to do that, it needs to know what are the values of e.g. mean execution duration of each of the atomic services. Moreover, for some specifications there is more than one atomic service that implements the service specification, e.g. implementation of *CheckDomain* service is offered by three different service providers.

In order to perform a choice of services, the values from service profiles and service ranking are required. In the profile, we compute and provide several non-functional properties. However, for simplicity, only three of them will be used in further description. These characteristics are: *price, execution duration,* and *accessibility*. The *accessibility* parameter is used by the negotiation subsystem for partner selection to filter the list of potential providers. For each relevant atomic service (including substitutes) the negotiation subsystem asks the service profiling subsystem for a matching profile. One example for such a query is shown in Listing 6.1.

It contains the following data:

Parameter defines which parameters will be put into the output data structure, the profile or the ranking of profiles.

ServiceIDList is a list of service implementation identifiers, for which parameters should be computed.

Listing 6.1. A sample service profiling query

```
query1 = new DspQuery(
    'Profile',
    '2',
    'Accessibility > 0.48',
    'ChargingMethod=per execution',
    '3',
    'Synthetic,Price',
    '1');
getServiceProfile (query1);
```

HavingQuan is a list of conditions constraining quantitative parameters, i.e. Response-Latency, MaxResponseLatency, MinResponseLatency, ExecutionDuration, MaxExecutionDuration, MinExecutionDuration, Price, MaxPrice, MinPrice, Reliability or Accessibility. Services that do not meet all of the conditions will not be included in the output.

HavingQual serves the same purpose as *HavingQuan* but is used for constraining qualitative parameters. i.e. PaymentMethod or ChargingMethod. Each condition consists of two parts, the qualitative parameter name and the string value.

Horizon restricts the time scope for analysing service instances. Only three values are allowed for the parameter, representing data not older than one month, data not older than half a year, or data not older than one year.

OrderBy is a list of quantitative parameters. If it is not empty, the output will be sorted in the order of ascending values of given parameters. If it is empty, Synthetic parameter is taken as a default ordering indicator.

Limit is an integer that defines the upper limit on the number of service profiles in the output. Set to 1, and used together with OrderBy may be employed to select the best service accordingly to a selected parameter set. If Limit is set to zero or not given, all the profiles will appear in the output.

In order to answer the presented query for services, the profiling subsystem uses specific profiling algorithms, as well as data from the service profiling repository. The service profiling repository is replenished continuously with information about the service executions in the form of the log files. The relevant information about service behaviour is derived from the log file and SLA contracts and stored in the repository in question. The result of the sample query from Listing 6.1 is shown in Listing 6.2.

The service profiling subsystem creates service profiles for each implementation of atomic service specification (e.g. for each implementation of CreateDomain service specification), and orders them according to the synthetic indicator value, which is an aggregated value derived from the available quality factors. The returned profile information can be expressed as XML document, as shown in he example Listing 6.2.

Similarly, profiles for all other services involved in a process can be created. They are sent back to the negotiation subsystem, and on the basis of these values, the negotiation subsystem chooses appropriate atomic services. Additionally, the service profiling subsystem offers the negotiation subsystem computed profiles about service providers. They are especially useful when existing services outside of the platform are considered in the negotiation process. The provider profile gives information on its reliability, accessibility etc. This information is then used to choose one service from the set of services having the same characteristics.

As another aspect a service profiling subsystem is the acquisition of data necessary to compute service and provider profiles. This data is used in order to create profiles of each of the atomic services involved in the process as described. By analysing changes in the repository, service profiling subsystems can suggest tuning possibilities and/or the re-negotiation of service composition.

Listing 6.2. A sample answer to a service profiling query

```xml
<?xml version="1.0" encoding="UTF-8" ?>
<ProfileData>
  <ServiceProfile>
    <BasicData>
      <WS-ID>2</WS-ID>
      <WS-Price>2.5</WS-Price>
      <WS-MinPrice>2.0</WS-MinPrice>
      <WS-MaxPrice>3.0</WS-MaxPrice>
      <WS-ExecutionDuration>21.5</WS-ExecutionDuration>
      <WS-ExecutionDurFulfilment>75.0</WSExecutionDurFulfilment>
      <WS-MinExecutionDuration>15</WS-MinExecutionDuration>
      <WS-MaxExecutionDuration>28</WS-MaxExecutionDuration>
      <WS-Synthetic>1.0</WS-Synthetic>
      <WS-SlaFulfilmentIndicator>0.88</WSSlaFulfilmentIndicator>
    </BasicData>
    <AdditionalData>
      <WS-PaymentMethod>credit card</WS-PaymentMethod>
      <WS-ChargingMethod>per execution</WS-ChargingMethod>
      <WS-Accessibility>1</WS-Accessibility>
      <WS-Reliability>1</WS-Reliability>
      <WS-ResponseLatency>1.5</WS-ResponseLatency>
      <WS-ResponseLatencyFulfilment>100</WSResponseLatencyFulfilment>
      <WS-MinResponseLatency>1</WS-MinResponseLatency>
      <WS-MaxResponseLatency>2</WS-MaxResponseLatency>
    </AdditionalData>
  </ServiceProfile>
</ProfileData>
```

A detailed architecture for service profiling is available in other studies [3], and the challenges of QoS computation [4], and problems with assessing reliability of Web services have also been discussed in other works [2]. The relation of service profiling to other components of service delivery platforms has also been discussed in related work [133, 134]. Future experiments and research results will determine the relevant functionality for a service profiling environment.

6.4 Fault Management Strategies

Beside the performance aspect of service monitoring and profiling in composition enactment, the detection and reaction to fault conditions plays also a major role. In order to assure an appropriate level of adaptability, the composition enactment unit should provide sophisticated strategies for fault management. These strategies start from re-binding of concrete atomic service and end with re-planning of the whole service composition. If an invoked atomic service fails, the fault management strategies can be categorised as described in the service delivery life cycle (see Sect. 2.3):

re-binding either stands for a SLA re-negotiation with the provider of an atomic
    service, or for the replacement of a service by re-selection.

re-planning denotes the creation of the whole service composition. The service com-
    position enactment is continued with its new definition.

In the context of re-binding, re-negotiation results in updating the SLA document. Re-selection usually happens if either re-negotiation was not possible or the
source of the failure was related to a functional problem. In this case the responsible component of a service provisioning infrastructure should try to find another
atomic service providers that match the service specification and new requirements.
Since this re-planning is the most advanced mechanism, it will be discussed in the
consecutive sections in detail.

6.4.1 Re-planning of a Service Composition

In order to re-plan a service composition, the authors propose a multi-step procedure that includes the termination of failed activities, the sound suspension of the
workflow, the generation of a new process definition, and the adequate process resumption.

Considering related work there are some approaches for automated re-planning,
but none of them explicitly take workflow suspension and resumption into account.
In [117] requests are matched against standard business processes to generate an execution plan. Every time a knowledge gathering action is executed the additional information is used to generate a new plan. Ontologies of domain services and domain
integration knowledge can be used as a model for workflow integration rules [15].
DYflow [214] avoids predefined process definitions and allows the dynamic composition of Web services to business processes by applying backward-chain, forward-
chain and data flow inference.

One of the main preconditions for process re-planning is the assumption that the
state of the process instance and all its activity instances does not change during
re-planning. This assumption may be satisfied if re-planning is proceeded by suspending a given process instance and followed by resuming it. These two functions
operate on process instance and activity instance entities and need to be represented
in their behavioural model.

The usual way of doing it is to define a new "suspended" state together with two
events: "suspend" which goes to and "resume" which goes from the defined state
[90, 1]. An implied assumption of this approach is that suspension is done only for
entities remaining in state "running". This assumption, however, seems to be too
restrictive in case of re-planning since re-planning may occur to an activity instance
remaining in any of its state (e.g. "scheduled").

To cope with the above problem it is possible to introduce two new states, which
enable or disable the workflow management system to process the mentioned entities. These states are called enabling states and are orthogonal to the remaining states
which called operational states. Regardless of the operational state in which a
given entity remains, at any time it is possible to suspend or to resume a process or

activity instance. If the suspend event occurs, the entity moves to state "disabled". In this state the functions operating on the entity may behave in a different way. Basically, the functions responsible for assignment or execution of the entities omit disabled entities. For example, activity instances (or tasks) remaining in states "scheduled + disabled" will not be displayed in the participants work lists. On the contrary, the functions responsible for completing or terminating entities will behave in a similar way as those for enabled activities do. Suspension of a process instance causes suspension of all its activity instances. In this case, the suspend event is also sent to all activity instances of a given process instance.

If the resume event occurs, a suspended entity moves back to state "enabled". This also triggers appropriate operation related to the entity operational state. For example, for activity instance remaining in state "running", this entity is re-run. Resuming of a process instance causes resuming of all its activity instances. In this case, the resume event is also sent to all activity instances of a given process instance. In addition, in the proposed approach the state "suspended" is not needed any more. Now, it is expressed as a combination of "running + disabled" states.

The process instance behavioural model presented in Fig. 6.6 consists of two group of states: operational and enabling ones. The state "new" is the operational state in which a process instance is created. If all its preconditions are satisfied, it starts its first activity and moves to state "running". Then it remains in this state until all its activity instances are finished and all its postconditions (if present) are satisfied. Afterwards it moves to the state "completed". At any time it is possible to terminate

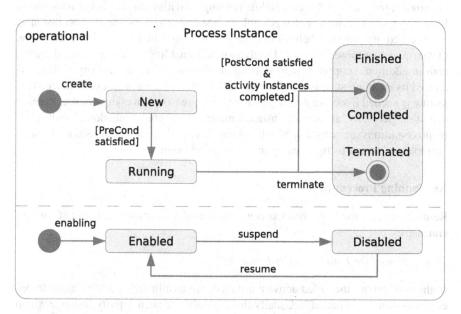

Fig. 6.6. Process instance behavioural model

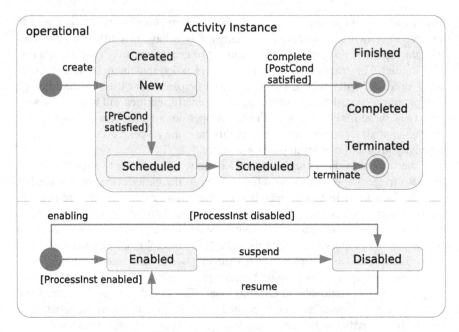

Fig. 6.7. Activity instance behavioural model

the process instance. In this case, all its running activities are also being terminated. In addition, at any time it is also possible to suspend or resume the process instance.

The activity instance behavioural model presented in Fig. 6.7 is an extension of the model proposed in [90]. Firstly, we add enabling states introduced earlier and, in addition, support it with starting conditions. When an activity instance is created its enabling state is the same as for the corresponding process instance. This feature is needed if we use the suspension technique based on completion of running activities. Secondly, an activity instance moves to the state "scheduled" only if all its preconditions are satisfied. Similar situation is with postconditions and the state "completed" which is triggered by the completion event.

Re-planning Procedure

Re-planning of a workflow process is a quite complex operation and consists of several steps:

Termination of the Failed Activity Instances

In the first step all the failed activity instances are terminated (i.e. they move to operational state "terminated"). Usually there is only one such activity instance which caused re-planning. However, it is also possible that during replanning some other activities that are still running (a suspending technique—see next section) will also fail. In that case re-planning must be terminated and then started once more with information about all failed activity instances (i.e. that which had failed before the first re-planning as well as those which have failed after the first re-planning started).

Process Instance Suspending

In the next step the process instance and all its activity instances are suspended. This results in changing the enabling state of these entities to the state "disabled". This operation is to assure that the mentioned entities will not change their state until re-planning is completed. Since an atomic activity may be executed as an application, for every instantiation of such activity it is also required to send a request for suspension to the corresponding application. If the application implements the suspend-operation then such request will be handled correctly. Otherwise, it is not possible to suspend properly the application and thus the activity instance. There are two possible techniques to cope with this situation: we may either leave the running application (activity instance) to complete its execution or terminate the running application (activity instance). The former technique allows the running applications to complete. If they complete before finishing the re-planning, they will move to state "completed". Then the workflow management system will evaluate the outgoing transitions and create new activity instances being the successors of the completed activity instances. Since the process instance remains in state "disabled", also the new activity instance will remain in this state and thus they will not be processed until the state changes to "enabled" (when the process instance is resumed). If the running application completes after finishing re-planning, the process will behave in the normal way. This is because resuming operation will change the enabling state of all activity instances to "enabled".

The former technique allows us not to waste the results of activity instances which have not failed but can not be suspended for re-planning. This is especially useful in case when the mentioned activities are still present in the new process definition and thus will have to be executed once again. Also using this technique we do not increase the constraints on the non-functional requirements such as response time or cost. On the contrary, if, during re-planning, such running application fails, it triggers a request for a new re-planning. In that case, we will have to prolong the re-planning operation (which may increase the time constraints on the process instance execution) and to ignore all the re-planning effort achieved so far (the input data for replanning has changed). The latter technique terminates immediately all running activity instances. This technique may avoid re-planning reiteration as it was pointed out for the former technique. However, using this technique it is possible to waste the results that may be retrieved and to re-execute the same application. In addition, some application may not support termination.

Generation of a New Process Definition

After suspending the process instance a new process definition is generated based on the current state of the case. This automated process generation works analogous to the initial generation of a process definition. The main difference is that instead of the initial state the current state is used as input. The current state is derived by starting with the initial state and retracing all effects of all currently executed or terminated activities. In this way, the current state reflects all previously unexpected effects of failing activities. Thus, these failures are automatically taken into account when using the current state to generate the new process definition. As a result, the new process definition describes a way of how to compensate the failed activity.

Process Instance Re-planning

Afterwards the old and newly generated process definitions are merged and, according to that merged definition, the process instance is prepared for resuming and further execution (continuation). In order to merge the old and new process definitions the activities present in both definitions must have the same identifiers (not changed during generation of the new definition). At the activity level re-planning is carried out in the following way:

- For activities present in both old and new process definitions no action is taken.
- For activities present only in the old process definition, in case the operational state was "completed" or "terminated", no action is taken. Otherwise they need to be terminated.
- For activities present only in the new process definition, a new activity instance needs to be created. In addition, for intermediate activities (one or more ingoing and outgoing transitions) all ingoing transitions required for the activities must be instantiated.

Process Instance Resuming

The final step for re-planning is to resume the re-planned process instance and continue it with the new, merged process definition. To resume the process instance at least one of its activity instances has to remain in a not finished state (i.e. new, scheduled or running). This precondition assures that after resuming the process instance will be executed. The resuming event causes that the enabling state of the process instance and all its activity instances is changed to Enabled. In addition, this event also triggers re-running of the activity instances remaining in state running.

The enactment of static service compositions is covered by a huge market of workflow engine products, according standards and competing technological trends. This chapter focussed on the identification and discussion of crucial enactment issues in the context of dynamic service provisioning environments. This included questions of composition monitoring, service profiling, and fault management strategies.

While the technologies and approaches for service composition enactment can be seen as mature, more advanced topics in the context of semantic services are still an issue. The chapter presented some possible strategies in relation to the book's use case scenario. Due to the ongoing research activities in this field, new results can be expected in the future. The next chapter will go down into technology and present current developments regarding infrastructures for service provision.

7

Service Infrastructure

Andreas Polze and Peter Tröger

7.1 Overview and Motivation

The enactment of service compositions demands a direct interaction with existing middleware technology, which provides the execution environment for service implementations. The service infrastructure forms the base for a service oriented distributed application. It combines all relevant functionalities for the development, installation, usage, and monitoring of single atomic services. Even though this aspect gained no explicit attention in the beginning of *service oriented architecture (SOA)* research and industry adoption, all existing SOA applications rely on such middleware functionalities. SOA vendors meanwhile started to introduce new or updated software component models in order to consider the specific demands of service environments on middleware technologies. Also the SOA reference model [123] describes service infrastructures as explicit concept to be considered.

Middleware acts as a conversion or translation layer, not only in an service oriented software architecture, but in all kinds of distributed systems. Custom-programmed middleware solutions have been developed for decades to enable one application to communicate with another one that runs on a different platform or comes from a different vendor. Today, there is a diverse group of products that offer packaged middleware solutions. The ongoing shift to communication technologies based on XML—commonly denoted as Web services—in these middleware platforms is the base for service infrastructures.

Due to the relevance of the basic technologies and protocols in service provisioning infrastructures, the following section explains some of the relevant aspects for today's service infrastructures.

7.2 Types of Middleware

There is a set of commonly accepted classes of middleware, which share some common principles in their functionality. These classes are not specifically related to

SOA environments, even though all of them are utilised in one or the other way also in service infrastructures. In general, a middleware layer allows an application to locate and interact with communication partners transparently across a network. It ensures the two basic goals of middleware stack, namely the interoperability and portability of such distributed applications. The interaction functionalities are de-coupled from the network services, and should scale up in capacity without losing function. Also reliability and availability functionality as part of middleware lowers the implementation efforts for single applications.

Most middleware frameworks provide a component model [186], in order to stan-dardise the packaging layout of software entities. Typical examples are the *Enter-prise Java Bean (EJB)* model, the *Corba Component Model (CCM)* or the .NET assembly format. Web service development makes no exception from the compo-nent oriented development, since it only represents another wire format (SOAP) and interface description language (WSDL) in the according component model. For this reason, Web service implementations can also benefit from the different functional-ities provided by the middleware framework. Sometimes these features are denoted as *middleware services* (like in CORBA), without any direct relation to the service term assumed in this book.

Middleware frameworks can be categorised in several ways, according to the pro-vided feature set or basic architecture. We rely here on the differentiation by Alonso et al. [10]:

Transaction Processing (TP) Monitors

The *Transaction Processing (TP)* monitor was perhaps the first product to be called middleware. Participating as third party beside the requesting client program and the utilised services in the network, a TP monitor ensures that interactions with mul-tiple services from one client are grouped by one transactional context. The client can decide to either commit or abort the transaction at any point in the interaction, which demands a coordinated transaction coordination for all services by a central entity.

A TP monitor can reliably and efficiently manage the resources needed by appli-cations that conform to the TP monitor's rules. CICS (Customer Information Con-trol System) and IMS/TM (a message based transaction manager) are the transaction processing workhorses of the mainframe environment. On UNIX systems, product like BEA's TUXEDO, BEA's TOP END, and IBM's Encina typically use TP moni-tors.

Messaging Middleware

Message Oriented Middleware (MOM) provides a point-to-point communication over a message broker, which enables the decoupling of message sending on producer side and message receiving on the consumer side. MOM is analogous to e-mail in the sense it is asynchronous and requires the recipients of messages to interpret their

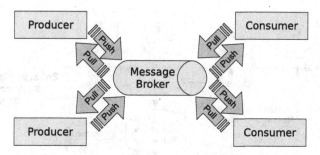

Fig. 7.1. Message oriented middleware

meaning. MOM provides a common interface and reliable transport between applications, based on queueing facilities in the broker and a standardised *Application Programming Interface (API)*. The messaging system may contain business logic that routes messages to the appropriate destinations and reformats the data as well. This includes the publish/subscribe communication pattern, where multiple receivers get the message from one producer (see Fig. 7.1).

The predominant messaging product for managing asynchronous communication between applications is IBM's MQSeries, which has been ported to all major server platforms. In conjunction with the Component Object Model (COM), Microsoft introduced its own messaging system, Microsoft Message Queue Server (MSMQ). There is also a variety of freely available and open source implementations for message brokers. These products are not interoperable in their message exchange, since the communication protocols between producer/broker and consumer/broker are specifically optimised for the according product. At least for consumers and producers based on Java, the industry agreed on the *Java Messaging Service (JMS)* [82] as common access API for products. Newer products meanwhile also adopt the *Web Services Notification (WSN)* specification [141], in order to allow a *SOAP* access to message broker functionality.

Message oriented middleware has gained an increased consideration with the *Enterprise Service Bus (ESB)* concept, initially proposed by Chappell [42]. The architecture concept is mainly proposed as solution for the integration of heterogeneous protocols and data formats in service oriented architectures. A ESB represents the extended version of a classical message broker, which supports not only the routing and queueing of incoming messages, but also the transformation of XML message payload data. All ESB products support a variety of adapters and proxies for legacy system integration. The ESB therefore acts as mediator between service requester and service provider. Product examples are the Sonic ESB, the IBM WebSphere ESB, or the Microsoft BizTalk Server.

Beside the central components for message routing and queueing, the ESB concept also includes the notion of an ESB container. This part of the architecture acts as execution environment for called services and legacy adapters. In most practical cases, these containers are part of an object based middleware product.

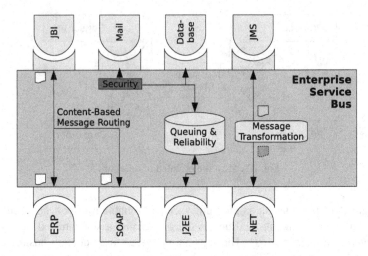

Fig. 7.2. Enterprise service bus

Object based Middleware

Remote Procedure Calls (RPCs) enable the logic of an application to be distributed across the network. Program logic on remote systems can be executed as simply as calling a local routine [179]. Classical examples for purely procedural remoting architectures are the *Distributed Computing Environment (DCE)* and the *Common Object Request Broker Architecture (CORBA)*. Distributed object systems are the most popular kind of middleware approach today. Beside CORBA, systems like *Distributed Component Object Model (DCOM)*, .NET, and *Java Platform Enterprise Edition (Java EE)* provide all facilities for interoperable and distributed object based applications. The still RPC based programming paradigms in such systems typically lead to synchronous interaction between processes (components/objects).

Since object based middleware stacks currently form the sole foundation of service infrastructures, they are discussed in the following section in more detail.

7.3 Middleware Technologies

Among the middleware categories presented in the previous section, distributed objects have the biggest potential to solve a wide range of challenges faced by designers of large software systems.

For our discussion, we separate distributed object architectures into two categories: component architectures and remoting architectures. We define component architectures as architectures that focus primarily on component packaging and cross-language interoperability. In contrast, remoting architectures focus primarily on support for remote method invocation on distributed objects. Component architectures are mainly relevant for service implementations to specify their packaging and deployment format. Remoting architectures can help in service environments by providing the networking programming model for client and service implementations. The following sections discuss the most prominent middleware platforms and component models in use today.

7.3.1 CORBA

CORBA is a language- and platform-neutral middleware technology that is based on a standardised communication protocol, an according interface definition language, and a set of standardised middleware services. CORBA is actively maintained by the *Object Management Group (OMG)* standardisation body. The OMG has been founded in 1989 as a consortium of eight companies (3Com, American Airlines, Canon, Data General, Hewlett-Packard, Philips Telecommunications, Sun Microsystems, Unisys). Today, the OMG exists as an international non-profit organisation of more than 800 software developers, network operators, computer vendors, research institutions, and commercial computer users.

The OMG organises its standardisation work by a central architectural model, the *Object Management Architecture (OMA)* [180]. It describes software architectures for application interoperability, independent of the applications' implementation languages, locations, operating systems, and hardware platforms. In this architecture, CORBA stands for a set of specifications which allow a language- and platform-independent communication of distributed software objects. The *Object Request Broker (ORB)* is the central element of this middleware concept (see Fig. 7.3). Comparable to a software bus, the ORB serves as universal communication means for various objects in heterogeneous distributed systems.

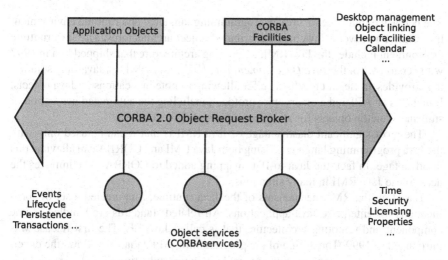

Fig. 7.3. Object management architecture

A CORBA object is independent from a programming language object, meaning that multiple CORBA objects can be implemented by one language object or vice versa. It is represented to the outside world by an interface with a set of methods. The description of this interface is provided in a language-neutral standardised language, the CORBA *Interface Definition Language (IDL)*.

A particular instance of an object is identified by an object reference. The client of a CORBA object acquires its object reference and uses it as a handle to make method calls, as if the object was located in the client's address space. The ORB is responsible for all the mechanisms required to find the object's implementation, prepare it to receive the request, communicate the request to it, and carry the reply (if any) back to the client. The object implementation interacts with the ORB through either an *Object Adapter (OA)* or through the ORB interface. In order to implement communication across machine boundaries, multiple ORB instances residing on different machines in the network interact typically using *Internet Inter-ORB Protocol (IIOP)* [94].

CORBA is frequently compared to Web service technology, claiming that XML based messaging and interface description are just re-invention of existing solutions in CORBA. Existing serious comparisons (like [10, 64, 136]) mostly conclude the same things. Web service stacks and CORBA stacks share well-known approaches for distributed middleware, such as language-neutral interface descriptions, data encoding rules and error handling support. However, the usage of XML in Web service mainly supports a coarse-grained document messaging approach, while CORBA is still intended for fine-grained RPC communication between client and server objects. Both technology stacks therefore have their advantages for different application domains.

7.3.2 Java SE & EE

The pervasive influence of Java as programming language and runtime environment has resulted in several Java based distributed object architectures. The Java runtime environment includes the Java RMI, a remoting architecture that shipped first in 1997 with version 1.1 of the *Java Development Kit (JDK)*. Java RMI is a Java-only solution that provides an elegant mechanism for allowing remote invocations on Java objects. It includes an API and a binary wire protocol, including the automated generation of stub and skeleton objects for a transparent remote object access.

The most significant disadvantage of Java RMI is that it can be used only with the Java programming language. Using both Java RMI and CORBA can alleviate this disadvantage. In fact, the Java-to-IDL mapping added to CORBA 3.0 eliminates the need to use Java RMI in many situations.

Based on the RMI mechanisms of the Java runtime, Sun created a set of specifications for enterprise Java applications. All related standards are bundled as one component and remoting architecture that is called Java EE. The first release was introduced in 1999. The design of the programming API's mainly follows the development of the Java language. One example is the introduction of *Java Annotations* for configuration in the latest version 5 of the Java EE middleware stack.

The included APIs are managed by the *Java Community Process (JCP)*, which produces *Java Specification Request (JSR)* documents for the different features. Different vendors can implement the specifications, which leads to portability for the Java EE applications and interoperability for their runtime environments, the application server. The specifications rely on a container concept, where each Java EE component is executed and managed by an application server, instead of running as own operating system process. The container provides the standardised APIs for the implementation, and handles relevant middleware features such as security, resource management and dynamic loading transparently for the implementation.

Figure 7.4 shows the basic architecture of a Java EE environment, which implements a classical 3-tier architecture. The client tier contains the different application clients, which either use native Java RMI technology or Web service protocols to call object functions. The third typical client is a Web browser, where the application server generates dynamic HTML pages.

All server-side functionality is hosted by an Java EE application server. Sun offers a certification process for Java EE implementations, where a particular application server vendor can prove its compliance to the standards. Typical implementations are IBM WebSphere, JBoss, or BEA WebLogic.

Each application server hosts either web components or business components. The web tier acts as presentation logic layer, and provides the front-end to the client application. All components are implemented based on the Java Servlet technology [80]. In the case of Web browser clients, these components generate HTML output

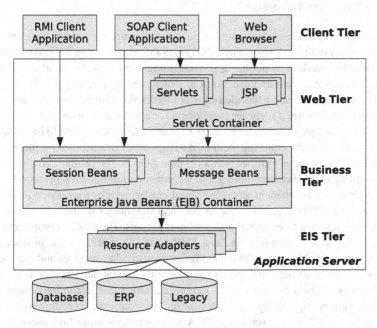

Fig. 7.4. Java EE architecture

based on an incoming HTTP request. In case of Web service clients, the components un-marshal the SOAP request data, and either forward it to the business logic or answer it by them self. Even though the latter approach does not confirm to the architectural idea of functional separation, it becomes more and more the pre-dominant approach in real infrastructures.

The business tier hosts the functional logic of the implementation, and is either called by web tier components or native RMI applications directly. These business components confirm to a dedicated software component model, the EJB architecture [56]. It defines the packaging format and demanded interfaces for the component, but also the set of available container functions for the implementation. An EJB typically provide an RMI interface, but can also offer a SOAP interface for Web service clients [81].

Application servers are typically executed on one machine, even though most products support a replicated operation for fault tolerance and scalable behaviour. Other features supported by application servers are transactional requests, legacy integration of existing infrastructure, authentication and authorisation, or messaging-style interaction [166]. Java EE application servers therefore form the base of service infrastructures in most cases. Many implementations of extended Web service specifications (see also Sect. 7.5) simply rely on existing implementations from application server products. Many open source projects complement the Java EE architecture with own container architectures [202] or useful libraries for XML handling or persistence management.

Service Component Architecture

In reaction on the wide-spread usage of Java middleware for service environments, the *Service Component Architecture (SCA)* was introduced as an initiative from different industry vendors. It defines a programming model for Java and C++, which supports the development and execution of distributed service oriented applications [22]. The concept relies on the idea of a configurable combination of base implementations, which form a software component for a particular business functionality. SCA extends the idea of *Business Process Execution Language (BPEL)* based service compositions, since the coupling technology is specified in a declarative manner, and can therefore be changed to other protocols than SOAP. The primary goal of SCA is the decoupling of service assembling and technical communication protocols.

SCA defines a component as collection of configurations for service implementation instances. This is a difference to classical definitions of the component term [186] with a relation to encapsulated software entities. Each SCA component consists of its implementation (e.g. in Java, PHP, COBOL or BPEL), the provided services (e.g. over SOAP or Java RMI), the references to other services and the specific attribute values. Multiple components can configure one implementation in different ways. This is realised by marking different data structures in the implementation, which are then configured by the SCA runtime environment, according to the component definition. The Java version of SCA realises this by using Java annotations as the programming language mechanism.

Multiple components can form a composite, by linking their provided services and references to each other. This approach is similar to the CCM and allows the late connection of components to achieve more flexible applications.

SCA considers the need for stateful service interactions with the concept of a conversational interface, which describes a set of operations to be used together. Again, the relationship between methods is expressed by attribution. The configured communication protocol then has the responsibility to relate state data and session identifiers to the according conversational interface. The session starts with the first call of a marked method, and ends after a given time or explicitly by calling a finalisation method.

SCA demands new service container implementations, which support the component configuration approach. It acts therefore as separate component model in addition to existing environments such as Java EE or CORBA. Vendors and SOA designers need to carefully weigh up the advantages and disadvantages of the different component frameworks.

Input and output data in SCA should be modelled after the *Service Data Objects (SDO)* concept [35]. An SDO contains a disconnected data graph, which is given to the client as tree structure. The client modifies the structure and the content of the data tree, and returns the result of the modification to the data source. Beside the data graph, SDO defines also a data object as node in the tree, and data access services as access API for the graph traversal and modification.

A data object contains a set of named properties, which either represent a value or a reference to another data object. Stubs for data objects are generated from static schema definitions, such as XML schema [65], SQL result structures, WSDL definitions for SOAP messages or UML models. The access API is based on the standardised XPath protocol [45], which allows the traversal and change of XML data structures. Graph changes are saved, and can be retrieved as change history afterwards.

7.3.3 DCOM

In the early 1990s, Microsoft has made a strong commitment to *Object Linking and Embedding (OLE)* as there solution for heterogeneous distributed environments. Although OLE allowed for interoperability among applications, component packaging and cross-language interoperability were insufficiently addressed by OLE. Microsoft addressed these issues with the subsequent *Component Object Model (COM)*, which became the foundation for a wide range of technologies, among them visual COM controls named ActiveX. COM is the dominant component architecture in use today. This is not too surprising since COM is the component architecture for today's most dominant desktop operating system—Microsoft Windows. Recently, Microsoft has coined the acronym COM+ to identify the bundling of the COM infrastructure with a number of component services. This is a similar development to the CORBA middleware, were packaging format and interoperability specifications are complemented with default services available for applications.

The DCOM is the distributed extension to COM that builds an object remote procedure call layer on top of DCE *Remote Procedure Call (RPC)* to support remote objects. Since the specification is at the binary level, it allows integration of binary components possibly written in different programming languages such as C++, Java and Visual Basic.

COM is a very mature component architecture that has many strengths. Thousands of third party ActiveX controls (in-process COM components) are available in the market today. Microsoft and other vendors have built many tools that accelerate development of COM based applications. Microsoft is also providing advanced services such as *Microsoft Transaction Server (MTS)* and *Microsoft Message Queueing Server (MSMQ)* to support development of enterprise multi-tier systems. However, due to the strict focus of Microsoft on the .NET platform for Web service technologies, DCOM has no relevant role in service oriented environments. In many real-world scenarios, the legacy integration of DCOM services in a SOA environment therefore becomes a major issue. For this reason, Microsoft has carried on many of COM's concepts into the new .NET framework, which has the potential to lift most of COM's limitations.

7.3.4 .NET

In an evolutionary sense, Microsoft's .NET [160] is the newest and most advanced component architecture available in the market today. As Java, .NET is based on a machine-neutral intermediate language format and just-in-time compilers .NET takes a fundamentally new and sound approach to cross-language interoperability as it starts with a common object model and type system applicable to all .NET languages (among them C#, C++, Visual Basic, Jscript, Eiffel#, Cobol, and Scheme). .NET extends COM as it makes meta-data—runtime type information, which was optional for COM components—mandatory for each .NET component (so-called assemblies).

.NET initially marked a departure from earlier component systems by requiring each component (assembly in .NET jargon) to carry meta-data. Meta-data is used by the system for integration with legacy technologies, such as COM, however, since component meta-data is extensible from the programming language level through the attribute construct, .NET allows the programmer to explicitly express component properties and requirements, such as security, resource usage, timeliness, or fault-tolerance assumptions.

The *Common Language Runtime (CLR)* forms the most important component of the framework. Comparable to the *Java Virtual Machine (JVM)*, the CLR activates objects, performs security checks on them, lays them out in memory, executes them, and garbage-collects them. Conceptually, the CLR and JVM are similar in that they are both runtime infrastructures that abstract the underlying platform differences. Microsoft has submitted the *Common Language Interop (CLI)*, which is a functional subset of the CLR, to *ECMA* for standardisation, so a third-party vendor could theoretically implement a CLR for additional operating system platforms.

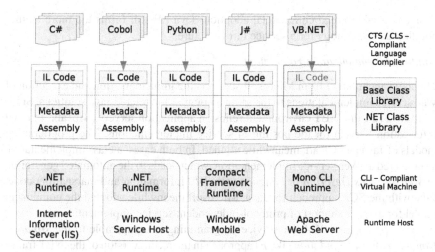

Fig. 7.5. .NET architecture

Figure 7.5 shows the relations among the different basic .NET concepts. Different language compilers generate *Intermediate Language (IL)* code, which relies on the standardised *Common Type System (CTS)* definition and the *Common Language Specification (CLS)*. Implementations can utilise either the standardised *Base Class Library (BCL)*, or its extended version provided with the Microsoft .NET framework. The relevant class library functions for service oriented environments (like XML processing or Web service development) are mostly not standardised in the BCL, and can therefore only be used with Microsoft's implementation of the .NET standards.

The application IL code and the meta-data information (like version, security settings, author information) form the assembly, a deployable binary software component similar to a Java JAR file. An assembly can be executed in different virtual runtime environments, as long as they fulfil the demands of the CLI specification, which also includes the CLS/CTS compliance. In difference to Java, Microsoft uses the same assembly format for software components on standard PCs and mobile devices. The Microsoft .NET runtime environment for PC's is realised as software library, which is used by a runtime host for the execution of .NET assemblies. By this strategy, different runtime hosts can realise different security and resource management strategies with the same runtime implementation.

Since all basic technologies are standardised at ECMA, it is meanwhile possible to run .NET assemblies also on non-Microsoft platforms. The most popular example is the Mono project, which provides a dedicated implementation of BCL and CLI-compliant runtime. This implementation can be embedded into the popular Apache Web server, which enables Unix platforms to act as runtime environment for .NET Web services or other implementations. However, most infrastructure in this area is still under development and should be carefully evaluated before usage. Due to its age and widespread commercial adoption, Java EE still forms the more mature middleware technology for a service infrastructure.

Windows Communication Foundation

The .NET technology from Microsoft supports the implementation and execution of Web service implementations to the same amount as the related Java solutions. Similar to Java EE, the .NET environment relies on application servers (BizTalk, Internet Information Server) for the hosting of service implementations. The programming models of Java and C# are meanwhile aligned. In both cases, a class implementation is annotated as Web service implementation, which leads to the automated generation of *Web Services Description Language (WSDL)* information and marshalling code. Like with the SCA approach for Java, Microsoft meanwhile adopted the component model for a better support of protocol-independent service implementations.

The approach of SCA for service programming is comparable to the *Windows Communication Foundation (WCF)* approach in the recent version of the .NET framework. Also here, functional service implementations are separated from the communication capabilities of the middleware. The components define there connection points by the attribution capability of the .NET programming languages, similar to the Java annotation mechanism used by SCA. WCF defines a service as combination of a service class, hosting environment and one or multiple endpoints. Each endpoint is defined as combination of *(A)ddress, (B)inding,* and *(C)ontract,* and is usually described by an WSDL file, even if the classical SOAP over HTTP transport mechanism is not used. WCF forbids any kind of direct interaction, even for in-process communication. Communication partners always access a local proxy for the remote peer, which allows the transparent addition of security, life cycle or reliability features without changing the implementation.

The address is needed in order to reach the service functionality represented by the end point. It maps to the `<service>` section of a WSDL definition, and usually contain a machine address and port number in the network.

The binding specifies all details of the message encoding of the wire, namely the message format, representation of data structures, and the utilises transport protocol (like HTTP). It maps to the `<binding>` and `<portType>` definitions in a WSDL file. WCF supports a rich set of protocols, like WS-I—compliant SOAP over HTTP, SOAP over TCP, SOAP over named pipes, or SOAP over message queues.

The contract specification describes the interaction patterns and behavioural aspects of the service. This is only related to functional aspects of the peer interaction, and should not be mixed up with the semantic description of service functionality. The according message types and exchange patterns are part of the WSDL sections `<portType>`, `<message>` and `<types>`. Examples are the service contract (supported operations), data contract (types passed to and from the service), or the fault contract (errors possibly raised). The service class must be implemented as .NET assembly, and can therefore be executed by the different runtime hosts shown in Fig. 7.5.

Every service instance in WCF is bounded to a context in the .NET runtime, which represents to session with the client. Similar to SCA, the server performs an implicit session management, taking care of lifetime issues and garbage collection efforts. The according semantics are not directly visible to clients.

Since .NET moves from its traditional remoting programming model to the WCF approach, this technology should be considered for the realisation of new Microsoft-compliant service implementations.

7.3.5 Summary

Some of the challenges solved by middleware frameworks include component packaging, cross-language interoperability, inter-process communication, and inter-machine communication. The distributed processing and distributed object architectures that have been introduced over the last decade exhibit different strengths and weaknesses based on their ability to meet these challenges.

Existing middleware platforms meanwhile always implement a large set of Web service protocols. Initially, these protocols just formed an extension of the already existing remoting paradigms. Well-known examples are the Web service programming with .NET Remoting [126] or the JAX-RPC specifications in Java [185]. This led to the general understanding of Web services as an RPC implementation, which does not fit to the intended use cases of the original protocols.

The multitude of different service programming models in the last years clearly shows that Web services should be discussed from there basic protocol functionalities, rather than taking a particular programming model as intended way of using these protocols. The following section therefore focusses on the Web service standards itself. Based on this knowledge, the interested reader should refer to the particular middleware framework documentation, in order to understand the mapping of original SOAP and WSDL concepts to a particular remoting architecture.

7.4 Web Service Technologies

Since the middle of the 1990s, XML was established more and more as the exchange format for structured data of any kind. With the parallel success of Internet and World Wide Web, developers and industry started to utilise XML not only for data exchange, but also for the creation of communication protocols. The two most prominent examples are SOAP and XML-RPC.

Meanwhile, industry has chosen XML communication protocols as the primary interoperability mechanisms for heterogeneous systems. Even though most authors stress the independence of SOA concepts from specific protocols and data formats, XML is the obvious realisation strategy today [139, 112].

Most people refer to XML protocols as Web services, even though the term is used in different and sometimes conflicting interpretations. A precise and technology oriented definition is offered by the *World Wide Web Consortium (W3C)* [30]:

> A Web service is a software system designed to support interoperable machine-to-machine interaction over a network. It has an interface described in a

machine-processable format (specifically WSDL). Other systems interact with the Web service in a manner prescribed by its description using SOAP messages, typically conveyed using HTTP with an XML serialisation in conjunction with other Web-related standards.

A SOA that is implemented on-top-of Web service technologies is named by some authors as *service oriented computing (SOC)* (see also Sect. 2.1.1). Middleware and service infrastructures are part of the basic services in such an architecture, and provide the atomic functionalities for a composed service. The management layer fulfils the relevant tasks for the surveillance of the infrastructure.

The technical realisation of the basic services demands interoperability to different providers. The common idea of using XML middleware technology is the standardised access to service functionality, regardless of the underlying implementation strategy. For this reason, all relevant protocols and description formats are managed by standardisation bodies such as the W3C, *Organization for the Advancement of Structured Information Standards (OASIS)*, and *Open Grid Forum (OGF)*. Similar to the traditional middleware presented in the last section, also Web service stacks achieve interoperability by a standardised interface description format—WSDL— and a standardised communication protocol—SOAP.

7.4.1 WSDL

The description of Web service interfaces is performed in WSDL [44]. A service is represented as a number of ports, where each of them groups a set of operations and can be therefore understood similar to a classical interface. Each operation is represented by messages. Each of the messages is structurally described by XML schema, a structure definition language for XML documents. A WSDL description can bind each port to a particular transfer protocol. Typical Web services are bounded to the SOAP protocol, but there is no problem to use WSDL with a completely different messaging protocol. Latest developments for the WSDL 2.0 specification try to consider the description of *Representational State Transfer (REST)* [68] interfaces with the same interface description language as for SOAP interfaces.

Listing 7.1 shows an example for a simple *HelloWorld* service, which requires no input and returns a string message. A useful approach for the analysis of such a WSDL description is to read it from the bottom to the top.

The `<service>` section describes the information needed to contact the service in the network. The WSDL file therefore not only describes the layout of the interface, but can also provide the technical information for sending a message. This is a difference to classical interface description languages such as in CORBA, where (static) interface definitions and (dynamic) runtime server information are separated.

The `<service>` section refers to a specific `<binding>`, which describes the mapping of the message structures to a particular transport protocol like SOAP. Especially the `style` and the `use` attribute declare the particular SOAP encoding used for the message transfer. Each binding relates to an `<operation>` definition from the `<portType>` section.

Listing 7.1. Example for a WSDL description

```xml
<?xml version="1.0"?>
<definitions name="HelloWorld"
  targetNamespace="http://troeger.eu/helloworld"
  xmlns:xsd="http://www.w3.org/2001/XMLSchema"
  xmlns:soap="http://schemas.xmlsoap.org/wsdl/soap/"
  xmlns="http://schemas.xmlsoap.org/wsdl/">
    <message name="HelloWorldInput"/>
    <message name="HelloWorldOutput">
      <part name="message" type="xsd:string"/>
    </message>
    <portType name="HelloWorldPortType">
      <operation name="helloWorld">
        <input message="HelloWorldInput"/>
        <output message="HelloWorldOutput"/>
      </operation>
    </portType>
    <binding name="HelloWorldSoapBinding" type="HelloWorldPortType">
      <soap:binding style="document" transport="..."/>
        <operation name="helloWorld">
          <soap:operation soapAction="http://troeger.eu/HelloWorld"/>
          <input><soap:body use="literal"/></input>
          <output><soap:body use="literal"/></output>
        </operation>
      </soap:binding>
    </binding>
    <service name="HelloWorldService">
      <port name="HelloWorldPort" binding="HelloWorldSoapBinding">
        <soap:address location="http://troeger.eu/helloworld"/>
      </port>
    </service>
</definitions>
```

Each `<portType>` summarises a set of operations and can therefore be compared to classical interface concepts from programming languages or interface definition languages. Each operation in the `portType` section consists of zero to one `<input message>` elements and zero to one `output message` elements. The messaging concept of WSDL supports different kinds of combinations, in order to express different styles of dependency between caller and callee. The server-side can either be specified to receive messages without responding (one-way), to send a response message for each incoming message (request-response), to trigger some message transfer by itself and wait for an answer (solicit-response), or to send a message to the client without expecting an answer (notification). Due to the support of different communication patterns, WSDL is not only feasible for classical request-response style service interfaces, but also for the description of Web services with a message based communication style. This is especially important for SOA frameworks using an ESB, where a central message broker routes and filters incoming messages to different consumers.

Each <message> definition in the WSDL file contains of different parts, which can either be based on simple types provided by XML schema, or on complex types defined in a separate types section. For the example in Listing 7.1, it can be seen that the service expects a request-reply communication style, even though the request message has no defined parts. A WSDL compiler creating client stub implementation would map this to an operation with no input parameters and one result parameter. However, these kinds of mappings are not centrally defined by language binding documents as given with CORBA. For this reason, the usage of WSDL for service interfaces can only help for interoperability, but not for portability of applications.

7.4.2 SOAP

The messaging protocol for a Web service is SOAP, a specification which is maintained by the W3C standardisation body. The standard defines a XML message format, a processing model, a number of encoding rules for application-specific data, the syntax of error information, and a number of conventions for implementing remote procedure calls [131].

A SOAP message is emitted by a *sender*, targeted at a ultimate receiver, and traverses multiple intermediaries on its way. In contrast to many informal descriptions of Web service technologies, SOAP must be understood as a pure messaging protocol without a close relation to the RPC programming paradigm. SOAP itself is also not bound to a particular underlying transport protocol, even though nearly all Web services implementations relied on the *HyperText Transfer Protocol (HTTP)* as communication facility in the past. Meanwhile, modern Web service protocol stacks support also other transport mechanisms, such as TCP or message queueing systems. The latter case is frequently referred to as 'SOAP over JMS', which expresses the usage of JMS programming interface in the Web service stack. Since JMS is not a wire protocol but an *API*, these Web service implementations still demand a classical message oriented middleware for the transportation of the message content.

As shown in Listing 7.2, the first part of a SOAP message is the optional message header, which allows the inclusion of meta-data in each message. This extensibility mechanism is the basis for all advanced Web service standards, like WS-Security or routing extension for SOAP messages. The mechanism relies on the basic idea of intermediaries, where each SOAP message might pass multiple machines on its way to the ultimate receiver. Each intermediary can process SOAP header elements, like user credentials, before it forwards the packet to the next node. This feature provides the prerequisite for many advanced service infrastructure technologies like the ESB concept. Intermediaries can be enforced to not ignore a particular header entry before they forward the message. This forms the base for policy-driven Web service mechanisms. Latest industry products provide complex intermediary implementations, which can control the SOAP message flow based on such policies and the understanding of header entries related to a centrally specified *Service Level Agreement (SLA)*.

Listing 7.2. Example for a SOAP message

```
<?xml version='1.0' ?>
<env:Envelope xmlns:env="http://www.w3.org/2003/05/soap-envelope"
              xmlns:wsse="..." xmlns:wsu="...">
  <env:Header>
    <wsse:Security>
      <wsse:UsernameToken>
        <wsse:Username>Peter</wsse:Username>
        <wsse:Password Type="wsse:PasswordDigest">
          489utdoghn=xf943=--höo8tgkl</wsse:Password>
        <wsse:Nonce>764gfkjhg8gJHGL=jb</wsse:Nonce>
        <wsu:Created>2008-03-01T06:44:03Z</wsu:Created>
      </wsse:UsernameToken>
    </wsse:Security>
  </env:Header>
  <env:Body>
    <p:itinerary xmlns:p="http://troeger.eu/reservation">
      <p:departure>
        <p:departing>Potsdam</p:departing>
        <p:arriving>Hawaii</p:arriving>
        <p:departureDate>2008-05-01</p:departureDate>
        <p:seatPreference>firstClass</p:seatPreference>
      </p:departure>
    </p:itinerary>
  </env:Body>
</env:Envelope>
```

The main part of the SOAP message is the *SOAP body*, which contains the XML payload to be transferred. For the marshalling of payload data, the SOAP specification distinguishes between messages for remote procedure calls (rpc-style) and messages for the transfer of structured documents (document-style). Both messaging styles can use different encodings of the payload data. With SOAP encoding, the structured payload data (like arrays or object graphs) is encoded according to rules from the SOAP specification. With literal encoding, the transmitted data follows a XML schema definition, and therefore acts a self-contained XML document. The chosen vocabulary for the different encoding approaches turned out to be confusing in the past—after all, the encoding does not mandate a particular kind of usage.

One major problem with Web services in the past was the missing support for all the encoding variations in the different toolkits. For some time, Java environments only supported the RPC/encoded style of Web services, while other toolkits has chosen to use the document/literal encoding with some slight extension (called document/wrapped encoding). The WS-I interoperability standardisation body was founded in 2003 by leading industry vendors, in order to solve this problem by restricting the original specifications. For this reason, the meanwhile established common way of encoding SOAP message payload is the document/wrapped style. This holds not only for XML document transmission, but also for remote procedure calls based on SOAP.

Binary data was originally intended to be transferred in a larger XML representation. Meanwhile, several specifications like *Message Transmission Optimization Mechanism (MTOM)* and *XML-binary Optimized Packaging (XOP)* support the transmission of the binary raw data together with the SOAP message. This decreases the amount of transferred data, which is specially important in document oriented SOA environments.

7.4.3 UDDI

The third basic building block for Web service architectures is the *Repository for Universal Description, Discovery and Integration (UDDI)* specification. It describes the necessary interfaces and data models of a directory for WSDL descriptions. Even though UDDI was initially designed to work as general business registry, it works nowadays mainly as background technology in service registries from different vendors. These products basically rely on the UDDI data model, while the access API's are complemented by less complex interfaces such as *Java API for XML Registries (JAXR)*.

The initial idea of UDDI—internet-wide central service registries—turned out to be a miss. The public open UDDI registries, created at the time of ongoing standardisation by SAP, Microsoft, and IBM, were closed in 2005. While the official announcement mainly argued with a finished test phase, it must be noted that the registries were simply without useful content for the public audience.

Service registries meanwhile have there major application in company-internal SOA installations, were company policies ensure consistent and valuable set of services in the registry (see also Sect. 8.2.1). The according products are constantly extended with additional governance and monitoring capabilities, in order to not only register, but also analyse and supervise the service landscape in a SOA installation.

7.5 WS-*

With the three basic specifications in hand, industry vendors and standardisation bodies immediately started to create advanced technologies and *API* definitions. The extensibility mechanism of SOAP allow the introduction of new message header elements, in order to implement extended features such as security, reliable messaging, state access or transactional messaging. The extended headers and their possible influence on the SOAP body are defined by documents from standardisation bodies, but sometimes are also published as pure industry proposals. The hype phase of Web service technology led to a huge number of such specifications, typically described as "WS-*" or "WS-hell". The main problem was (and still is) the existence of conflicting and under-specified SOAP and WSDL extensions from different interest groups. In many cases, multiple specifications solve the same type of problem in different ways. Figure 7.6 shows a possible classification of the WS-* specification landscape.

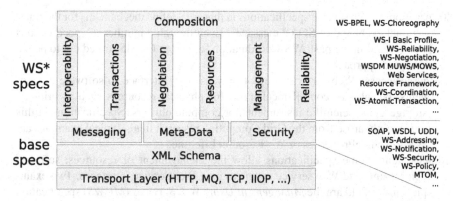

Fig. 7.6. Classification of Web service specifications

The figure categorises the different specifications based on their technical dependencies, instead of referring to the intended usage stated in the according document. A dependency between two specifications is given when one specification refers to elements from the other specification. A typical example is the usage of WS-Addressing functionalities in higher-layer specifications such as WS-Security. The typical classes are:

Messaging: The basic messaging protocol in Web service environments is SOAP, which acts obviously as technical base for all other specifications. Some extensions of SOAP, like the MTOM, the WS-Addressing or the WS-Notification specification optimise SOAP for new use cases.

Meta-Data: The meta-data of Web services is described in WSDL. All extensions aiming on an improved meta-data description realise this by an extension of the WSDL description format. Typical examples are WS-Policy or WS-Addressing. The UDDI specification also falls into this category, since it enables the management and standardised search for Web service meta-data.

Security: Comparatively many specifications refer in their technical description to elements from the WS-Security standards. In most cases, the integration is an optional mechanism to ensure end-to-end security between sender and ultimate receiver. WS-Security stands for the combination of several basic specifications, like the *X.509 Token Profile* or the SOAP With Attachments (SWA) Profile.

Interoperability: Different implementations of SOAP, WSDL, and UDDI had interoperability problems in the initial years of Web service technology. This was (and still is) partly reasoned by the degrees of freedom in XML schema, but also by the incomplete, erroneous and misleading standardisation documents. Because of these interoperability issues, a consortium of industry vendors works since 2002 in the *Web Service Interoperability Organization (WS-I)* for correcting, restricting or improving existing Web service specifications. The resulting *profile* definitions for existing standards are meanwhile considered by all major Web service products.

Transactions: Web service specifications in this area define mechanisms for the transactional exchange of SOAP messages. Even though a number of specifications
was created in the past, WS-Coordination [67] from OASIS turned out to be the
accepted approach.

Resource access: Web services are not only used as interface to software components, but also as control mechanism for physical resources such as printers,
storage units, scientific instruments, or compute clusters. Specifications in this
area mainly arose from the Grid Computing research field. Typical examples are
WS-ResourceProperties or Ws-ResourceLifetime.

Management: Some specifications allow the management of resources, software
components and Web service instances over Web service interfaces. Two examples in this field are the *Management Using Web Services (MUWS)* specification
and the *Management Of Web Services (MOWS)* specification.

Reliability: In order to allow a reliable transfer of messages, SOAP extensions from
this class support the utilisation of existing reliability middleware (such as
TIBCO or IBM MQSeries) over Web service interfaces. Typical features considered by these specifications are transmission acknowledgements and repeated
transfers. One of the currently established specifications is WS-Reliability [95].

Technical details of all specification classes are provided by different publications [64, 10], even though the original standards document is always the best source
of information. A long-time study of the authors discussed in the next section gives
an initial impression of the current adoption rate for the different specifications.

7.5.1 Empirical Analysis

In the context of the *Adaptive Services Grid (ASG)* project (see Sect. 9.1) the authors
analysed publicly available Web service descriptions for their technical properties.
The goal of this study was a better understanding of the frequently cited "service
landscape", in order to identify relevant Web service specifications and interoperability problems. Even though most SOA architectures and services are intended for
public access from the Internet, the study can still show relevant developments.

For the inspection of public Web service descriptions, different sources for WSDL
data where used. The search engine *Google* was queried for results with the file type
"wsdl". This query was repeated several times, until no more new results were available. The same kind of crawling was performed with the *Yahoo* search engine. The
second kind of information source were the public Web service listings *xmethods.net*
and *strikeiron.com*. All sites with an available WSDL description were additionally
crawled for more descriptions. The data retrieval was repeated on a weekly base from
June 2007 to January 2008.

The constantly repeated crawling procedure led to 5523 unique WSDL files from
public sources in 6 months of evaluation time. Duplicate content and invalid XML
was ignored. Even though many of the identified service descriptions do not represent
a really callable endpoint, they give a first understanding of the technology adoption
in the field:

- The unification of the different SOAP encoding in use to the document/literal encoding (as intended by WS-I) is not completed so far. 33% of the WSDL files specified the RPC/encoded SOAP style for their service, which is primarily used by Java Web service implementations with the *JAX-RPC* toolkit. 54% of the WSDL files specified the WS-I-conformant document/literal encoding. The remaining ones either specified an illegal or no encoding.
- 92% of the WSDL definitions contained no additional information about the endpoint of the Web service (<[ns:]address location=>). Under the assumption of real service descriptions, this shows the demand for additional usage information with such a service. This might not lead to a problem with manually implemented Web service clients, but it complicated the enabling process as described in Sect. 4.2. The detailed analysis further showed that in most such cases the service demands the usage of specific client libraries, transport protocols, or non-standardised SOAP header extensions. In many cases, the fetched WSDL was also only intended as example code fragment.
- 55% of the WSDL definitions contain XML elements from the extended Web service specifications described in the last section. This was identified by testing the name space declarations of XML elements. The most prominent specifications are the different versions of WS-Addressing (17%), WS-Security (16%), the WSRF specifications (15%), WS-Policy (11%), WS-Notification (9%), WS-BPEL (7%), WS-MetadataExchange (5%), and WS-Trust (3%).

The statistic confirms the identified demand for manual integration or adapter implementations on the level of the service infrastructure. Even though automated service composition and discovery remains the ultimate goal of semantic service provisioning architectures, the practice still requires a lot of manual "plumbing" tasks. The adoption rate of WS-* specifications slowly increases, even though real-world usage is only identifiable for a few of the available specifications. Service infrastructures need to consider this investigation, mostly by shielding the higher layers (like service composition and profiling) from the ever-changing technical Web service standards. The service infrastructure as autonomous part must therefore always be considered in a service oriented environment.

7.6 Future Trends

Distributed systems—such as service oriented applications and their infrastructures—are inherently very dynamic, which can make them difficult to program. Resource management is a prerequisite for predictable system behaviour, but is often not enough for most distributed applications. The abstractions offered by various middleware frameworks—with or without Web service protocols—can be used to provide resource management in a distributed system at a high level.

Starting in late 1990s, distributed systems research has begun to focus on providing comprehensive Quality-of-Service (QoS), an organising concept referring to the behavioural properties of an object or system, to help manage the dynamic nature of distributed systems. The goal of the research is to capture the application's high-level QoS requirements and then translate them down to low-level resource managers. QoS can help runtime adaptation. But it also helps the applications evolve over their lifetime to handle new requirements or to operate in new environments, issues more in the domain of software engineering but also of crucial importance to users and maintainers of distributed systems.

Recent middleware frameworks, like the CORBA 3.0 Component Model (CCM), or the Microsoft .NET framework, allow the expression of non-functional component properties, such as resource requirements, timing and security constraints, or fault-tolerance assumptions on the component level using language constructs or component meta-data. The according fulfilment mechanism from operating system and virtual runtime environment can help to realise *Quality of Service (QoS)* demands on service execution from higher layers in a service provisioning stack. As one example, the ASG project investigated the dynamic usage of Grid Computing resources for reliable service execution at the service infrastructure level [193, 194]. Future efforts in both research and industry products will further concentrate on this interconnection of high-level SOA approaches and existing middleware technologies.

8

Service Engineering Methodology

Joachim Bayer, Michael Eisenbarth, Theresa Lehner, and Kai Petersen

8.1 Motivation

Today, enterprises have to keep pace with increasing business changes in every sphere—customer preferences, competition, technology, economic conditions, sourcing and development strategy, distribution and service models, regulatory requirements, pricing models, and market scope. According to statements of most CEOs, their companies are neither responsive enough to these changing business conditions nor agile enough to pursue new market opportunities [25]. Further, in the IDC study from January 2004, 89% of respondent business executives rated IT as a critical or important factor in the overall success of their business.

The service oriented paradigm provides enterprises' IT solutions to be more flexible and agile. IT solutions based on a service oriented architecture consists of a framework for integrating business process and supporting IT infrastructure as secure, standardized components, called services, that can be reused and combined to address changing business priorities [25].

Thus, a service platform is the solution for today's enterprises and their increasing business changes. In order to establish the solution in an enterprise the specific engineering processes have to be integrated. And applications, services and domain ontology (see Fig. 8.1) have to be engineered. Services provide a specific kind of functionality which are described syntactically as well as semantically. The specification comprises the attributes and their values according to concepts from the domain ontology.

8.2 Service Engineering Process

As each engineering process is product-related our service engineering process depends on the applications that will be developed. Service providers engineer services

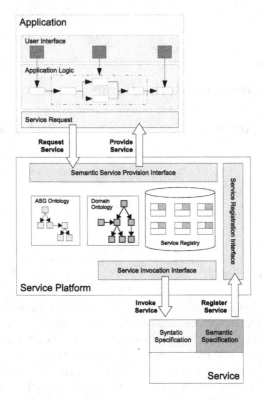

Fig. 8.1. Products used for service provisioning

that fulfil the requirements of a variety of service consumers in order to realize service oriented applications. Service consumers often share common requirements, but at the same time require consumer specific solutions. In order to satisfy the needs of a large customer base, the service provider requires an engineering methodology that allows for developing consumer specific service applications of high quality within a short time to market. By drawing on methods and techniques from product line engineering which is a successful paradigm for achieving this goal, the service provider can be supported in providing services that can be tailored and reused between different applications.

The benefit of service reuse is illustrated in the Fig. 8.2. When not reusing services in order to support several number of applications that share commonalities (e.g., all applications need to support credit card payment) and variable parts (e.g., some applications also would like to support debit card payment), the cumulative number of services is higher. Consequently, a higher number of services needs to be maintained and monitored which leads to additional effort. From the development perspective, exploiting variability and commonality for leads to shorter times to market and higher quality [156, 46].

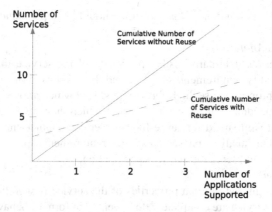

Fig. 8.2. Benefits of service reuse

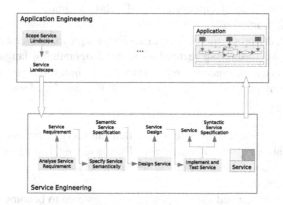

Fig. 8.3. The application and service engineering process

The engineering process for service oriented applications is divided in application engineering and service engineering as shown in Fig. 8.3. Application engineering consists of the phases service landscaping and service scoping.

- *Service Landscaping*
  During application engineering, the needs of the service consumers interacting directly with the application are identified and documented as high level requirements. Based on these requirements, a set of services is identified which fulfils these requirements, referred to as the service landscape.
- *Service Scoping*
  Scoping is a method that helps to focus investments on reuse where they pay off in the best possible way [172]. Applying scoping to services, scoping helps to make the following decisions at different stages of the engineering process:
  1. Which applications should be supported by the service provider?
  2. Which technical domains are required to support the selected applications and what are the boundaries of the domain?

  3. Which services and their compositions should be implemented in a reusable way?

- *Requirements Analysis*
  In this phase, the externally visible properties of the service in form of functional and quality requirements are specified. For capturing the requirements of services, we propose to use the KobrA method [14] which allows to specify components independently of the environment in which they are used, which makes this approach well suited for reuse-focused service engineering. The output of the requirements analysis phase is a service requirements specification as UML class diagrams and semantic service specification.

- *Service Design*
  In service design, the internal properties of the service is specified. That is, the internals of a service are completely documented in form of behaviour expressed as UML activity diagrams. Furthermore, services constituting one service on the requirements level are documented as UML class diagrams.

- *Service Implementation*
  In this phase, the properties defined in service design are implemented and compiled using the underlying technologies and programming language. Furthermore, the service interface in *Web Services Description Language (WSDL)*, as well as the semantic service description using *Web Services Modeling Language (WSML)* is generated.

- *Service Testing*
  The goal of service testing is to assure that the service implementation fulfils the functional and quality requirements. During testing, test cases are generated based on external and internal properties of the service.

- *Service Registration*
  When the service passed the test phase, it is registered to become accessible for invocation in the service application

Following subsections deal with the application engineering activities that scopes the service landscape and all service engineering activities. The methods as well as the artefacts used in the activities are described in more details.

8.2.1 Service Landscaping

Requirements engineering is a key area in successful software engineering and software development. Requirements engineering deals with system requirements, which are specifications of the services a system should provide, the constraints on the system and additional background information, which is required to develop the system. Requirements engineering is the systematic process concerned with the elicitation, understanding, analysis and documentation of the system requirements. Requirements engineering itself is called an "engineering" process as the process itself is used in practical and systematic way where trade-offs have to be made to find the best solution [111].

Identification of the Service Landscape

Considered from a requirements engineering point of view, the major benefit for providers is the identification of valuable applications and the required services. Whatever application would be valuable to develop depends on the application domain an end service consumer wants to have supported and what kind of business process are used in that domain. Business process analysis is therefore a major activity in an application engineering oriented requirements engineering approach. After the decision for developing a specific application has been made, it is up to the requirements engineering approach to identify the required services out of the service landscape. Within an Application Engineering process [190], three activities are related to requirements engineering. These activities are identification of sources for requirements, elicitation of requirements and analysis of requirements.

In the first activity, identification of sources for requirements, we propose to structure the context in which the service oriented application will be employed. Structuring the context helps to assure that important sources of requirements are not overlooked in order to arrive at a complete service landscape. The context can be subdivided in four facets that should be considered when looking for requirements sources. These are the *object facet*, *IT and system facet*, *usage facet* [138] and *development facet* [97, 155]. Within these facets, sources for requirements are the relevant stakeholders as well as specific types of documentation.

- *Object facet*
  The object facet is a source for objects that should be represented by the service application. An object can be a person or role (e.g., driver of a limousine in the travel booking domain), a material object (e.g., the limousine) or an immaterial object (e.g., the time and price of for the limousine usage). Relevant sources for requirements are domain experts for the domain in which the application will be used, existing systems, domain specific documentation as well as laws and regulations. Examples for requirements sources in the travel booking domain are travel agents, existing flight booking systems and laws related to tourism.
- *IT and system facet*
  The IT and system facet represents the systems (hardware and software) with which the service oriented application will interact. Furthermore the companies IT strategies and the maintenance of systems are considered. Sources for requirements in the IT facet are system administrators, technical documentation of components, and documentation of IT strategies. In the context of service orientation, sources for requirements are for example experts on middleware and grid technologies as well as documentation on standards for the implementation of services (like XML, WSDL and *SOAP*). Furthermore, existing services are identified within this facet which will interact with the newly developed services.
- *Usage facet*
  In this facet, the users and usage scenarios are represented. Sources for requirements on how the system will be used are relevant user groups, domain specific specifications and existing user interfaces. Examples in the travel agency do-

main are travel agents interacting with the system, documentation of business processes within travel agencies and user interfaces used in these agencies.

- *Development facet*
  The development facet is concerned with the development process of the service oriented application. Sources for requirements are roles involved in defining, using and managing the development process. Furthermore, existing standards, previous experience from post mortem analysis of finished projects and best practices should be considered when defining the development process. A source for best practices are for example process maturity models like CMMI [188].

When the sources are identified, the requirements are elicited from these sources. A variety of methods exist to elicit requirements from the relevant stakeholders. Such methods are focus groups, interviews, observation, workshops, studies of documentation, use of prototypes and questionnaires. A systematic review [52] was conducted to determine which technique is the most efficient one. The conclusion of the review was that structured interviews seem to be best suited to elicit requirements. Furthermore, not only interviews or documents should be considered when eliciting requirements. In addition, existing service repositories can be used to enrich the requirements specification in the early requirements engineering process. As proposed by Zachos et al. [211], the requirements analyst together with service consumers formulates search queries for service registries based on an existing requirements specification. When querying the service register, services are returned that in some form are related to the initial requirements specification. The descriptions of the returned services are explained to the relevant stakeholders who (together with the requirements engineer) use this information to either refine the existing requirements or add new requirements to the initial requirements specification. Thereafter, the process is repeated iteratively. That is, the updated requirements specification is used to define new search queries and the retrieved service descriptions are used as input to help further refine the requirements and so forth.

Drawing the Service Landscape

The major output of the Service landscaping is the service landscape that depicts a list of all services that have been identified during the application engineering and specifies the change requests to the domain and service ontologies that arise due to the semantic impact of the identified required services. Services can be graphically documented by using the graphical element as shown in Fig. 8.4. For each service

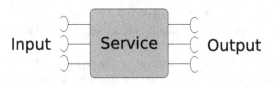

Fig. 8.4. A service element

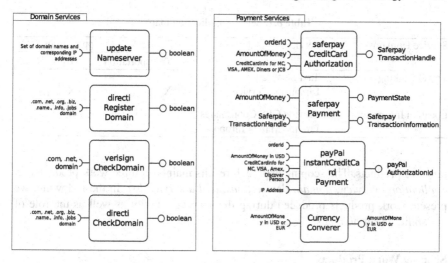

Fig. 8.5. An example service landscape

such an element is drawn representing the service. An example service landscape is depicted in Fig. 8.5. This type of diagram is intended to give an overview and a summary of the identified services that are required to implement the envisioned application. The simple notation facilitates the reduction of complexity, since the number of available services might be high. The diagram also serves as means for communication with service engineers.

The service landscape addresses only the service need of the envisioned application without considering the providers service portfolio. The different identified services are categorized in order to identify services offered by the platform and services that have to be implemented (i.e. serving as input for service engineering). According to this categorization, three situations are feasible for identified services:

- The identified service does already exist and is available in a platform executable form.
- The identified service does already exist, but must be re-engineered for platform execution.
- The identified service does not exist and must be engineered.

8.2.2 Service Scoping

The goal of the scoping activity is to define the service portfolio of a service provider. It is not unusual that a service provider is specialized in a single domain (e.g. flight-booking). But even then there might be multiple infrastructures. In order to exploit the benefits of service reuse, it is a key issue to develop the right set of services in a reusable manner at the right level of genericity. If the chosen scope is inappropriate, either effort will be wasted on domains and services that will not be sufficiently used or the developed services will not be able to adequately support the required

Table 8.1. Service application map

Service Domains	Services	Tourist Service applications	
		Transportation	Travel Route
Travel booking	Taxi Service	X	
	Limousine Service	X	X
Location Information	Provide GPS Coordinates		X
	Provide Map24 Infopoint		

range of products. The scoping approach results mainly in three work products: *an application overview, domain descriptions, and a service list.* In the following, we present work products produced during the scoping activity as well as the role of variability in service reuse.

Scoping Work Products

The *application overview* provides an overview of the products or applications the organization can provide or support by providing services. It is thus a conjecture on the side of the service provider regarding future applications that the infrastructure will be used for. It gives a characterization of the applications in terms of the major functionalities or user tasks they provide or shall support. The *domain descriptions* provide a break-down of the applications functionality in terms of the major technical areas relevant to it. The third work product is a *list of the services* that are provided by the identified domains. As result of the scoping activities, a service-application map is created. The development of the service-application map is also a final consistency-checking step that may lead to restructuring of the domains. Inconsistencies and especially conflicting services and infrastructure constraints can be identified with the help of this map. The map is also a good structuring mechanism to show the relationship between services and applications and helps to identify commonly used services in applications and rather rarely used services. The following table shows an example of a service-application map.

The example map in Fig. 8.1 shows that the service provider aims to support two tourist applications. He offers two services for transportation embedded in the providers travel booking domain. Additionally, the application, which displays a travel route to a customer will require the support of a GPS coordinate service.

The services identified and listed in the service landscape that are currently not available must be developed and engineered. To fill the gap of the required services for the application development, the service engineering process is initialized.

The Role of Variability for Service Reuse

Variability can be defined as the ability to customize or change a system [200]. For example, a payment service is able to support different payment options, depending on the needs of the application in which the service is used. One application might

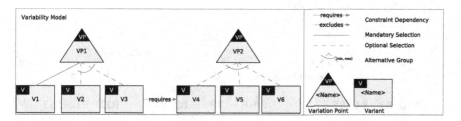

Fig. 8.6. Notation of the orthogonal variability model

require credit card, debit card and cheque while another application requires pay pal and debit card. The degree of customizability of a service or a composition of services determines how well the service or its composition can be reused in different service applications. A service that is able to support all types of different payment options has a high degree of genericity.

Variability is documented in so called variability models. In this chapter, we use the orthogonal variability model [36] to show which role variability plays in order to facilitate reuse in service oriented applications. The orthogonal variability models documents what varies (variants) and how it varies (variation points). Figure 8.6 shows the notation used for the orthogonal variability model. Variation points are represented by triangles and variants are represented by boxes. Variants and variation points are related to one another, represented by either solid or dashed lines. A solid line means that the variant is mandatory to select while a dashed line means that the selection is optional. A service that is able to realize the requirements associated to all the variants has a high degree of genericity. That is, the service can be reused in a variety of different applications. When looking at the service map in the previous section, we can see that the limousine service is used in different applications. Sometimes, this is only possible when the service can be customized to the specific needs of the application. Between different variants as well as variants and variation points, so called constraint dependencies are documented. If one variant requires the selection of another variant, then this is expressed by a requires dependency. On the other hand, if variants are mutually exclusive, this is expressed by an exclude dependency. The variants of the orthogonal variability model are related to requirements which need to be fulfilled to implement the variant.

In order to determine how well certain compositions can be reused, Petersen et al. [153] propose to calculate the coverage of the orthogonal variability model in order to determine how well a service or a set of services can be reused in different applications. Thereby, the variability model documents the variability between the applications that shall be supported by services. Figure 8.7 illustrates how the coverage of the variability model is defined. If the requirements related to a variant are fully fulfilled by a service or composition of services, then the variant is covered. If all variants related to a variation point are covered, then the variation point is covered. Consequently, the service compositions allows the selection of all variants and thus provides a high degree of genericity. Finally, the overall variability model is covered, if all its variation points are covered. The service provider can use these

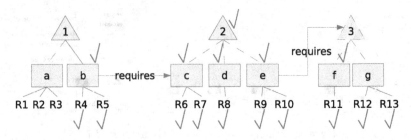

Fig. 8.7. Coverage of the orthogonal variability model

calculations when having different alternatives of service compositions in order to determine which composition provides the best reuse potential.

Formally, the variability model *OVM* is defined as the tuple of variation points *VP* and variants *V*.

$$OVM := (VP, V), \quad V := \{v_1, \ldots, v_n\}, VP := \{vp_1, \ldots, vp_m\}. \quad (8.1)$$

To calculate the coverage of different elements of the variability model like variants, variation points and the overall orthogonal variability model, [153] define different mappings documenting how the elements of the variability model are related to each other.

They define a mapping *VMap* (see Formula (8.2)) of variants to a power set of requirements. The mapping *VMap* delivers all requirements that needs to be fulfilled so that the variant is fully implemented.

$$VMap : V \to \wp(R), \quad R := \{r_1, \ldots, r_p\}. \quad (8.2)$$

The Mapping Variability Dependency *VD* gives all variants which related to a variation point. In the example, *VD*(2) delivers the variants c, d and e.

$$VD : VP \to \wp(V). \quad (8.3)$$

The mapping *SMap* delivers all requirements that are covered by a given service.

$$SMap : S \to \wp(R), \quad S := \{s_1, \ldots, s_q\}. \quad (8.4)$$

The mappings describing the relations between services, variation points, variants and requirements can now be used to calculate the coverage of the OVM. The mapping *VCover* is used to calculate the coverage of a variant v by a set of services S, resulting in a value between 0 and 1. In particular, we calculate the arithmetic average as the number of requirements covered by the set of services divided by the total number of requirements related to the variant.

$$VCover : V \times \wp(S) \to [0..1], \quad (8.5)$$

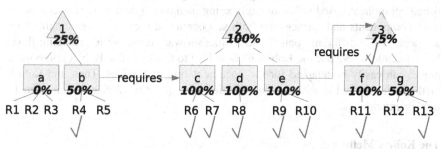

Fig. 8.8. Calculation of coverage

$$VCover(v, S') = \frac{|\cup_{s \in S'} SMap(s) \cap VMap(v)|}{|VMap(v)|}. \tag{8.6}$$

The mapping *VPCover* calculates the coverage of a variation point *vp* for a given set of services *S'*. For this mapping, a function is defined which calculates the sum of the coverage of all variants related to a variation point divided by the number of variants associated to the variation point.

$$VPCover : VP \times \wp(S) \to [0..1], \tag{8.7}$$

$$VPCover(vp, S') = \frac{\sum_{v \in VD(vp)} VCover(v, S')}{|VD(vp)|}. \tag{8.8}$$

The mapping *VMCover* determines the coverage of the OVM by a set of services *S'*. The function for this mapping calculates the sum of coverage of all variation points that are part of the OVM divided by the number of variation points related to the OVM.

$$VMCover : \wp(S) \to [0..1], \tag{8.9}$$

$$VMCover(S') = \frac{\sum_{vp \in VP} VPCover(vp, S')}{|VP|}. \tag{8.10}$$

In Fig. 8.8 an example of the calculation of variability coverage is shown.

8.2.3 Requirements Analysis

The starting point for service engineering is the service landscape, capturing all required services on one hand and the domain ontology on the other. The goal of service requirements analysis and the subsequent service design is to identify and define the required services in terms of their functional and non-functional properties. This includes the interaction between the service and its environment (i.e., user or invoking application) along with exchanged data, as well as services used along with exchanged data.

The similarity of software components and services suggest the use of established component based software engineering methods to document services. Software components and services are both self-contained pieces of functionality that are deployed in different context's to realize software reuse while providing flexible applications. We use the KobrA method [14] to this end. The KobrA component model can easily be adapted for the documentation of services. Then, the KobrA method can be used to support the activities subsequent to service design, namely implementation and testing.

The KobrA Method

The KobrA method represents a synthesis of several advanced software engineering technologies, including product line development, *Component Based Software Development (CBSD)*, frameworks, architecture centric inspections, quality modelling, and process modelling. These have been integrated in the KobrA method with the basic goal of providing a systematic approach to the development of high quality, component based application frameworks.

All products in the KobrA method are organized around, and oriented towards, the description of individual components. This means that, as far as possible, there are no global or system-wide products; all products (and accompanying processes) are defined to carry information only related to their particular component. The advantage is that components (and the products that describe them) can then easily be separated from the environment in which they were developed and therefore can be reused independently. This characteristic makes the KobrA method well-suited to be used for service engineering.

Applications in the KobrA method are represented as a set of components organized in the form of a tree. Each component is described at two levels of abstraction, a specification, which defines the component's externally visible properties and behaviours, and thus serves to capture the contract that the component fulfils, and a realization, which describes how the component fulfils this contract in terms of contracts with lower level components. Components are modelled as a mixture of textual and UML-based (graphical) models. The advantage of using the UML is that frameworks and associated application are independent of any particular programming language or component technology.

The transformation of an application into an executable form is carried out in a distinct set of activities that are essentially orthogonal to the design activities. The implementation activity takes UML models and maps them, through a series of well-defined refinement and translation steps into an executable representation (e.g., high-level source code). Finally, the build activity actually creates binary load modules ready for deployment in the target environment.

We use the KobrA component specification as a basis for the service requirements specification and the semantic service specification and the KobrA component realization as a basis for the service design.

Service Requirements Specification

The service requirements specification describes the externally visible properties of a service. The information captured in the service requirements specification is used as a basis for the service specification and, thus, for service identification, selection, composition, negotiation, contracting, invocation, monitoring, and failure recovery.

To fulfil this task, the service requirements specification must contain the complete information on a number of different aspects of a service, namely structure and quality. The structure of a service captures the service's choreography. The choreography is the complete syntactical information about a service, that is, the signatures of its operations. The signature of an operation captures the name by which a service can be called, as well as the types of input and output data, respectively. The functionality of a service captures the externally visible effects of the operations provided by a service. Finally, the quality of a service captures quality aspects of the service execution, referred to as quality of service.

The information documented in a service requirements specification is the complete information that is necessary to use a service. The internal structural information of a service is captured in UML class diagrams. A service is denoted as a class with stereotype «`service`»; the different operations with their signatures are given as methods of such a service class. An example of how to document structural information of a service is presented in the context of service design.

The quality of service is documented considering a variety of different quality aspects. For example, different quality requirements need to be fulfilled by the service, like performance, reliability or security. Quality of service is documented by the *Profile for Modeling Quality of Service and Fault tolerant Characteristics and Mechanisms* [76] (UML QoS profile). The UML QoS profile provides a framework that allows to document and quantify quality requirements. The advantage of the framework is that it allows to define a quality reference model tailored to the specific needs on the company and project level. In order to define the quality of service, Rinke and Weyer [162] propose a lightweight process which considers the previously introduced four context facets as sources for quality requirements.

Figure 8.9 shows how quality requirements can be documented. In the first step, quality characteristics are defined. A quality characteristic is a quantifiable aspect of a service (like performance) and is documented as a class stereotyped as «`QoSChar-acteristic`». Furthermore, quality of service dimensions are defined and stereotyped as «`QoSDimension`» [76]. A quality of service dimension quantifies a quality of service characteristic. For example, the quality dimension latency can be quantified as maximum latency. The definition of a QoS Characteristic can be made more specific by inheritance. Based on a more abstract definition of the QoSCharacteristic for Latency (e.g., Latency4Composition), we can define what latency means on a more detailed level (e.g., Latency4Encryption). That is, we for example define that the maximum latency should be considered for Encryption and that the maximum latency is measured in seconds. For other services, we might require other definitions for latency and thus create further sub-classes. When we have defined the quality of service, we can annotate the quality requirement within the requirements

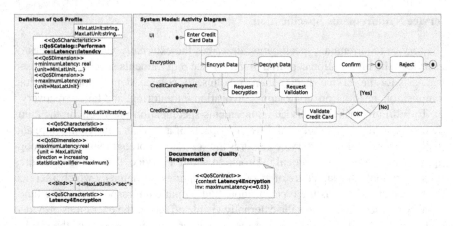

Fig. 8.9. Documentation of quality requirements

specification as a comment. Within the comment, we use the stereotype «QoSCon-straint» introduced in [76]. In our example, the activity *encrypt data* in the activity diagram documenting the behaviour of a service for online payment should have a maximum latency of 0.03 seconds. The annotation refers to the definition of how to quantify the quality requirement, i.e., Latency4Encryption.

Semantic Service Specification

The semantic specification of a service describes the effects of invoking that service (see Sects. 3.4 and 4.3). That is, it describes what happens when an operation of the service is invoked. This information is captured in operation schemata that describe for each operation of a service the pre-conditions and assumptions that must be fulfilled before the respective operation can be invoked, as well as the post conditions and effects that can be guaranteed after the execution. For example, in order to pay with credit card using an online payment service, the pre-condition is that data submitted to the service has to be encrypted for security reasons. An example for a post condition is that the credit card data has been successfully validated and the credit card is either rejected or accepted.

8.2.4 Service Design

The service design describes the internal properties of a service. The information captured in the service requirements specification and in the semantic service specification is used to describe how a service provides the properties given in the service specification. The design thus captures a service's orchestration, as well as other services that are required by a service.

The service design documents the internal structure of a service, its behaviour, as well as related quality aspects. The internal structure describes the internal structure of a service along with sub-services a service requires to fulfil its task. This internal

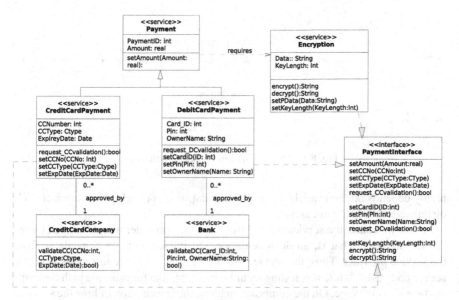

Fig. 8.10. Documentation of the internal service structure

structure must be related to the externally visible structure captured in the service requirements specification. The behaviour describes how a service provides its functionality by showing the respective algorithms. The quality aspects described in the service realisation document how relate the quality asserted in the service specification captured in the service specification is provided.

The information documented in a service design describes the internals of a service completely. The internal structure is, like the external structure, captured in UML class diagrams. Actually, the internal class diagram is a refinement of the external one, relating the internal to the external structure. The example in Fig. 8.10 shows how a payment service is structured. It consists of several services, like one service for encryption, and different services for payment (payment by credit card and payment by debit card). The operations for accessing the payment service are defined in the *PaymentInterface*.

The behaviour of a service describes the functionality of a service. It might be documented using UML activity diagrams, in which the different sub-services that are used by a service are represented by swim lanes, as shown in Fig. 8.11.

Input for implementing a service is the service design and the domain-specific ontology. The result is a service implementation and a service specification, as described in Sect. 3.4.

8.2.5 Service Testing

The implemented service then needs to be tested. Inputs for testing are the service implementation, the service design, and the service specifications. What can be tested

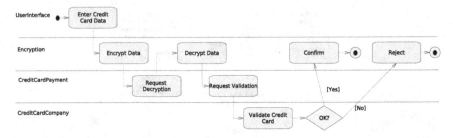

Fig. 8.11. Documentation of service behaviour

highly depends on the availability of documentation and development artefacts. We distinguish two different cases:

In the first case, the service offered by the service provider was developed by the service provider. That is, all documentation and implementation is available from the service provider. Thus, the service provider is able to derive test cases from the source code using white box testing techniques [195], like for example path coverage or statement coverage. On the composition level, the information of how the services are composed is available to the service provider, including the flow in which services are executed. Here, path testing can be applied as well [17].

In the second case, the service provider uses services of other service providers, i.e., the service provider has the role of an service integrator. Therefore, the internal structure of the service is not available to the service provider, as other service providers avoid to make their implementations public [215]. In consequence, testing has to be done based on the available interface and documentation of the service. That is, black box testing techniques have to be applied based on the available service specification. In addition to that, test cases can be automatically derived from WSDL [17]. To conduct tests based on WSDL, four coverage criteria are proposed by Bai et al. [17]. These are part coverage, message coverage, operation coverage and flow coverage.

- Part coverage: Each part, which is mapped to a parameter, should be covered by at least one positive and negative test case.
- Message coverage: In WSDL, one distinguishes between input and output messages. One input message should be at least covered by one positive and negative test case and an output message is covered if each equivalent class is covered by at least one test case.
- Operation coverage: Each operation should be covered by one negative and positive test case.
- Flow coverage: Based on the parameter data sets of operations (i.e., input and output parameters) the dependencies between different services can be identified and a flow of service execution can be generated. The flow is covered if each path is covered by one positive and one negative test case.

However, this situation is not always desirable because of two reasons. The first reason is that tests only derived from specification (i.e., black box testing) is not adequate to achieve adequate testing [74]. Secondly, when a service is changed, regression testing becomes necessary. However, as the internals of a service are not available, the change might stay unnoticed and is not tested properly. To avoid this problem, [215] propose to offer testing as a service in itself where only trusted service providers are allowed access to the internal structure of services.

8.3 Summary

In this chapter, we presented the development life cycle in order to develop services to support service based applications. Thereby, we focused on how to develop services considering service reuse in order to produce services in shorter time to market and with high quality. The phases presented are requirements engineering for services, service design, service implementation and test and service registration. Within the development process, we proposed different methods that can be used in the service development process. These are for example frameworks for structuring the context to arrive at complete service maps, scoping, variability to facilitate service reuse, UML as a means for documenting and designing service based systems with respect to functional and quality properties as well as a guideline which testing techniques should be used in the context of services. All the previous chapters together with this chapter have given a full overview on how semantic service provisioning is intended to work. The next chapter will give a short overview on the Adaptive Services Grid project which was the major basis for our finding and this book.

9

Application and Outlook

Dominik Kuropka, Harald Meyer, Peter Tröger, and Mathias Weske

Even though semantic service provisioning is still a hot research topic,[1] many projects and collaborations already gained a tremendous amount of experiences. This chapter sketches the prototype experiences from one of these projects, the European integration project ASG, which was also the starting point for this book. The chapter further discusses possible next steps for advanced service provisioning platforms.

9.1 Adaptive Services Grid Project

The ASG project with 22 partners from 7 countries was funded by the European Commission in the Sixth Framework Programme. It developed a prototypical architecture for semantic service provisioning platform to identify relevant components and their responsibilities, as well as the interactions between them. The reference architecture was validated by a prototypical implementation, in collaboration with industrial partners.

The research of relevant semantic service technology and according possible use cases led to three focus points:

- *Seamless integration of heterogeneous existing services*: Mechanisms for service enabling reduce the maintenance and modification costs for large numbers of existing services and functionalities. This has the potential to ease integration of services and data formats.
- *On-demand creation of service compositions*: Current service integration, based on manual programming, makes it hard to cost-effectively maintain and modify a complex service world. Semantic service provisioning lifts the interface to services from a manual to a logical level, and supports service composition based on automated tools. The adaptive service composition implies a cost reduction in service provision.

---

[1] http://www.nessi-europe.com.

- *Reliable service provision with assured quality of service*: The future service world will be based on global and dynamic services, which can be composed to answer the needs of complex service requests. Dynamic service re-enactment, re-binding or re-composition provide reliable solutions for non-reliable services by adapting to changes and failures, thus provides the end-customer with a reliable service delivery.

These three features sum up typical expectations on a semantic service provisioning platform. They therefore formed also the conceptional frame for components in the ASG platform.

One relevant issue with the design of such a platform is the role of the service consumer. Most discussions with third parties about the ASG concepts raised the question of how the generated composed services are accessed. In the concept of ASG, end-user applications or back-end systems act as service consumers. They send a semantic service request to the platform. This request is syntactically similar to a semantic service description. However, while the description gives details about a existing service, a semantic service request specifies a desired service. The platform tries to find a service or a composition of services which are able to meet a posed request.

End-users only interact with the platform through the front-end applications, which formulate the ontology-compliant semantic queries. The main reason for this approach is the inherent complexity of semantic description languages, which conflicts with the commercial demand for domain-specific and user friendly interfaces. In conclusion needs very application domain or usage scenario not only a proper domain ontology definition, but also a matching front end application which formulates the semantic queries. These applications take the data from the user and build a semantic service request out of them either by using a template, or by assembling a request out of given building blocks.

The ASG approach for semantic service provision platforms relieves the business functionality developer from dealing with discovery and composition of services. Additionally to this, it raises the reliability by providing failure handling on the basis of service re-binding and re-composition.

Beside the interaction with the end user, the service platform is also coupled to integrated atomic services from other parties. Also this part of the architecture raises a set of questions:

How can a mapping between heterogeneous data formats and protocols of integrated services be realized? In which way are domain ontology and functional service descriptions coupled? How to realise monitoring and negotiation functionality for existing services, which are demanded by service profiling and composition?

The main concept for achieving this is the introduction of a adaptation layer for atomic services, the service infrastructure [194]. It provides a unified invocation, monitoring and deployment interface for internal atomic, as well as proxy services.

9.1.1 ASG Software Architecture

The ASG architecture and according prototype implementation consists out of five logical components, *Facade, Dynamic Service Composition, Semantic Service Discovery, Adaptive Process Management,* and *Service Infrastructure,* as shown in Fig. 9.1.

The *Facade* component provides programmatic interfaces that can be used by external applications or tools. It provides two major interfaces, for the composed service consumers and for the service integration tooling.

The domain ontology, which is the foundation for the description of services and for the semantic service requests, can be accessed and uploaded via the *Facade*. The domain ontology describes the concepts that are of relevance in the application domain of the platform. These concepts can describe data objects and their relation to each other like for example defining an invoice as a structure consisting out of an address, an order and an amount to be transferred. Furthermore, the ontology can define relationships which are usually not directly represented in usual information systems, but which are useful to describe the functionality of services.

Regarding the books use case scenario, an example would be the relationship "domainNameServers" between a domain name and a list of servers. With such a relationship, the functionality can be formally described. The effect of the example service is that for the entered domain name, a list of servers will be returned which have the domain name registered.

To be usable, services have to be registered in the platform. This registration happens via an external *Service Integration Tool* that uses the programmatic interface

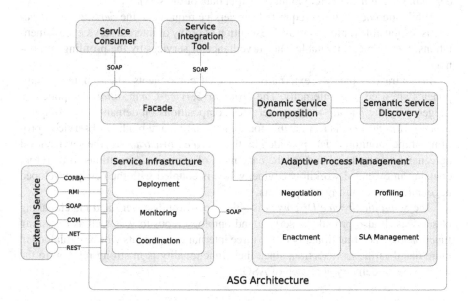

Fig. 9.1. The ASG reference architecture

of the *Facade*. The following information needs to be provided to properly register a service: input, preconditions, output, effects, non-functional properties, and the proxy code.

All invocations of external services are conducted via proxies, which are stored and executed in the service infrastructure component. The major task of the proxies is the provision of translations between protocols and mediation of data types, according to an XML-Schema [208] which is derived via rules from the domain ontology. This ensures that the data is compatible and can be exchanged between services during composition enactment without manual mediation.

In case that the service to be registered is not accessible via Web service protocols, the proxies are also responsible for a protocol translation. In summary, the proxies handle the technical and data format issues of service integration, while the description of input, preconditions, output, and effects are used for the semantic integration.

The input of a service specifies the required input of a service by referring to the domain ontology. Preconditions can be defined that have to hold for the input. For example, it can be defined that credit card data which are the input of a service, have to be the data of the customer and not someone's else data. Similar to this, the output defines the output data of a service while the effects can specify additional hints about the meaning and influence of the output on the further execution.

Two functionally different services may exist that have the same input and output, even though they provide different functionality. Such differences can be modelled adequately by preconditions and effects. Also non-functional properties can be defined for a service. However these properties are only applicable if they are not depending from the concrete input or output data of the service [4].

While the *Facade* takes requests from service requesters, the *Service Infrastructure* is responsible for the controlled execution of proxy or internal service implementations. Furthermore, it enables the surveillance of services by the profiling component.

In contrast to the two externally connected components, the remaining components are used only internally. The *Dynamic Service Composition* component is triggered by the *Facade* to create services compositions on demand. The *Adaptive Process Management* is responsible for the negotiation and binding of services, profiling of the monitored data provided by the *Service Infrastructure*, the service level agreement management and for the enactment of service compositions. It therefore contains an extended workflow engine, which is coupled with the newly developed negotiation and profiling components.

The *Semantic Service Discovery* is able to perform discovery and matchmaking of services. It also provides a service and ontology repository as well as reasoning functionality. The functionality of the three internal components will be explained in more detail in the next section, since their functionality is in strong relation to the whole service delivery approach of ASG.

9.1.2 Use Case Scenario

The described architecture of a semantic service provisioning platform was implemented by the ASG project on the basis of existing 'real-world' services. In order to work with a realistic set of services and composition problems, the project implemented an Internet service provider (ISP) scenario from one of the industrial partner. This scenario is also used all through the book.

The ISP is specialized on products like domain registration and web hosting, and intended to use the ASG platform for a combined usage of B2B services. In order to realize its Web hosting products, this company uses remotely accessible services from companies such as VeriSign or PayPal. The resulting Web hosting purchase service is offered to resellers. One motivation for the usage of a dynamic service composition platform is the necessary adaptation to the external service landscape. Utilized third party functionality, like the ordering of domain names, changes constantly in price and quality. This leads to expensive continuous adaptions of the Web hosting service implementation, which was now intended to be replaced by a dynamically created service composition.

One benefit for the resellers is, that they do not need to deal with the individual integration of the various basic services, as shown in Fig. 9.2. Instead, the reseller uses the interface of the composed service as provided by the ASG platform.

Figure 9.3 shows an already bound service composition, which is automatically created by the ASG platform. Translated to natural language, the semantic service requests which is the origin of the composition looks like this: "Given the following domain x and the following user data y the goal state to achieve is that the domain is registered at an registrar, our name server is updated, a web hosting account is created, and a default forwarding for the domain is set up." Both, the (Directi and Verisign) services for domain registration and the Plesk server management service expect as precondition that the existence of a domain is checked prior their execution. Therefore, a domain checking service is executed at the beginning of the service composition. The server management service can naturally only be executed on existing web hosting accounts, therefore a web hosting account is created before a domain is created. Figure 9.3 shows how the service composition is recovered in case the Denic service for domain checks fails. In this case, the platform searches for a semantically equivalent service like from Verisign and replaces (re-binds) the failed service.

Figure 9.4 shows how re-planning can affect a service composition. In the ASG scenario, two proxy services for real-world payment services with test accounts were used: PayPal and SaferPay. While PayPal can handle the payment activities in one step, the SaferPay payment service which needs two steps for this task. Both alternatives are semantically equivalent and can be therefore replaced by each other. The ASG platform reacts on the outage of the PayPal service with an according partial adoption of the composed service implementation.

Further details about the conceptional design and the prototype implementation of ASG are available from the project home page and the according publications, such as [165, 190, 134, 133, 129, 194, 69].

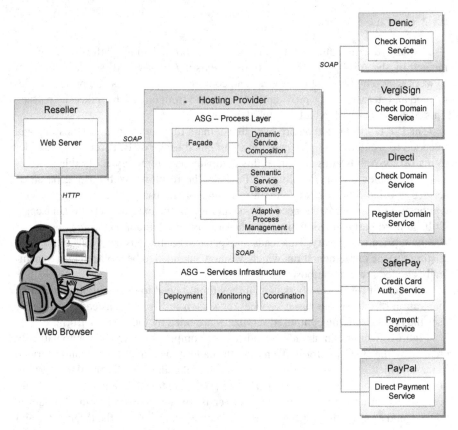

Fig. 9.2. ISP scenario for ASG platform

9.2 Outlook

There is no doubt that future applications will use more and more existing software systems, so that the integration of functionality from various source systems will be one of them most important factors in system development. Furthermore, there is little doubt that the integration of functionality from heterogeneous sources will be based on services, i.e., well-specified units of functionality with a business value. Specifically in the Web services world, there are accepted standards for syntactic specifications of services and also of service compositions.

Doubt increases when it comes to rich service specification languages that can express functional and non-functional aspects beyond syntax. While recently different approaches emerged from the research community, there is no completely satisfying language proposal that is both pragmatic and formally sound. Formal soundness is required if runtime service composition without human intervention is aimed at. Unfortunately, specifying a sufficiently complex functionality in a mathematically precise way is hard, to say the least. The halting problem from theoretical computer

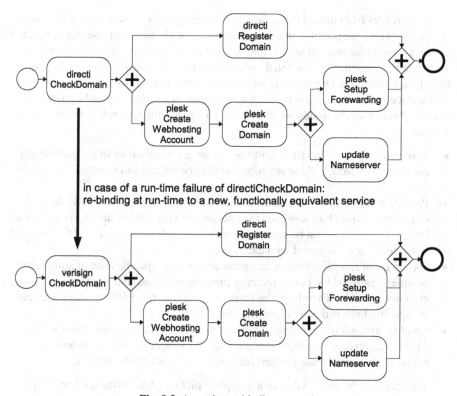

Fig. 9.3. A service re-binding example

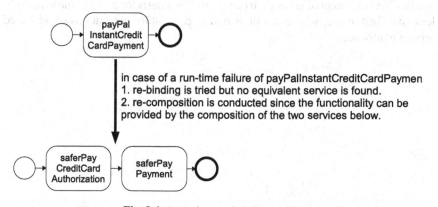

Fig. 9.4. A service re-planning example

science determines that it is not possible to devise an algorithm that determines for given program and input data whether the program terminates, not to speak about application semantics.

Experiences from the Adaptive Services Grid project show that complete semantic specifications are possible in a narrow application domain. In these domains, the concepts can be formalized and related to each other in a domain ontology, the services can be semantically annotated and integrated, so that they be discovered, composed, and enacted in an adaptable way. Experiences also shows that not all aspects of a service based application requires a high level of adaptability and dynamic behaviour. From this discussion we can derive an agenda for research in service engineering

- *Research methodology*: Real-world use cases are required to shape the research questions. Answers to these questions need to be refined and validated by the use cases.
- *Vertical completeness*: Use cases need to stretch multiple levels of systems design, ranging from business level to conceptual levels and, eventually, to software levels. An approach can be successful only if the solutions developed for the different levels are integrated with each other.
- *Specification completeness*: A complete and precise specification of sufficiently complex real-world services requires massive overhead and is, in many cases, even not possible. Therefore, the level of detail and precision in which services are specified needs detailed investigation.
- *Level of dynamicity*: We state that dynamic behaviour does not come for free. Therefore, detailed investigations are required to specify where the level of dynamicity provided by the devised service platform is actually required.

This book is the first to devise a complete picture of an advanced service provisioning platform that facilitates the specification, dynamic discovery, composition, and flexible enactment of services. It can be used as a basis for tackling the hard problems sketched above, whose solutions will impact future generations of advanced service platforms.

References

1. W. Aalst, B. van Dongen, J. Herbst, L. Maruster, G. Schimm, A. Weijters. Workflow mining: A survey of issues and approaches. *Data and Knowledge Engineering*, 47:237–267, 2003.
2. W. Abramowicz, J. Gwizdala, T. Jakubowski, M. Kaczmarek, A. Kliber, M. Kowalkiewicz, D. Zyskowski. A survey of qos computation for web service profiling. In S. Dascalu (editor), *Proceedings of the ISCA 18th International Conference on Computer Applications in Industry and Engineering*, 2005.
3. W. Abramowicz, M. Kaczmarek, M. Kowalkiewicz, D. Zyskowski. Architecture for service profiling. *Proceedings of 2006 IEEE Services Computing Workshops (SCW 2006)*, 2006.
4. W. Abramowicz, M. Kaczmarek, D. Zyskowski. Duality in web services reliability. In *Proceedings of the Advanced International Conference on Telecommunications and the International Conference on Internet and Web Applications and Services*, page 165, 2006.
5. Active Endpoints, Adobe, BEA, IBM, Oracle, SAP. *Web Services Human Task (WS-HumanTask), Version 1.0*, 2007.
6. Active Endpoints, Adobe, BEA, IBM, Oracle, SAP. *WS-BPEL Extension for People (BPEL4People), Version 1.0*, 2007.
7. S. Agarwal, S. Handschuh, S. Staab. Annotation, composition and invocation of semantic web services. *Journal on Web Semantics*, 2(1), 2004.
8. R. Akkiraju, J. Farrell, J. Miller, M. Nagarajan, M. Schmidt, A. Sheth, K. Verma. *Web Service Semantics: WSDL-S*. World Wide Web Consortium (W3C), November 2005. W3C Member Submission, 7 November 2005. Available from http://www.w3.org/Submission/WSDL-S/. http://www.w3.org/Submission/WSDL-S.
9. H. Alani. TGVizTab: An ontology visualisation extension for Protégé. In *Proceedings of the Workshop on Visualization Information in Knowledge Engineering (K-CAP)*, 2003.
10. G. Alonso, F. Casati, H. Kuno, V. Machiraju. *Web Services—Concepts, Architectures and Applications*. Data-Centric Systems and Applications. Springer-Verlag, New York, 2004. ISBN 3-540-44008-9.
11. T. Andrews et al. Business process execution language for web services version 1.1. Technical report, BEA, IBM, Microsoft, SAP AG, Siebel Systems, 2003.

12. A. Andrieux, K. Czajkowski, A. Dan, K. Keahey, H. Ludwig, T. Nakata, J. Pruyne, J. Rofrano, S. Tuecke, M. Xu. *Web Services Agreement Specification.* Globus Alliance, USC, ISI, Univa, IBM, ANL, NEC, HP, Platform Computing, August 2004. http://www.gridforum.org/Public_Comment_Docs/Documents/Public_Comment_2004/WS-AgreementSpecification_v2.pdf.

13. A. Andrieux, K. Czajkowski, A. Dan, K. Keahey, H. Ludwig, T. Nakata, J. Pruyne, J. Rofrano, S. Tuecke, M. Xu. *Web Services Agreement Specification (WS-Agreement).* Globus Alliance, USC, ISI, Univa, IBM, ANL, NEC, HP, Platform Computing, September 2006. http://www.ogf.org/Public_Comment_Docs/Documents/Oct-2006/WS-AgreementSpecificationDraftFinal_sp_tn_jpver_v2.pdf.

14. C. Atkinson, J. Bayer, C. Bunse, E. Kamsties, O. Laitenberger, R. Laqua, D. Muthig, B. Paech, J. Wust, J. Zettel. *Component-Based Product Line Engineering with UML.* Addison-Wesley Professional, Reading, 2001. ISBN 0201737914.

15. V. Atluri, S. A. Chun. Handling dynamic changes in decentralized workflow execution environments. In *14th International Conference on Database and Expert Systems Applications,* 2003.

16. A. Avizienis, J. Laprie, B. Randell. Fundamental concepts of dependability. Technical report, UCLA & LAAS & Newcastle University, 2001.

17. X. Bai, W. Dong, W.-T. Tsai, Y. Chen. Wsdl-based automatic test case generation for web services testing. In *Proceedings of the International Workshop on Service-Oriented System Engineering (SOSE 2005),* pages 1–6, 2005.

18. M. S. C. Bartolini. Management by contract. Technical report, Hawlett Packard, 2004. http://www.hpl.hp.com/techreports/2003/HPL-2003-186R1.pdf.

19. S. Battle, A. Bernstein, H. Boley, B. Grosof, M. Grüninger, R. Hull, M. Kifer, D. Martin, D. L. McGuinness, S. McIlraith, G. Newton, D. D. Roure, M. Skall, J. Su, S. Tabet, H. Yoshida. *Semantic Web Services Framework (SWSF).* World Wide Web Consortium (W3C), 2005. http://www.w3.org/Submission/2005/07.

20. BEA, IBM. *BPELJ: BPEL for Java,* 2004.

21. S. Bechhofer, F. van Harmelen, J. Hendler, I. Horrocks, D. L. McGuinness, P. F. Patel-Schneider, L. A. Stein. *OWL Web Ontology Language Reference—W3C Recommendation 10 February 2004.* World Wide Web Consortium (W3C), February 2004. W3C Recommendation 10 February 2004. http://www.w3.org/TR/owl-ref/.

22. M. Beisiegel, H. Blohm, D. Booz, M. Edwards, O. Hurley, S. Ielceanu, A. Miller, A. Karmarkar, A. Malhotra, J. Marino, M. Nally, E. Newcomer, S. Patil, G. Pavlik, M. Raepple, M. Rowley, K. Tam, S. Vorthmann, P. Walker, L. Waterman. SCA Service Component Architecture—Assembly Model Specification v1.0. Open Service Oriented Architecture Collaboration, March 2007. http://www.osoa.org/.

23. D. Berardi, D. Calvanese, G. De Giacomo, M. Mecella. Composition of services with nondeterministic observable behavior. In *Proceedings of the 3rd International Conference on Service Oriented Computing (ICSOC'05), Lecture Notes in Computer Science,* vol. 3826, pages 520–526. Springer, New York, 2005.

24. J. Bettin. Model-driven software development. *MDA Journal,* 13(4), 2004.

25. N. Bieberstein, S. Bose, M. Fiammante, K. Jones, R. Shah. *Service-Oriented Architecture (SOA) Compass: Business Value, Planning, and Enterprise Roadmap (The developerWorks Series).* IBM Press, 2005. ISBN 0131870025.

26. B. Bloch et al. Web services business process execution language version 2.0. Technical report, OASIS, 2005. http://www.oasis-open.org/committees/download.php/14616/wsbpel-specification-draft.htm.

27. A. Blum, M. Furst. Fast planning through planning graph analysis. *Artificial Intelligence,* 90:281–300, 1997.

28. M. Boddy. Imperfect match: PDDL 2.1 and real applications. *Journal of Artificial Intelligence Research*, 20:133–137, 2003.
29. E. P. Bontas. *A Contextual Approach to Ontology Reuse: Methodology, Methods and Tools for the Semantic Web*. Ph.D. thesis, Freien Universität Berlin, 2006.
30. D. Booth, H. Haas, F. McCabe, E. Newcomer, M. Champion, C. Ferris, D. Orchard. Web Services Architecture. World Wide Web Consortium (W3C), February 2004. http://www.w3.org/TR/ws-arch/.
31. R. J. Brachman. What IS-A is and isn't: An analysis of taxonomic links in semantic networks. *IEEE Computer*, 16(10):30–36, 1983.
32. R. J. Brachman, D. L. McGuinness, P. F. Patel-Schneider, L. A. Resnick, A. Borgida. *Living with CLASSIC: When and How to Use a KL-ONE-Like Language*, Morgan-Kaufmann, San Mateo, 1991, pages 401–456.
33. R. J. Brachman, J. Schmolze. An overview of the KL-ONE knowledge representation system. *Cognitive Science*, 9(2):171–216, 1985.
34. R. Brafman, J. Hoffmann. Conformant planning via heuristic forward search: A new approach. In S. Z. Sven Koenig, Shlomo Zilbe Koenig (editors), *Proceedings of the 14th International Conference on Automated Planning and Scheduling (ICAPS-04)*, pages 355–364. Morgan-Kaufmann, San Mateo, 2004.
35. S. Brodsky, R. Patel. Service Data Objects. *JSR 235*, December 2003.
36. S. Bühne, K. Lauenroth, K. Pohl. Modelling requirements variability across product lines. In *Proceedings of the 13th IEEE International Requirements Engineering Conference (RE 2005)*, pages 41–52, 2005.
37. S. Burbeck. The tao of e-business services—the evolution of web applications into service-oriented components with web services. Technical report, IBM Software Group, October 2000. http://www.ibm.com/developerworks/webservices/library/ws-tao/.
38. F. Buschmann, R. Meunier, H. Rohnert, P. Sommerlad, M. Stal. *Pattern-Oriented Software Architecture, Volume 1: A System of Patterns*. Wiley, New York, August 1996. ISBN 0471958697.
39. G. Carter. *LDAP System Administration*. O'Reilly, 2003.
40. F. Casati et al. Adaptive and dynamic service composition in eflow. Technical report, Hawlett Packard, 2000. www.hpl.hp.com/techreports/2000/HPL-2000-39.pdf.
41. D. Chapman. Planning for conjunctive goals. *Artificial Intelligence*, 32(3):333–377, 1987.
42. D. A. Chappell. *Enterprise Service Bus. Theory in Practice*. O'Reilly, July 2004. ISBN 978-0596006754.
43. P. P. Chen. The entity-relationship model—toward a unified view of data. *ACM Trans. Database Syst.*, 1(1):9–36, 1976.
44. E. Christensen, F. Curbera, G. Meredith, S. Weerawarana. Web services description language (wsdl) 1.1. Technical report, World Wide Web Consortium, 2001. http://www.w3.org/TR/2001/NOTE-wsdl-20010315.
45. J. Clark, S. DeRose. XML Path Language (XPath) Version 1.0, November 1999.
46. P. Clements, L. Northrop. *Software Product Lines: Practices and Patterns (The SEI Series in Software Engineering)*. Addison-Wesley Professional, Reading, 2001. ISBN 0201703327.
47. E. F. Codd. *The Relational Model for Database Management: Version 2*. Addison-Wesley, Reading, 1990.
48. M. Comuzzi, B. Pernici. An architecture for flexible web service QoS negotiation. In *EDOC*, pages 70–82, 2005.
49. Congress of the United States. Public company accounting reform and investor protection act (sarbanes-oxley act), 2002. Pub. L. No. 107-204, 116 Stat. 745.

50. S. Conrad, W. Hasselbring, A. Kosche. *Enterprise Application Integration. Grundlagen–Konzepte–Entwurfsmuster–Praxisbeispiele.* Spektrum Akademischer Verlag, October 2005. ISBN 978-3827415721.

51. B. Curtis, M. I. Keller, J. Over. Process modeling. *Communications of the ACM*, 35(9):75–90, 1992.

52. A. M. Davis, Ó. D. Tubío, A. M. Hickey, N. J. Juzgado, A. M. Moreno. Effectiveness of requirements elicitation techniques: Empirical results derived from a systematic review. In *Proceedings of the 14th International Conference on Requirements Engineering (RE)*, pages 176–185. IEEE, New York, 2006.

53. F. de Boer, M. Bonsangue, R. van Buuren, L. Groenewegen, S. Hoppenbrouwers, M.-E. Iacob, H. Jonkers, M. Lankhorst, E. Proper, A. Stam, L. van der Torre, G. V. van Zanten. Concepts for architectural description. Technical report TI/RS/2003/007, Telematica Institute, December 2004. ArchiMate Deliverable 2.2.1 v4.0.

54. J. de Bruijn, H. Lausen, R. Krummenacher, A. Polleres, L. Predoiu, M. Kifer, D. Fensel. *The Web Service Modeling Language WSML—WSML Final Draft 5 October 2005.* Digital Enterprise Research Institute (DERI), October 2005. WSMO Final Draft D16.v0.21. http://www.wsmo.org/TR/d16/d16.1/v0.21/.

55. G. Decker, O. Kopp, F. Leymann, M. Weske. Bpel4chor: Extending bpel for modeling choreographies. In *Proceedings of the IEEE 2007 International Conference on Web Services (ICWS)*. IEEE Computer Society, New York, July 2007.

56. L. DeMichiel, M. Keith, Enterprise JavaBeans 3.0 (Final Release). *JSR 220*, May 2006. http://www.jcp.org/en/jsr/detail?id=220.

57. W. E. Deming. *Out of the Crisis.* MIT Press, Cambridge, 1982.

58. M. Do, S. Kambhampati. Sapa: A multi-objective metric temporal planner. *Journal of Artificial Intelligence Research*, 20:155–194, 2003.

59. J. Domingue, L. Cabral, F. Hakimpour, D. Sell, E. Motta. IRS-III: A platform and infrastructure for creating WSMO-based Semantic Web services. In *Proceedings of the Workshop on WSMO Implementations (WIW 2004)*. Frankfurt, Germany, 2004.

60. B. Dournaee. *Introduction to ebXML*, June 2004. http://dev2dev.bea.com/pub/a/2004/12/ebXML.html.

61. K. Erol, D. S. Nau, V. Subrahamnian. Complexity, decidability and undecidability results for domain-independent planning: A detailed analysis. Technical report CS-TR-2797, UMIACS-TR-91-154, SRC-TR-91-96, University of Maryland, 1991.

62. K. Erol, D. S. Nau, V. Subrahamnian. Complexity, decidability and undecidability results for domain-independent planning. *Artificial Intelligence*, 76(1–2):75–88, 1995.

63. H. L. et al. Web service level agreement language specification. Technical report, IBM, 2003. http://www.research.ibm.com/wsla/.

64. I. M. et al. *Service-orientierte Architekturen mit Web Services. Konzepte–Standards–Praxis.* Spektrum Akademischer Verlag, 2007. ISBN 978-3827418852.

65. D. C. Fallside, P. Walmsley. XML Schema Part 0: Primer Second Edition. W3C Recommendation, October 2004.

66. J. Farrell, H. Lausen. *Semantic Annotations for WSDL and XML Schema (SAWSDL).* World Wide Web Consortium (W3C), August 2007. http://www.w3.org/TR/sawsdl.

67. M. Feingold, R. Jeyaraman. Web Services Coordination (WS-Coordination) Version 1.1. OASIS Open, April 2007.

68. R. T. Fielding, R. N. Taylor. Principled design of the modern Web architecture. *ACM Trans. Inter. Tech.*, 2(2):115–150, 2002. ISSN 1533-5399. doi:10.1145/514183.514185.

69. M. Flehmig, P. Tröger, A. Saar. Design and Integration of SLA Monitoring and Negotiation Capabilities. Adaptive Services Grid Project—Deliverable D5.II-7, August 2006.

70. M. Gelfond, V. Lifschitz. The stable model semantics for logic programming. In R. A. Kowalski, K. Bowen (editors), *Proceedings of the Fifth International Conference on Logic Programming*, pages 1070–1080. MIT Press, Cambridge, 1988.

71. J. Gennari, M. A. Musen, R. W. Fergerson, W. E. Grosso, M. Crubzy, H. Eriksson, N. F. Noy, S. W. Tu. The evolution of Protégé: An environment for knowledge-based systems development, 2002. http://citeseer.ist.psu.edu/545954.html.

72. A. Gerevini, A. Saetti, I. Serina. Planning through stochastic local search and temporal action graphs. *Journal of Artificial Intelligence Research*, 20:239–290, 2003.

73. M. Ghallab, D. Lau, P. Traverso. *Automated Planning: Theory and Practice*. Morgan Kaufmann, San Mateo, 2004.

74. J. B. Goodenough, S. L. Gerhart. Toward a theory of test data selection. *IEEE Transactions on Software Engineering*, 3(3), 1975.

75. B. N. Grosof, I. Horrocks, R. Volz, S. Decker. Description logic programs: Combining logic programs with description logic. In *Proc. Intl. Conf. on the World Wide Web (WWW-2003)*. Budapest, Hungary, 2003.

76. O. M. Group. Uml profile for modeling quality of service and fault tolerance characteristics and mechanisms (version 1.0), 2006.

77. T. Gruber. A translation approach to portable ontology specifications. *Knowledge Acquisition*, 2(5):199–220, 1993.

78. T. Gruber. Toward principles for the design of ontologies used for knowledge sharing. *International Journal on Human-Computer Studies*, 43(6):907–928, 1995.

79. X. Gu, K. Nahrstedt, R. Chang, C. Ward. Qos-assured service composition in managed service overlay networks, 2003.

80. M. Hall, L. Brown. *Core Servlets and JavaServer Pages, Vol. 1: Core Technologies*. Sun Microsystems Inc., 4150 Network Circle, Santa Clara, CA 95054, USA, second edition, 2004.

81. G. Hambrick. The EJB advocate: SOA applications using Java EE. *WebSphere Journal*, November 2006.

82. M. Hapner, R. Sharma, J. Fialli, K. Stout. *JMS specification*. Sun Microsystems Inc., 4150 Network Circle, Santa Clara, CA 95054 USA, 1.1 edition, April 2002.

83. J. Heinsohn, D. Kudenko, B. Nebel, H.-J. Profitlich. An empirical analysis of terminological representation systems. *Artificial Intelligence*, 2(68):367–397, 1994.

84. M. Hepp, F. Leymann, J. Domingue, A. Wahler, D. Fensel. Semantic business process management: A vision towards using semantic web services for business process management. In *IEEE International Conference on e-Business Engineering (ICEBE 2005)*, pages 535–540. Beijing, China, 2005.

85. M. Hepp, D. Roman. An ontology framework for semantic business process management. In A. Oberweis, C. Weinhardt, H. Gimpel, A. Koschmider, V. Pankratius, B. Schmizler (editors), *eOrganisation: Service-, Prozess, Market-Engineering*, volume 1 of *Proceedings of the 8th International Conference Wirtschaftsinformatik 2007*, pages 423–440. Universitaetsverlag Karlsruhe, Karlsruhe, February 28–March 2, 2007.

86. A. Hess, E. Johnston, N. Kushmerick. Assam: A tool for semi-automatically annotating semantic web services. In *Proceedings of the International Semantic Web Conference 2004*, pages 320–334. Springer, New York, 2004.

87. J. Hoffmann. Metric-FF planning system: Translating "ignoring delete lists" to numeric state variables. *Journal of Artificial Intelligence Research*, 20:291–341, 2003.

88. J. Hoffmann, R. Brafman. Contingent planning via heuristic forward search with implicit belief states. In *Proceedings of the 15th International Conference on Automated Planning and Scheduling (ICAPS-05)*. Morgan Kaufmann, San Mateo, 2005.

89. J. Hoffmann, B. Nebel. The FF planning system: Fast plan generation through heuristic search. *Journal of Artificial Intelligence Research*, 14:253–302, 2001.

90. D. Hollingsworth. The workflow reference model version 1.1, technical report wfmc-tc-1003. Technical report, Worflow Management Coalition, 1995.

91. I. Horrocks. Using an expressive description logic: Fact or fiction? In A. G. Cohn, L. Schubert, S. C. Shapiro (editors), *KR'98: Principles of Knowledge Representation and Reasoning*, pages 636–645. Morgan Kaufmann, San Francisco, 1998.

92. M. N. Huhns, M. P. Singh. Service-oriented computing: Key concepts and principles. *IEEE Internet Computing*, 09(1):75–81, Jan/Feb 2005.

93. IBM, SAP. *WS-BPEL Extension for Sub-processes BPEL-SPE*, 2005.

94. O. M. G. Inc. CORBA Components—v3.0 Full Specification, June 2002. http://www.omg.org/cgi-bin/doc?formal/02-06-65.

95. K. Iwasa. Web Services Reliable Messaging TC—WS-Reliability 1.1. OASIS Open, November 2004.

96. K. Jank et al. Adaptive service grid deliverable d3.k-1: Initial service creation analysis and requirements (part 1), 2005.

97. M. Jarke, K. Pohl. Establishing visions in context: Toward a model of requirements processes. In *Proceedings of the 14th International Conference on Information Systems (ICIS 1993)*, pages 23–34, 1993.

98. N. Jennings, P. Faratin, A. Lomuscio, S. Parsons, C. Sierra, M. Wooldridge. Automated negotiation: Prospects, methods and challenges. *International Journal of Group Decision and Negotiation*, 10(2):199–215, 2001.

99. J. M. Joachim Miller. Mda-guide version 1.0.1, 2003. http://www.omg.org/docs/omg/03-06-01.pdf.

100. N. Karten. Establishing service level agreements, 2006. http://www.nkarten.com/sla.html.

101. A. Keller, G. Kar, H. Ludwig, A. Dan, J. L. Hellerstein. Managing dynamic services: A contract based approach to a conceptual architecture. In *Proceedings of the 8th IEEE/IFIP Network Operations and Management Symposium (NOMS 2002)*, 2002.

102. G. Keller, M. Nüttgens, A.-W. Scheer. Semantische Prozessmodellierung auf der Grundlage Ereignisgesteuerter Prozessketten (EPK). Arbeitsbericht Heft 89, Institut für Wirtschaftsinformatik Universität Saarbrücken, 1992.

103. U. Keller, R. Lara, A. Polleres, I. Toma, M. Kiffer, D. Fensel. WSMO discovery. Working Draft D5.1v0.1, WSMO, 2004. http://www.wsmo.org/TR/d5/d5.1/v0.1/.

104. M. Kifer, G. Lausen. F-logic: A higher-order language for reasoning about objects, inheritance, and scheme. In *SIGMOD Conference*, pages 134–146, 1989.

105. M. Kifer, G. Lausen, J. Wu. Logical foundations of object-oriented and frame-based languages. *Journal of the Association for Computing Machinery*, 42(4):741–843, 1995.

106. E. Kim, Y. Lee. Quality model for web services. Technical report, OASIS Web Services Quality Model TC, 2005. http://www.oasis-open.org/committees/wsqm/.

107. J. Kim, M. Spraragen, Y. Gil. An intelligent assistant for interactive workflow composition. In *IUI '04: Proceedings of the 9th International Conference on Intelligent User Interface*, pages 125–131. ACM Press, New York, 2004. ISBN 1-58113-815-6.

108. C. Kirwin. *The Oxford Companion to Philosophy*, chapter Reasoning, page 748. Oxford University Press, 1995.

109. S. C. Kleene. *Mathematical Logic*. Dover, New York, 2002.

110. H. Knublauch, R. W. Fergerson, N. F. Noy, M. A. Musen. The Protégé OWL plugin: An open development environment for semantic web applications. In *Proceedings of the 3rd International Semantic Web Conference (ISWC), LNCS*, vol. 3298. Springer, New York, 2004.

111. G. Kotonya, I. Sommerville. *Requirements Engineering: Processes and Techniques. Worldwide Series in Computer Science.* Wiley, New York, 1998. ISBN 0471972088.

112. D. Krafzig, K. Banke, D. Slama. *Enterprise SOA. Service Oriented Architecture—Best Practices.* Prentice-Hall PTR, Englewood Cliffs, December 2004. ISBN 131465759.

113. C. W. Krueger. *Software Product-Family Engineering—5th International Workshop, PFE 2003, Siena, Italy, November 4–6, 2003. Revised Papers,* volume 3014/2004 of *LNCS,* chapter Towards a Taxonomy for Software Product Lines, pages 323–331. Springer, 2004.

114. D. Kuropka. *Modelle zur Repräsentation natürlichsprachlicher Dokumente— Information-Filtering und -Retrieval mit relationalen Datenbanken.* Logos Verlag, Berlin, 2004.

115. B. Laasri, H. Laasri, S. Lander, V. Lesser. A generic model for negotiating agents. *International Journal on Intelligent and Cooperative Information Systems,* 1(2):291–317, 1992.

116. J.-C. Laprie, B. R. anf Carl Landwehr. Basic concepts and taxonomy of dependable and secure computing. *IEEE Transactions on Dependable and Secure Computing,* 1, January–March 2004.

117. A. Lazovik, M. Aiello, M. Papazoglou. Planning and monitoring the execution of web service requests. In *1st International Conference on Service-oriented Computing (IC-SOC'03),* 2003.

118. F. Leymann. The influence of web services on software: Potentials and tasks. In *34th Annual Meeting of the German Computer Society.* Ulm, Germany, September 20–24, Springer, Berlin, 2004.

119. F. Leymann, D. Roller. *Production Workflow: Concepts and Techniques.* Prentice-Hall, Englewood Cliffs, 2000.

120. Z. Liu, M. S. Squillante, J. L. Wolf. On maximizing service-level-agreement profits. In *EC '01: Proceedings of the 3rd ACM Conference on Electronic Commerce,* pages 213–223. ACM Press, New York, 2001. ISBN 1-58113-387-1. doi:http://doi.acm.org/10.1145/501158.501185.

121. J. W. Lloyd. *Foundations of Logic Programming.* Springer, New York, 1993.

122. A. R. Lomuscio, M. Wooldridge, N. R. Jennings. A classification scheme for negotiation in electronic commerce. *Lecture Notes in Computer Science,* 1991, 2001.

123. C. M. MacKenzie, K. Laskey, F. McCabe, P. F. Brown, R. Metz. Reference model for service oriented architecture 1.0, committee specification 1. http://www.oasis-open.org/, August 2006.

124. C. Malu, C. Fabio, D. Umeshwar, S. Ming-Chien. Intelligent management of slas for composite web services. *Lecture Notes in Computer Science,* 2822, 2003.

125. D. Martin, M. Burstein, J. Hobbs, O. Lassila, D. McDemott, S. McIlraith, S. Narayanan, M. Paolucci, B. Parsia, T. Payne, E. Sirin, N. Srinivasan, K. Sycara. *OWL-S: Semantic Markup for Web Services,* December 2003. W3C Member Submission, 22 November 2004. Available from http://www.w3.org/Submission/OWL-S/. http://www.daml.org/services/owl-s/1.0/owl-s.html.

126. S. McLean, J. Naftel, K. Williams, *Microsoft .NET Remoting.* Microsoft Press, 2002. ISBN 0-7356-1778-3.

127. J. Mendling, G. Neumann, M. Nüttgens. Towardsworkflow pattern support of event-driven process chains (epc). In M. Nüttgens, J. Mendling (editors), *XML4BPM 2005, Proceedings of the 2nd GI Workshop XML4BPM – XML Interchange Formats for Business Process Management at 11th GI Conference BTW 2005,* Karlsruhe, Germany, March 2005, pages 23–38.

128. H. Meyer. Calculating the semantic conformance of processes. In *Proceedings of the Advances in Semantics for Web Services 2007 Workshop (semantics4ws)*, 2007.

129. H. Meyer, D. Kuropka, P. Tröger. ASG—techniques of adaptivity. In *Proceedings of the Dagstuhl Seminar on Autonomous and Adaptive Web Services*, 2007.

130. P. Mika, D. Oberle, A. Gangemi, M. Sabou. Foundations for service ontologies: Aligning owl-s to dolce. In *The 13th International World Wide Web Conference Proceedings*, pages 563–572. ACM, New York, May 2004.

131. N. Mitra, Y. Lafon. SOAP Version 1.2 Part 0: Primer (Second Edition)—W3C Recommendation. World Wide Web Consortium (W3C), April 2007.

132. A. Mocan, E. Cimpian. An ontology-based data mediation framework for semantic environments. *International Journal on Semantic Web and Information Systems (IJSWIS)*, 3(3), 2007.

133. M. Momotko, M. Gajewski, A. Ludwig, R. Kowalczyk, M. Kowalkiewicz, J. Y. Zhang. Towards adaptive management of qos-aware service compositions—functional architecture. In *4th International Conference on Service Oriented Computing*, Chicago, 2006.

134. M. Momotko, M. Gajewski, A. Ludwig, R. Kowalczyk, M. Kowalkiewicz, J. Y. Zhang. Towards adaptive management of QoS-aware service compositions. *International Journal of Multiagent and Grid Systems*, 2007.

135. B. Motik, R. Rosati. A faithful integration of description logics with logic programming. In *Proc. of IJCAI-07*, pages 477–482, 2007.

136. P. Murray, E. Golluscio. CORBA and Web Services. *Cape Clear Software Whitepaper*, July 2002. http://www.omg.org/news/whitepapers/.

137. K. L. Myers et al. PASSAT: A User-centric Planning Framework. In *Proceedings of the 3rd International NASA Workshop on Planning and Scheduling for Space*. AAAI, Houston, TX, USA, 2002.

138. J. Mylopoulos, A. Borgida, M. Jarke, M. Koubarakis. Telos: Representing knowledge about information systems. *ACM Transactions on Information Systems*, 8(4):325–362, 1990.

139. Y. V. Natis. Service-oriented architecture scenario. *Gartner Research*, AV-19-6751:6, April 2003.

140. J. V. Neumann, O. Morgenstern. *The Theory of Games and Economic Behaviour*. Princeton University Press, Princeton, 1944.

141. P. Niblett, S. Graham. Events and service-oriented architecture: The OASIS Web Services Notification specifications. *IBM Systems Journal*, October 2005. ISSN 0018-8670. doi:10.1007/s10208-008-9024-2.

142. K. Nichols, S. Blake, F. Baker, D. Black. Definition of the differentiated services field (ds field) in the ipv4 and ipv6 headers. RFC 2474 (Proposed Standard), December 1998. DiffServ specification, Updated by RFCs 3168, 3260. http://www.ietf.org/rfc/rfc2474.txt.

143. J. Nitzsche, T. van Lessen, D. Karastoyanova, F. Leymann. $bpel^{Light}$. In *Proceedings of the 5th International Conference on Business Process Management (BPM 2007)*, pages 214–229. Springer-Verlag, New York, September 2007.

144. R. L. Nord (editor). *Welcome to the Third Software Product Line Conference—SPLC 2004*. Springer, New York, 2004.

145. D. Oberle. *Semantic Management of Middleware*. Springer, New York, 2006.

146. D. Oberle, S. Lamparter, S. Grimm, D. Vrandecic, S. Staab, A. Gangemi. Towards ontologies for formalizing modularization and communication in large software systems. *Journal of Applied Ontology*, 2006.

147. D. Oberle, S. Staab, A. Eberhart. Semantic management of distributed web applications. *IEEE Distributed Systems Online*, 7(5), 2006.

148. Organization for the Advancement of Structured Information Standards (OASIS). *Introduction to UDDI: Important Features and Functional Concepts*, October 2004. http://uddi.org/pubs/uddi-tech-wp.pdf.

149. Organization for the Advancement of Structured Information Standards (OASIS). *Web Services Business Process Execution Language (WS-BPEL)*, 2004.

150. Organization for the Advancement of Structured Information Standards (OASIS). *Web Services Business Process Execution Language Version 2.0 Primer*, 2007. http://docs.oasis-open.org/wsbpel/2.0/Primer/wsbpel-v2.0-Primer.pdf.

151. M. P. Papazoglou, D. Georgakopoulos. Introduction. *Commun. ACM*, 46(10):24–28, 2003. ISSN 0001-0782.

152. S. Parsons, C. Sierra, N. Jennings. Agents that reason and negotiate by arguing. *Journal of Logic and Computation*, 8(3):261–292, 1998.

153. K. Petersen, J. M. Zaha, A. Metzger. Variability-driven selection of services for service compositions. In *WESOA 2007*, 2007.

154. M. Pistore, F. Barbon, P. Bertoli, D. Shaparau, P. Traverso. Planning and monitoring Web service composition. *Lecture Notes in Computer Science*, 3192:106–115, Jan 2004.

155. K. Pohl. *Requirements Engineering. Grundlagen, Prinzipien, Techniken*. Dpunkt Verlag, 2007.

156. K. Pohl, G. Böckle, F. J. van der Linden. *Software Product Line Engineering: Foundations, Principles and Techniques*. Springer, New York, 2005. ISBN 3540243720.

157. D. G. Pruitt. *Negotiation Behaviour*. Academic Press, New York, 1981.

158. H. Raiffa. *The Art and Science of Negotiation*. Harvard University Press, Cambridge, 1982.

159. J. Recker, M. Indulska, P. Green. Extending representational analysis: Bpmn user and developer perspectives. In *Proceedings of the 5th International Conference on Business Process Management (BPM 2007)*, pages 384–399. Springer-Verlag, New York, September 2007.

160. J. Richter. *Applied Microsoft .NET Framework Programming*. Microsoft Press, 2002. ISBN 0-7356-1422-9.

161. C. Ringelstein, T. Franz, S. Staab. The process of semantic annotation of web services. In J. Cardoso (editor), *Semantic Web Services—Theory, Tools, and Applications*. Idea Publishing Group, USA, 2007.

162. T. Rinke, T. Weyer. Defining reference models for modelling qualities: How requirements engineering techniques can help. In *Proceedings of the 13th International Working Conference on Requirements Engineering: Foundation for Software Quality (REFSQ 2007)*, pages 335–340, 2007.

163. D. Roman, U. Keller, H. Lausen, R. L. Jos de Bruijn, M. Stollberg, A. Polleres, C. Feier, C. Bussler, D. Fensel. Web service modeling ontology. *Applied Ontology*, 1(1):77–106, 2005.

164. D. Roman, H. Lausen, U. Keller. *Web Service Modeling Ontology (WSMO)*, 2005. WSMO Working Draft D2v1.2. http://www.wsmo.org/TR/d2/v1.2/.

165. D. Roman et al. Requirements analysis on the asg service specification language. Deliverable d1.1-1, DERI Innsbruck, 2005.

166. D. Rossi, E. Turrini. Analyzing the impact of components replication in high available J2EE clusters. In *ICAS/ICNS*, page 56, 2005.

167. T. W. Sandholm. *Multiagent Systems—Distributed Rational Decision Making*. MIT Press, Cambridge, 1999.

168. J. Schaffner, H. Meyer, C. Tosun. A Semi-automated orchestration tool for service-based business processes. In *Proceedings of the 2nd International Workshop on Engineering Service-Oriented Applications: Design and Composition*, Dec 2006.

169. J. Schaffner, H. Meyer, M. Weske. A formal model for mixed initiative service composition. In *Proceedings of the IEEE International Conference on Services Computing (SCC 2007)*, pages 443–450, 2007.

170. A.-W. Scheer. *ARIS—Vom Geschäftsprozeß zum Anwendungssystem.* Springer, fourth edition, 2002.

171. A.-W. Scheer, O. Thomas, O. Adam. Process modelling using event-driven process chains. In M. Dumas, W. M. P. van der Aalst, A. H. M. ter Hofstede (editors), *Process-Aware Information Systems*, pages 119–146. Wiley, Hoboken, 2005.

172. K. Schmid. A comprehensive product line scoping approach and its validation. In *Proceedings of the 22rd International Conference on Software Engineering (ICSE)*, pages 593–603. ACM, New York, 2002.

173. M. Schmidt-Schauß, G. Smolka. Subsumption in KL-ONE is undecidable. In R. Brachman (editor), *Principles of Knowledge, Representation and Reasoning: Proceedings of the First International Conference of Knowledge Representation and Reasoning*, pages 421–431. Morgan Kaufmann, San Mateo, 1991.

174. W. Shen, Y. Li, H. H. Genniwa, C. Wang. Adaptive negotiation for agent-based grid computing. *Journal of the American Statistical Association*, 97(457):210–214, 2002.

175. C. Sierra, N. Jennings, P. Noriega, S. Parsons. A framework for argumentation-based negotiation. In *Proc. 4th International Workshop on Agent Theories, Architectures and Languages*. Rode Island, USA, 1997.

176. E. Sirin, B. Parsia, J. Hendler. Filtering and selecting semantic Web services with interactive composition techniques. *IEEE Intelligent Systems*, 19:42–49, 2004.

177. E. Sirin, B. Parsia, D. Wu, J. Hendler, D. Nau. HTN planning for Web service composition using SHOP2. *Journal of Web Semantics*, 1(4):377–396, 2004.

178. H. Smith, P. Fingar. *Business Process Management: The Third Wave.* Meghan-Kiffer Press, Tampa, FL, USA, first edition, 2003.

179. P. G. Soares. On remote procedure call. In *Proceedings of the 1992 Conference of the Centre for Advanced Studies on Collaborative Research (CASCON)*, pages 215–267. IBM Press, 1992.

180. R. M. Soley, C. M. Stone. Object Management Architecture Guide Rev. 3.0, June 1995. http://www.omg.org/cgi-bin/doc?ab/97-05-05.

181. J. F. Sowa. *Knowledge Representation: Logical, Philosophical, and Computational Foundations.* Brooks Cole Publishing Co., Pacific Grove, 2000.

182. S. Stein, K. Barchewitz, M. El Kharbili. Enabling business experts to discover web services for business process automation. In C. Pautasso, T. Gschwind (editors), *2nd Workshop on Emerging Web Services Technology*, pages 19–35. Halle, Germany, November 2007.

183. S. Stein, K. Ivanov. Epk nach bpel transformation als voraussetzung für praktische umsetzung einer soa. In W.-G. Bleek, J. Raasch, H. Züllighoven (editors), *GI Software Engineering 2007*, volume 105 of *Lecture Notes in Informatics (LNI)*, pages 75–80. Gesellschaft für Informatik (GI), Hamburg, Germany, March 2007.

184. M.-A. Storey, M. Musen, J. Silva, C. Best, N. Ernst, R. Fergerson, N. Noy. Jambalaya: Interactive visualization to enhance ontology authoring and knowledge acquisition in Protégé. In *Proceedings of the Workshop on Interactive Tools for Knowledge Capture (K-CAP)*, 2001.

185. Sun Microsystems. Java API for XML-based RPC 1.1. *JSR-101*, October 2003.

186. C. Szyperski. *Component Software—Beyond Object-Oriented Programming.* Addison-Wesley/ACM Press, 1999. ISBN 0-201-17888-5.

187. A. Tate. Generating project networks. In *Proceedings of the Fifth Joint Conference on Artificial Intelligence*, Cambridge, MA, USA, pages 888–893. Morgan Kaufmann, San Mateo, 1977.

188. C. P. Team. Capability maturity model integration (cmmi) version 1.1, cmu/sei-2002-tr-029. Technical report, Carnegie Mellon Software Engineering Institute, 2002.

189. R. Ten-Hove, P. Walker. Java Business Integration (JBI). *JSR 208*, August 2005.

190. J. B. Theresa Lehner. Adaptive service grid deliverable d6 iii-7: Asg application and service engineering approach, 2006.

191. M. V. Thomas Stahl. *Modellgetriebene Softwareentwicklung, Techniken, Engineering, Management*. Dpunkt Verlag, 2004.

192. T. F. TMF. Sla management handbook, volume 2, concepts and principles—gb917 v2.5, r2.5, 2005. http://www.tmforum.org/browse.aspx?catID=1722&linkID=30755.

193. P. Tröger. *Dynamische Ressourcenverwaltung für dienstbasierte Software-Systeme*. Ph.D. thesis, Universität Potsdam, November 2007.

194. P. Tröger, H. Meyer, I. Melzer, M. Flehmig. Dynamic provisioning and monitoring of stateful services. In *Proceedings of the 3rd International Conference on Web Information Systems and Technologies (WEBIST 2007)*, pages 434–438, March 2007. ISBN 978-972-8865-77-1.

195. W. T. Tsai, J. Gao, X. Wei, Y. Chen. Testability of software in service-oriented architecture. In *Proceedings of the 30th Annual International Computer Software and Applications Conference (COMPSAC 2006)*, pages 163–170, 2006.

196. R. van Buuren, S. Hoppenbrouwers, H. Jonkers, M. Lankhorst, G. V. van Zanten. Architecture language reference manual. Technical report TI/RS/2003/030, Telematica Institute, April 2006. ArchiMate Deliverable 2.2.2b v4.1.

197. W. van der Aalst, A. ter Hofstede, B. Kiepuszewski, A. Barros. Workflow patterns. *Distributed and Parallel Databases*, 14(3):5–51, 2003.

198. W. M. van der Aalst. Verification of workflow nets. In *ICATPN '97: Proceedings of the 18th International Conference on Application and Theory of Petri Nets*, pages 407–426. Springer-Verlag, London, 1997. ISBN 3-540-63139-9.

199. A. van Gelder, K. Ross, J. S. Schlipf. The well-founded semantics for general logic programs. *Journal of the ACM*, 38(3):620–650, 1991.

200. J. van Gurp, J. Bosch, M. Svahnberg. On the notion of variability in software product lines. In *IEEE/IFIP Working Conference on Software Architecture (WICSA 2001)*, pages 45–54, 2001.

201. L. von Bertalanffy. *General System Theory*. Braziller (George) Inc., New York, 1976.

202. C. Walls, R. Breidenbach. *Spring in Action*. Manning Publications, second edition, 2007. ISBN 1933988134.

203. S. Weibel, J. Kunze, C. Lagoze, M. Wolf. Dublin core metadata for resource discovery. RFC 2413, IETF, September 1998.

204. M. Weske. *Business Process Management: Concepts, Languages, Architectures*. Springer, New York, April 2007.

205. F. Wolff, D. Oberle, S. Lamparter, S. Staab. Economic reflections on managing web services using semantics. In *EMISA-2005—Enterprise Modelling and Information Systems Architectures*, October 24–25, 2005.

206. W. A. Woods. What's in a link: Foundations for semantic networks. In D. Bobrow, A. Collins (editors), *Representation and Understanding. Studies in Cognitive Science*, pages 35–82. Academic Press, New York, 1975.

207. M. Wooldridge. *Intelligent Agents: An Introduction to Multiagent Systems*. Wiley, New York, 2002.

208. World Wide Web Consortium. *XML Schema Part 0: Primer Second Edition—W3C Recommendation*, October 2004. http://www.w3.org/TR/xmlschema-0.
209. World Wide Web Consortium (W3C). *OWL Web Ontology Language Semantics and Abstract Syntax—W3C Recommendation 10 February 2004*, February 2004. W3C Recommendation 10 February 2004. http://www.w3.org/TR/owl-semantics/.
210. World Wide Web Consortium (W3C). *RDF Primer—W3C Recommendation 10 February 2004*, February 2004. W3C Recommendation 10 February 2004. http://www.w3.org/TR/REC-rdf-syntax/.
211. K. Zachos, N. A. M. Maiden, X. Zhu, S. Jones. Discovering web services to specify more complete system requirements. In *Proceedings of the 19th International Conference on Advanced Information Systems Engineering (CAISE)*, pages 142–157. Springer, New York, 2007.
212. L. Zeng, B. Benatallah, H. Lei, A. N. D. Flaxer, H. Chang. Flexible composition of enterprise web services. *Electronic Markets—Web Services*, 13:141–152, 2003.
213. L. Zeng, B. Benatallah, H. Lei, A. H. H. Ngu, D. Flaxer, H. Chang. Flexible composition of enterprise Web services. *Electronic Markets*, 13(2), 2003.
214. L. Zeng, B. Benatallah, H. Lei, A. H. H. Ngu, D. Flaxer, H. Chang. Flexible composition of enterprise Web services. *Electronic Markets—Web Services*, 13, 2003.
215. H. Zhu, A framework for service-oriented testing of web services. In *Proceedings of the 30th Annual International Computer Software and Applications Conference (COMPSAC 2006)*, pages 145–150, 2006.

Index